ADVANCE PRAISE FOR *COLD CASE NORTH*

"*Cold Case North* is an enthralling search for intimate answers and broader social accountability. Essential reading."
—DAVID CHARIANDY, author of *I've Been Meaning to Tell You*

"Like too many cases involving missing and murdered Indigenous people, authorities failed to ensure that Brady and Halkett's deaths were properly investigated. This book helps get to the bottom of the fate of these two men and demonstrates why investigators should never dismiss the knowledge of Indigenous Peoples." —DARREN PRÉFONTAINE, author of *Gabriel Dumont*

"*Cold Case North* is part true crime thriller, part gripping mystery about the disappearance of Métis legend James Brady and Absolom Halkett in northern Saskatchewan. It is also about Indigenous knowledge, investigative incompetence, and the stuff of legend." —PAUL SEESEQUASIS, author of *Blanket Toss Under Midnight Sun*

"A fascinating search for the truth, *Cold Case North* unravels the layers of a decades' old mystery. It is about how communities hold knowledge for generations, and how missing loved ones are never forgotten." ——̶V̶E̶R̶̶ETTE, author of *River Wom̶*

COLD CASE NORTH

The Search for **JAMES BRADY**
and **ABSOLOM HALKETT**

MICHAEL NEST

with **DEANNA REDER** *and* **ERIC BELL**

Printed and bound in Canada at Imprimerie Gauvin. The text of this book is printed on 100% post-consumer recycled paper with earth-friendly vegetable-based inks.

COVER AND TEXT DESIGN: Duncan Campbell, University of Regina Press
COPY EDITOR: Dallas Harrison
PROOFREADER: Rachel Taylor
INDEXER: Siusan Moffat
COVER ART: "Lake Island" by Chad/Adobe Stock.

Library and Archives Canada Cataloguing in Publication

TITLE: Cold case north : the search for James Brady and Absolom Halkett / Michael Nest with Deanna Reder and Eric Bell.

NAMES: Nest, Michael Wallace, author. | Reder, Deanna, 1963- author. | Bell, Eric (Park warden), author.

DESCRIPTION: Includes bibliographical references and index.

IDENTIFIERS: Canadiana (print) 20200276751 | Canadiana (ebook) 20200276832 | ISBN 9780889777491 (softcover) | ISBN 9780889777545 (hardcover) | ISBN 9780889777507 (PDF) | ISBN 9780889777521 (EPUB)

SUBJECTS: LCSH: Brady, Jim, 1908-1967. | LCSH: Halkett, Absolom, -1967. | LCSH: Missing persons,— Investigation,—Saskatchewan,—Case studies. | LCSH: Missing persons,—Saskatchewan,—Case studies. | LCSH: Cold cases (Criminal investigation),—Saskatchewan,—Case studies.

CLASSIFICATION: LCC HV6762.C2 N47 2020 | DDC 363.2/336097124,—dc23

10 9 8 7 6 5 4 3 2

University of Regina Press, University of Regina
Regina, Saskatchewan, Canada, S4S 0A2
tel: (306) 585-4758 fax: (306) 585-4699
web: www.uofrpress.ca

We acknowledge the support of the Canada Council for the Arts for our publishing program. We acknowledge the financial support of the Government of Canada. / Nous reconnaissons l'appui financier du gouvernement du Canada. This publication was made possible with support from Creative Saskatchewan's Book Publishing Production Grant Program.

Canada Council   Conseil des Arts   Canadä
for the Arts   du Canada

For Frank Tomkins
(1927–2019)

indians

indians go missing
they tell the family
indians go missing
everyday
blue suits shrug
no sense looking
they said
he'll turn up when
he gets bored
or broke

indians drown
the family finds out
happens everyday
this land floods
with dead indians
this river swells
freezes
breaks open
cold arms of ice
welcomes indians

indians get drunk
don't we know it
do stupid things
like being young
like going home alone
like walking across
a frozen river
not quite frozen
and not making it
to the other side.

—KATHERENA VERMETTE[1]

CONTENTS

MAPS

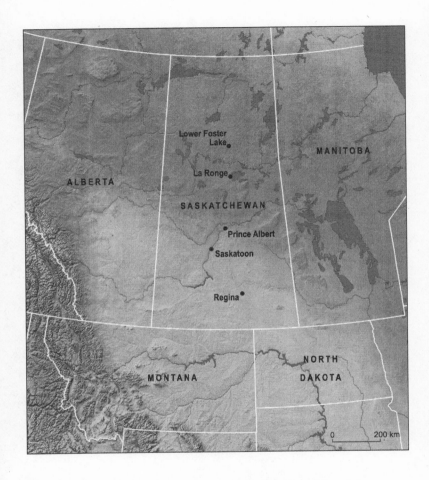

Saskatchewan in relation to Canada with detail of La Ronge and Lower Foster Lake
Map by Weldon Hiebert.

1
A QUINTESSENTIAL CANADIAN STORY

I do not remember June 1967 when Jim Brady and Abbie Halkett disappeared in the bush in northern Saskatchewan without a trace. I would have been too young. But I do remember my mother telling me about this mystery, how two local men living in her hometown, La Ronge, were dropped off by plane at a lake an hour north so that they could go prospecting. When their boss came by a week later to check on them, he found that their camp had been set up, their beds had been slept in, and cups half full of tea sat next to their extinguished campfire. Jim and Abbie were nowhere to be found.

The story of their disappearance was one of many that my mother told me and my brother. We lived away, and these stories connected us to our Cree and Métis relatives and life in northern Saskatchewan. Even as kids we would sit around drinking tea with Mom as she related this world to us through words, sometimes news that she'd heard from one of our nine aunties and uncles or dozens of cousins, sometimes her memories of family members and friends, in La Ronge and beyond.

Since our dad was in the army and we lived in a variety of military bases across western Canada, I knew La Ronge only in the summer, when my parents would use holidays to return home to see family members. Even so, I was amazed that there was any place north of this small town, which to my child's imagination after countless long drives over gravel roads to get there seemed to be as far north as anyone could go. At some point as a teenager, I took a look at a world map and was shocked to see La Ronge listed, as though it were any other world city, positioned just halfway up the province, almost smack dab in the middle of Saskatchewan. Yet I knew it as a place unlike any other, with only a few hundred residents, many of them my cousins or families of people that my mother grew up with.

Whenever Mom told me about the disappearance, she included a different detail, as when she told me that oddly around the time that Jim and Abbie disappeared it had been snowing— not impossible in northern Saskatchewan in June. There were no footprints from Jim and Abbie recording that they had left the camp and no footprints of anyone, human or animal, arriving at it. About a week after they were dropped off, their boss was scheduled to check in on them and replenish their supplies; he, along with the pilot who flew him in, were the first to make tracks in the snow. I always imagined, though it could not be true, that the boss reached out to the cups left by the campfire and felt that the tea was still warm.

Mom told me that the police had decided that Jim and Abbie had gotten lost in the bush, a point that made my mother sneer. It's not impossible to become disoriented anywhere, and the terrain where Jim and Abbie made camp was difficult. But they were men who had grown up on the land and knew how to read it. Even alone, each man had a lifetime of skills that would have allowed him to make his own way back to their campsite; with the two working together, it would have been impossible to get lost for long.

My mother didn't mention that both men had high public profiles. She didn't mention that James Brady was one of the "Famous Five" who had helped to establish the Métis Association of Alberta. She never mentioned, and likely did not know, two of the five, Felix Callihoo and Joseph Dion. Mom did know a fourth member, Malcolm Norris, though more as Jim's old friend than as an activist. She referred to him as Old Mac Norris to distinguish him from his son with the same name. And she knew the fifth member, Pete Tomkins Jr., as Mr. Tomkins, a close family friend because Mrs. Tomkins was a friend of my kohkum and their son Frank married my Auntie Irene. To Mom, Jim Brady was the man who lived in a little cabin in the middle of town, right next to Uncle George, Auntie Jane, and my cousins.

Mom never mentioned that Abbie Halkett had been a band councillor for the Lac La Ronge Indian Band, though family members lived on the reserve. At the time of Abbie's disappearance, my Auntie Bella and Uncle Edmund lived on the reserve with their kids, near Auntie Jane's mom, Amelia Sanderson. The only time that Mom mentioned Abbie was when he had sought out my kohkum for medical help. When she told me about that, Mom always referred to him not as Abbie but as Absolom, and so separate were these stories from each other that it took me years to realize that the two names referred to the same man.

Mom told me that at some point the police had determined that Jim and Abbie had gotten so lost in the bush that they had decided to try to walk out, a point that made my mother snort in derision. Well, not exactly snort. It's a gesture that I always think of as Cree and involves an exhaling of breath and a curling of the lip at the same time as rolling one's eyes. She explained that the police thought that Jim and Abbie had tried to walk out, and then she exhaled, with accompanying facial gestures, to articulate a word so aspirated that it is hard to write out but is close to *neee*. I understood why. When I tried as a child to explain the land around La Ronge to others and mentioned that it was in Saskatchewan, people would assume that it was on the plains and ask me if I missed the open sky. It was as though they had never heard of the bush and muskeg and water that begin about an hour outside Saskatoon, around Prince Albert, and extend north. It is unthinkable that anyone who knew that land would try to walk out of it.

Sometimes Mom would tell me that, even though the RCMP called off the search for Jim and Abbie a couple of weeks after the disappearance, their friends and community members continued to look for them all summer. And they came up with nothing. When I asked Mom what had happened to Jim and Abbie, she told me that the UFOs must have taken them. That seemed to be more logical than any of the theories that I had heard up until then.

Mom and Dad saw Uncle Frank and Auntie Irene a lot when I was growing up. Part of this was because Dad had been in the army with Frank's brother Jimmy as members of the Princess Patricia's Canadian Light Infantry or PPCLI. Dad had known the Tomkins family longer than he had known Mom. Part of this was also because, though Mom had four brothers and five sisters, she was closest to Irene.

Yet, though Uncle Frank had talked passionately about his theories of how Jim and Abbie disappeared, it wasn't until just before Mom passed on in 2000 that I first heard Uncle Frank tell the story. I was with my cousin Janet and little cousin Crystal, and I had asked Auntie Irene a question about Absolom Halkett; Uncle Frank interjected to say that he was the one to talk to about Abbie, with a conviction that surprised me. He then launched into the precise story of the days leading up to Jim and Abbie's disappearance, complete with details to support his theories and suspicions. He was convinced that the prospectors had found a sizable deposit worth millions of dollars and had been murdered in order to cut them out of the claim. Uncle Frank was certain that the police were corrupt, either shielding the murderer or simply happy that Indigenous "troublemakers" like Jim and Abbie were out of the way.

Once Auntie Irene passed on in 2005, I visited Uncle Frank at his home in Saskatoon several more times, sometimes alone and sometimes with family members. Usually my cousin Connie was there, helping her dad, and in recent years my cousin Pat too. Frank shared his stories about family members, about his grandfather, Peter Tomkins, who had been a prisoner-of-war at Batoche. He talked about the fact that his grandmother had been Poundmaker's widow. He talked about his work with the Saskatchewan Métis Association and their visit to England in the early 1980s to advocate for the inclusion of Métis rights in the 1982 Constitution of Canada. Frank talked about his memories of Brady and Norris. Regardless, at some point he always returned to the details of Jim and Abbie's disappearance and often told me that it wasn't too late to conduct a search. He was confident that the RCMP theories were wrong, that their murders had taken place, that their bodies could be found in Lower Foster Lake, and that the lake was so cold that their bodies would still be intact, even after almost half a century.

When I completed my PhD in 2007, Uncle Frank became convinced that as a researcher I would be able to follow up on his leads, find equipment to search the lake, and locate Jim and Abbie. As an Indigenous woman who teaches Indigenous literatures, I understand the responsibilities of our stories. Although it seems to me that a typical literature professor has only to study and teach well, people who teach Indigenous literatures struggle under a higher level of accountability; each time Frank told me about the disappearance, he was emphasizing my responsibility to him and to the story that he was sharing with me.

I did what I could, which truthfully was very little. Over the years, I talked to others who knew this story, and in fact one of my second-year students was Brady's great-niece, and she researched and wrote about the mystery for her final paper. I wrote about Uncle Frank's theories, as one star in the constellation of family stories, as a way to give it some attention. I followed social media and noted that my cousin Vanessa was part of a youthful contingent in La Ronge who didn't believe the official story of the disappearance—that Jim and Abbie had gotten lost and come to a bad end. It is one thing, after all, to get lost and perish, even together. It is another to get lost, perish, and manage to hide any evidence of your remains. I researched the history as best I could, trying to make sense of northern mining in the 1960s, without much luck. I researched the details of marine archaeology and became overwhelmed when I looked at the cost of sonar.

This came to a head in the summer of 2016 when Frank, at this point almost ninety years old, called me explicitly

Frank Tomkins at age ninety, March 2017. *Photo credit: Deanna Reder.*

to come to visit him so that we could strategize how to find Jim and Abbie. I never articulated to Frank what anyone who knew me would realize. Although I have been able to find documents written by Indigenous authors hidden in archives, no one would ever think that I have any skill to find bodies lost in lakes. I can organize conferences and literary awards, but I do not think that I have the ability to lead searches on land or under water. No one would mistake me for an outdoorswoman. On top of that, I was finally at a point when all three of my kids were raised, and I was pouring myself into my work in a field that hadn't even existed when I was an undergraduate. I knew that, if I had endless amounts of time, I could research anything, but I was pressed for time and not sure where to begin. Still, I did what I could with my limited skill set. I contacted Cree filmmaker Tasha Hubbard, who gave me the name of a well-respected camera operator so that I could take good-quality footage of Frank telling this story. I wrote out a research plan that included looking into mineral rights and hiring an underwater search team, with as much confidence as if I had sketched out a plan to fly to the moon. I tried to figure out how to proceed.

A great deal of luck struck when in February 2017 an acquaintance from Australia emailed me. Michael Nest and I had met a few years earlier, when he was visiting family in Vancouver, to talk about shared research interests. During our first meetings, I learned that, though he currently lived in Sydney, he had completed his doctoral work in New York City and travelled several times a year to Africa as an anti-corruption researcher in the mining sector. I told my husband that it was so much fun talking to Michael because he was such an international citizen, with a composure and memory that I associate with PBS broadcasts. The author of three books, Michael has an amazing ability to talk knowledgeably about a vast array of topics, from the debilitating effects of the mining of coltan on the economies and environments in African countries to the state of Indigenous politics in Australia. He told me that his partner had decided to begin a PhD at McGill University, so they were stopping en route to see family in Vancouver before moving to Montreal. In fact, his partner's elderly mother was going to move with them, and so, except for occasional business trips, he was going to work from home in Montreal so that he could help his mother-in-law adjust to a new life with them in a new city. We planned to visit when he was in town and catch up.

I remember that a storm had begun the day that we had planned to meet, making it difficult for us to visit in person. Instead, we were on the phone when it suddenly hit me that he was moving to Canada, where he knew very few people and would have more time on his hands than he normally would, and I knew him enough at that point to guess that this story would intrigue him. I began to tell him about Uncle Frank and Jim and Abbie, partly because the fiftieth anniversary of their disappearance was looming and partly because it is the quintessential Canadian story to tell a newcomer. Two Indigenous men, well known in their communities and in the prime of their lives, go out onto the land for work and vanish. The authorities conduct a cursory investigation, posit that it was the fault of the missing, decide that the location is too isolated to continue a search, and determine that the case is unsolved and likely unsolvable. Meanwhile, Métis and Cree members of Jim's and Abbie's communities are certain that there has been foul play. They see the various individuals and forces in society that might have been threats to Jim and Abbie, though the fact that one of those threats might be the authorities themselves means that they don't know whom to trust. The pain of the loss resonates through more than just the Brady and Halkett families; the loss of these two leaders leaves communities devastated for generations. Meanwhile, mainstream Canada barely remembers Jim or Abbie, never mind that they disappeared and were never found.

Knowing that I couldn't solve this mystery alone, and knowing that Michael would be able to follow up on Uncle Frank's theories about a stolen mining claim, I asked him for help. Although I knew that I could cover some research expenses, I couldn't offer Michael payment for his time. And I didn't have a well-thought-out plan on how to proceed even though I did suggest that this story would make a good book. I just knew that Michael would be able to help and that, if we came to an impasse, he knew enough about Indigenous protocols that he would understand if we needed to walk away.

Michael and I decided to meet in Saskatoon in March 2017 to interview Uncle Frank. A voracious researcher, Michael was already up to speed on all of the documentation that he could find about the case. Later in the year we planned a second trip to Saskatchewan for August 2017, where we would again meet with Uncle Frank and drive to La Ronge.

Another strike of good fortune! My cousin Eric Bell, my Auntie Bella's middle son, was just on the cusp of retirement and likely had more time to spare than he ever had in his working life. He invited us to stay with him and his wife, Wanda. I was honoured for this generous welcome, especially since they didn't know Michael, and even though Eric would know about the mystery he hadn't yet heard all of Uncle Frank's deductions. And Wanda, busy in her last few years working at the local high school, was encouraging and supportive, likely more aware than we could have been that Eric would find the mystery irresistible.

At this first visit, I actually didn't know my cousin Eric very well, though I knew him by reputation. He, along with Wanda, is known to have taken good care of family members, including his father and his youngest brother. Eric and Wanda are devoted grandparents. He's an accomplished hunter, annually going with his son Jordan to hunt moose, both of them taking one each and then a third that they share with Elders in the community. Eric is as comfortable on the lake as he is on the land. And, except for childhood years in residential school and then Lethbridge College, he has spent his entire life in the North. He started the Emergency Medical Services in La Ronge and has attended, or directed his staff, to every mishap or tragedy in the community. He is exactly the right person to be with in challenging situations. Plus he knows pretty much everybody, or at least every family, in La Ronge and the surrounding areas. If there was a historical figure about whom we had questions, Eric knew a way to reach out.

It became a bit of a game. When I mention that Michael and I had the opportunity to visit with Cree writer Harold Johnson before we arrived in La Ronge, Eric, of course, knows who he is. Later, while out on the boat with Eric, Michael, and two Lac La Ronge Band members, Thompson Mckenzie and Stanley Roberts, they talk about where Cree territory ends and Dené territory begins; I pipe up to say that I know that there are Dené to the west of La Ronge, near Ile a la Crosse, because that is where Dené poet Tenille Campbell is from. Suddenly Eric is attentive and asks, astonished, "How do you know Tenille Campbell?" I know her, of course, as a young doctoral student and poet; it turns out that she is a good friend of Eric's new daughter-in-law and was present at Jordan and Trudy's recent wedding. Since I know only one other Dené person, and want to see how much further we can play the game, I ask Eric if he knows Dogrib writer Richard Van Camp, who grew up in the Northwest Territories. "Oh, you mean Jack Van Camp's son?" Eric and Wanda met Jack in their early years together when they lived in Fort Smith. His knowledge of the community and its people goes on and on.

Indeed, it is only with Eric's involvement, his intelligence, his standing in the community, and his understanding of the story that we are able to get as far as we have, even as we keep asking permission along the way to continue. In Saskatoon, we have the chance to consult with Abbie Halkett's only child, Rema, and she expresses relief that someone is finally taking up the search again. On that first trip to La Ronge, we want to get in touch with one of Jim Brady's daughters, Anne Dorion, to make sure that she and her family are okay with us beginning this search. Now, La Ronge isn't a large place, and I didn't think she would be difficult to find, plus I knew that she worked at the local high school with Wanda. But we take it as a good sign that Anne lives about five doors down from Eric and Wanda. We call, and Michael and I find ourselves walking down the street and sitting on her backyard swings talking to her about what we know and what we are looking for. She asks us questions and tells us that for her this story is from so long ago, and she no longer thinks about it, but she understands our desire to keep looking. I suspect that she is relieved that Eric is involved, even as we still are not sure at this point what we will find. We only know that we need to start and that others want us to start. And so we begin.

Deanna Reder
Vancouver, May 2020

PART 1
LAST KNOWN
POSITION

Last known position: the starting point
for a search and rescue mission.

2
CIRCLING

Friday, June 16, 1967. Berry Richards is flying north from Otter Lake, Saskatchewan, in a Cessna 180 from Athabaska Airways. The weather is clear, and he is headed for the northeast end of *Middle* Foster Lake, where his two employees have been dropped off. Richards wants to check their prospecting work on a uranium claim and to restock their camp. He hasn't had an update from them for nine days, but that is not unusual, and he knows what his men want—a typical list of fresh food supplies. From the air, Richards cannot see their tent, but he asks the pilot to land the float plane on the lake, and they motor over to the obvious camping spot. Nothing. Richards and the pilot walk across the portage to the next lake. Still nothing. It is bizarre.

They take off and circle the area with an ever-larger radius, a common search technique from the air in good weather when it is easy to maintain a focal point so as not to go over the same ground twice. The pilot looks out the left window, Richards out the right. Just as they are about to give up, Richards spots something at the top end of *Lower* Foster Lake. The plane dips down, and Richards recognizes his company's white tent. They land, and there is the camp, fifteen metres back from the lakeshore, twelve kilometres south from where it is supposed to be.

The camp is eerily quiet. The shack-tent, made of wooden walls, a floor, and a frame roof with canvas stretched over it, is deserted. Inside is a radio transceiver and battery, a gas stove, a loaf of bread, half a pound of butter, and some fresh meat that has started to spoil. A yellowed map lies on a bed. A short distance away a hole has been dug for a toilet, which looks like it has been used four times, so the camp has been occupied for perhaps two days. Almost nothing has been taken or eaten, which shows that the men have not been there long and that, wherever they have gone, they have carried very little with them. Their canoe, compasses, geology map, axes, and Geiger counters are missing, suggesting that they have packed light to do some preliminary sampling work. There is no sign of a struggle, but something is seriously wrong.

Taking off again, Richards and the pilot circle around and spot the men's canoe near the mouth of a creek more than 200 metres northeast of the camp.[1] It is beached, tied to a birch stump, with the motor lifted, and appears to have been abandoned. Not only are the two employees on the wrong lake, but also they have completely vanished.

Richards radioes La Ronge and sets off the alarm.

* * *

When some people go missing, they disappear quietly and completely from memory: isolated men and women with no friends or family members. This has not been the case for James Brady and Absolom Halkett—or, as the community of La Ronge knows them, Jim and Abbie. Canada has had more extensive searches, and people more famous than they have vanished, but the mysteriousness of the circumstances makes it the North's greatest missing persons cold case.

Wikipedia's "List of People Who Disappeared Mysteriously: Pre-1970" features Jim and Abbie along with others who vanished without a trace, such as art collector and heir Michael Rockefeller in New Guinea, aviatrix Amelia Earhart over the Pacific Ocean, and explorer Percy Fawcett in Amazonia. *The Globe and Mail* ran an obituary of Brady in its "Died This Day" column in 2003, thirty-six years after he vanished.[2] In 2009, the *Regina Leader-Post* profiled the men in an article on historical Saskatchewan missing persons cases.[3] Two websites dedicated to unsolved murders and missing persons have entries for Jim and Abbie, websleuths.com and unsolvedcanada.ca. As a mystery, Jim and Abbie's disappearance ranks with the best of them.

Ongoing interest in the case is fuelled by Jim's legendary status as one of the Métis* "Famous Five": Felix Callihoo, Joseph Dion, Malcolm Norris, Pete Tomkins Jr., and Jim. Whereas Louis Riel is known as the Métis leader and activist of the nineteenth century, the Famous Five are the ones who breathed new

---

* In what is now Canada, there are three distinct Indigenous Peoples: First Nations, Inuit, and Métis. The genesis of Métis identity lies in the fur trade during the eighteenth and nineteenth centuries, especially around the Red River catchment in Manitoba, and originally evolved out of intermarriage between First Nations mothers and European fathers. Métis inherited values, beliefs, languages, and customs from all of their ancestors and adapted them over the centuries to create distinct kinship ties and culture.

life into Métis politics and activism in the twentieth century. All but one had remarkable lives but unremarkable deaths. Jim went on that prospecting trip in June 1967 with fellow activist and Lac La Ronge Indian Band Councillor Abbie Halkett and never came back. "Missing" is the official verdict of the Royal Canadian Mounted Police (RCMP) report. But rumours swirl to this day of secret mining interests and foul play despite what the Mounties say.

During our research, we came across nine people who tried to investigate what had happened: Deanna's Uncle Frank (Frank Tomkins); Lloyd Mattson, a friend of Jim's (who also teamed up with Frank); Murray Dobbin, a journalist and scholar; Harold Johnson, a Cree writer and lawyer; Tom "Tracker" Charles, a Cree spirit guide who co-hosts *The Other Side*, a show about paranormal experiences on the Aboriginal Peoples Television Network (APTN); a Lac La Ronge Indian Band employee; a police officer; a Saskatchewan government employee; and a television producer. Their efforts ran aground on a lack of hard evidence of motive, murder, or . . . anything. The absence of a crime scene or body that could yield forensic information about the cause of death, a suspect, or a specific location—and therefore movements into and out of that location—added immeasurably to the challenge.

Uncle Frank's ability to investigate was eventually incapacitated by age, but with terrier-like obsession Frank never let go of his theory that Jim and Abbie had been murdered. He impressed upon Deanna and other family members the injustice, the wrongness, of the presumed "disappearance."

Deanna and I formed a team with her cousin Eric Bell to try to investigate what had happened. I would do most of the paper-based research and writing, guided by Deanna and Eric and their knowledge of the case, the location, and the individuals involved. Eric would be the man on the ground who knew the country and had connections to all of the families in this story. Right from the start, we thought that our search had the potential to become a book that could help to explain to people why there have been so many misgivings about the verdict that Jim and Abbie were "missing" and how we went about establishing our own doubts about the official verdict through our research. I kept copious notes and started to draft text early in the process.

Our ultimate goals were to crack the cold case and, most importantly, to find the bodies of Jim and Abbie and return them to their families. If they had been murdered, we wanted to find evidence of that and, if possible, identify both a suspect and a motive. We also wanted to understand the RCMP's actions and whether their efforts had helped, or hindered, finding out what had happened to the men. We believed that there was truth in Uncle Frank's theory; although we didn't understand the connections among all of the people whom Frank alleged had been involved, we decided to use it as the starting point for our search.

3
RECOVERY

I n his book about the lives and work of James Brady and Malcolm Norris, Murray Dobbin writes that part of his purpose is to "contribute to the recovery of twentieth century Métis history, so long ignored and discounted by Canadian historians."[1] *Recovery* was also a salient word for our own project. But we had some grim questions to ask ourselves. What would we find? And, whatever we found, what could it tell us about how Jim Brady and Abbie Halkett had died?

There were two main possibilities, neither one leaving room for niceties. The first possibility was that Jim and Abbie had been "consumed by bears," as Corporal Clyde Conrad, the RCMP officer in charge of the official search for the men, prosaically put it.[2] If we were extraordinarily lucky, then we would find their bones. Also, a bear would not eat their compasses, Geiger counters, or axes, so they were other possible "finds" of the first possibility. The second possibility was more confronting: we would find their bodies. Doing so would not be straightforward. In June, the time of year when Jim and Abbie had disappeared, it wouldn't take long for a body to attract ravens and other scavengers. If the bodies were left on land, then ravens in the sky would have attracted the attention of the search parties, which meant that, if they had been murdered, whoever had killed them must have covered up their bodies. But in the North, even in June, it would be difficult to dig a grave big enough for two bodies, especially in a hurry if the ground hasn't fully softened. One of Jim and Abbie's former employers, Bill Knox, bluntly explained the solution: "There is only one way to get rid of a body like that and that's to open the stomach up and fill it full of stones and tie it up again and sink it to the bottom of the lake."[3]

Deanna discussed the possibility that Jim and Abbie had been "buried" in Lower Foster Lake with Dr. Rudy Reimer, an archaeologist from Skwxwú7mesh Úxwumixw (Squamish Nation) and a professor at Simon Fraser University, who co-hosts the APTN program *Wild Archaeology*. He told Deanna that lakes in the North are cold, so if bodies are in deep water there is a chance that they could be preserved even fifty years later.

Dr. Reimer's advice reminded me of a story about Lake Tahoe in the United States. That lake is cold and deep—at 500 metres, it's the fourth deepest lake in North America. In 1994, Donald Widecker went on a dive in the lake. His diving buddy noticed him sinking quickly, his respirator out of his mouth, but he was unable to rescue him. Seventeen years later, in 2011, a group of divers came across Widecker's body stuck in a crevice in an underwater cliff, eighty-two metres below the surface. Widecker was still in his wetsuit, wearing his scuba gear and air tank. A police officer involved in the recovery explained that at that depth the temperature is a constant two to three degrees Celsius, and "because he had a wetsuit on he was protected from the elements and was just remarkably preserved. From a pathological stand-point it's pretty incredible. Literally, it's a little spooky."[4] Nearly two decades after drowning, Widecker's body was perfectly intact.

The Lake Tahoe story gave me hope, but if we did find Jim and Abbie I wondered what their bodies could tell us about how they had died. Luckily Saskatchewan is just about the best place in the world to be a corpse wanting to tell a story, thanks to its pioneering chief pathologist from the 1920s, Frances McGill. Under her tutelage, modern forensic pathology was born on the Canadian prairies: "Dr. Frances McGill was the first person in the world to make this science a regular part of police investi-gations. Dr. McGill travelled by any means necessary, including dogsled and floatplane, throughout the vast province to inves-tigate suspicious deaths. Known as the Sherlock Holmes of Saskatchewan, she applied her training as a medical doctor to study crime scenes and protect and preserve evidence in ways that had never before been done."[5] It gave me confidence that, if we found Jim and Abbie, it would be Dr. McGill's legacy guiding the Saskatchewan authorities.

There was a lot of archival work to do to track down infor-mation about Jim and Abbie, about the search, and about busi-ness or other interests linking the key people involved—all of which might offer clues to motives for foul play, if that is what happened. However, no paper-based research would substitute for talking to people who knew the men and had direct knowl-edge of the search or for visiting the locations: the town of La Ronge, where Jim and Abbie lived, and Lower Foster Lake itself.

One of the first communications that I make is to Sergeant Geoff Bennett, of the RCMP's Historical Case Unit in Saskatche-wan, asking for any tips on how to proceed. He advises me that

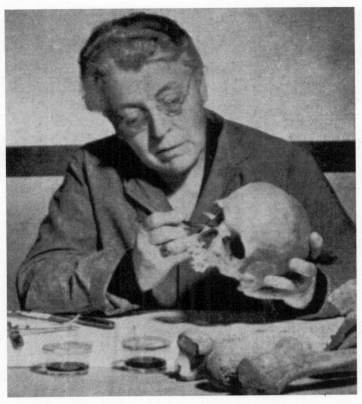

Dr. Frances McGill in her laboratory. *Source: Provincial Archives of Saskatchewan, call no. R-A12654.*

there are obvious difficulties with looking into a fifty-year-old missing persons investigation and suggests gathering whatever information is available publicly and speaking with surviving witnesses and family members. He cautions me that a major problem with investigations this old is that there are only a few people left with clear recollections of events, and they sometimes find it difficult to separate personal (first-hand) memories from rumours that they have heard over the years.[6]

With Sergeant Bennett's advice ringing in my ears, I wonder about my ability to track down family members, let alone surviving witnesses. But it is amazing how many people are still around and very much alive fifty years later: friends, family members, and colleagues of Brady and Halkett; people who knew their employer, Bill Knox, and other figures in the stories surrounding their disappearance; and people who participated in the search. Three are in their nineties (including Uncle Frank), and no one is under sixty, but they are spritely and sharp. I will become impressed by these tough old characters.

Speaking with witnesses and family members means travelling to Saskatchewan, and Deanna and I plan our initial trip to Saskatoon for March 2017 to interview Uncle Frank. We have to wait five months, but at the end of summer, in August 2017, we will also finally head to La Ronge to interview people about the disappearance—when clues about Jim and Abbie will come thick and fast, some of them hidden for decades in plain sight.

4
NOT JUST ANOTHER INDIAN

I have an outsider's view of northern Saskatchewan, coloured predominantly in shades of brown and white connected to its winters, though this is probably unfair. Amid this colour scheme, one image stands out. I heard repeatedly that in La Ronge Jim Brady had a little cabin that he had built himself—a tar-paper shack sixteen feet by twenty feet—full of books, and suddenly colours and ideas burst forth. Red books. Red ideas. His home was a beacon of learning that saw Jim through the winter and where he educated his friends, acquaintances, and drop-ins from far and wide. He had one of the best private libraries in the province with about 4,500 books, including revolutionary texts, classic nineteenth-century novels, poetry, sociology, race politics, philosophy, and political biography.

One of the challenges of writing about Jim is that in death his reputation has become so burnished. Everything that I read and everyone whom I meet who knew him have only praise. The terms used are consistent: "intelligent," "dedicated," "learned." But somewhere in all of this enthusiasm the man himself is missing. As a writer, I want to feel his presence and get a sense of those personal contradictions that we all have. The available sources are interviews, including our own, with people who knew Jim; his own writings and other people's writings about him; government documents that talk about the organizations that Jim helped to establish; and photographs.

A more complex individual emerges from sifting through these materials. The easy part is the activism that started when Jim was a young man in Alberta. He grew up in St-Paul-des-Métis (now just St. Paul), 200 kilometres east of Edmonton. Jim was a master strategist at planning campaigns to influence political debates, and, in a rare combination, he had the personality and skills to do grassroots organizing of Indigenous people around basic needs. Over several decades, he gained a reputation for his dedication to Indigenous causes, his erudite explanations of dispossession and struggle, his personal integrity, and his quiet magnetism. But Jim was also self-confident and sometimes stubborn, reluctant to change course once he had made up his mind.

Jim loved his people—their generosity, their knowledge, their willingness to find consensus and to engage in dialogue, and their sense of kinship. He told a professor at the University of Regina that "among Indians and Metis there is a sort of a loose fraternity. If you haven't got it, well they have, so all you have to do is go looking for them. I don't know a soul here outside of you people and the people at the University, but I'll bet you I won't starve in this town as long as there are any Indians or natives around. I'll just find out where they are and who they are and that's it, I'll be all right."[1]

Brady is not at the forefront of younger generations' consciousness, but he was a giant of Indigenous activism—and the history of community activism generally—in the North, helping to establish the Métis Association of Alberta, the Métis Association of Saskatchewan, and the Métis Association of La Ronge, as well as Indigenous fishing and timber cooperatives, credit unions, and adult education classes. Brady also had a profile across Canada. The *Globe and Mail* obituary described him as a "prospector and Métis leader born at Lac St. Vincent, Alta., on March 11, 1908; grandson of one of Louis Riel's soldiers; self-educated in politics and history; became leader among Métis of northern Alberta and Saskatchewan."[2]

To Métis and First Nations people, Jim was a hero and an educator:

> People would come here [to La Ronge]; sociologists (and one from Africa) . . . would drop in the hotel and ask [the hotel owner], "Have you seen Mr. Brady?"
>
> "You mean the Jim Brady in the little cabin?"
>
> "Yes, that's him."
>
> "Native?"
>
> "Yes, that's him."
>
> And [local white people] would be astounded to think this doctor in sociology and so on would be wanting to come and see such a poor individual in La Ronge. . . . To them, he was just another Indian on the street.[3]

This story—the visit of an African professor in the 1960s to seek the advice and wisdom of an Indigenous man in northern Canada—is exemplary. Because of his leadership and understanding, Jim was a magnet for people who wanted to make sense of the world.

For Indigenous people, he was also a bridge to the wider world of ideas and places, books being his key instrument. Anne Carrière-Acco, a Métis writer from Cumberland House, told how when she was a girl Jim stored some of his books in her father's warehouse and "told us we could read his books and we all did. . . . I read all the French classics. He had all of them. All the important books of that time; in the 1950s. Everything you had to read and it was a self-education. At the same time, it opened the world to us in a totally different way. When you read about Paris, you start wondering? Is it true you know, or is this a fantasy?"[4] Carrière-Acco added that Jim "was all about economic development, self-realization, self-actualization and self-determination. And we understood that language because you can say it in Cree."[5]

Even though for decades Jim had the energy to be an activist, by all accounts he was also pragmatic—even cynical—about people and what they could achieve. Surely it was the cynic in him that made him such a good strategist: he knew which battles to pick, never losing sight of the larger war. Jim was an "anti-leader," the smart behind-the-scenes guy who cast a shrewd eye at the malleable crowds and always kept a piece of himself private. His reserve and the difficulty that others had figuring him out have great appeal. In his activist work, Jim didn't want to be a frontman for the Métis. He was happy to leave that to his close colleague and friend, Malcolm Norris, who was formidable in this role.

The different angles of Jim's personality come through in different contexts. In the political context, Jim was tough and strategic, though these skills made him enemies. Politicians, civil servants, and clergy tried to expose his leftist politics to undermine his organizing of independent Métis associations, and the Hudson's Bay Company was against his efforts to establish independent Indigenous control of the fur trade. He was also targeted on the street. In Lac La Biche around 1937, "after distinguishing himself with particularly effective heckling at a political meeting, [Jim] was attacked by six local men outside the hall. The conclusion of the story, 'six men lying on the ground' may be an exaggeration, but it leaves little doubt about Brady's prowess as a fighter. He was big and powerful, prided himself on keeping physically fit, and was a boxer of some talent."[6]

To friends, family members, and people with good intentions, Jim was warm and welcoming. Tony Wood, a friend, said that to white people Jim "was another Indian, but to me he was someone I took so many of my problems to. And after you talked it over with Brady, you better believe it, he straightened you out and put you on the right track. . . . He would analyse your marriage and everything that went wrong with it, as well as your life and many other things."[7] James Carriere, a colleague, described him as "talkative and sociable" and how they went to parties together: "[Jim] was a great man to serve you a hot toddy any time. . . . Anything that you wanted to talk about, he was right there. And you'd talk about history right there. He was 100 percent and the first thing he'd come out with a bottle and 'Let's talk it over. Let's talk then.' And he could read all night and he could talk all night if you gave him a chance."[8] Sometimes Jim *did* talk all night. Carriere told of a time when they were out in the bush and slept under the stars by a campfire: "[Jim] used to like that, you know, sitting by the campfire Indian style. He would cross his legs like that and sit by the fire and talk."[9]

Jim shared his warmth and love, having several children with at least a couple of women. A stepdaughter, Isabelle, recalls how her mother, Cecilia, said that she had found her soulmate in Jim and that he was "loved very much by our family."[10] He had another daughter, Emma Jean, with Rema Bird, though that relationship did not endure. Jim supported both women and their children financially from the late 1950s until he died.

Two of Uncle Frank's daughters have childhood memories of Jim as always happy and great with kids and like a brother even though he was a lot older. The memory that I like the most is from his daughter Anne, who remembers him buying a tricycle for her sister Ruth's birthday and how they all used to ride it around. It is a universal picture: laughing little kids riding in circles around their proud dad.

Although Jim was sociable, he also craved periods of solitude and enjoyed being at home, where he would bury himself in a book, if he hadn't lent it to someone else. He liked to collect poetry—favourite topics being war, revolution, workers, and humour—and his wide reading included newspapers, of course, out of which he would cut recipes and household hints.

Photographs of Jim from the Second World War reveal other aspects of his character. In the Glenbow Archives in Calgary, there is one of him in military uniform looking youthful (at the time actually thirty-six) and determined: off to war to fight fascism. Jim spent eleven months as a gunner in a French-speaking regiment in combat in France, Belgium, the Netherlands, and Germany over 1944 and 1945. He enlisted late because initially

Jim Brady, 4th Medium Regiment, Royal Canadian Artillery, in the Netherlands, 1944. *Source: Glenbow Archives, NA-3517-2 Archives and Special Collections, University of Calgary.*

the government refused to let communists join the war effort. A second photograph also shows him in uniform, only this time it is after the war, and Jim has the exhausted face of someone who has seen too much. A later picture, from 1950, shows him in a clean white shirt, work pants, and boots, lounging on the roof of a barge next to a beautiful young woman, looking totally relaxed—clearly in another chapter of life after the war.

In keeping with the political atmosphere in Canada in the postwar period, Jim was tight-lipped about his political party affiliations. He joined the Cooperative Commonwealth Federation (CCF) after moving to Deschambault Lake, northern Saskatchewan, from Alberta in April 1947 (he was discharged from the army in Calgary in 1946). The CCF had swept to power in the Saskatchewan provincial election in 1944. But Jim was also a communist and joined the Canadian Communist Party's front, the Labor-Progressive Party, in 1947.* Communism had gained support across Canada in the 1920s, 1930s, and into the 1940s, and Jim thought that its ideology of a working class that ran its own enterprises independently of rich people was a good model for workers and Indigenous communities alike. This occasionally conflicted with his CCF membership. Although Saskatchewan's CCF government had social-democratic policies, it kept a distance from communism to increase its appeal to centre voters.[11] If you were known to

---

* The Canadian Communist Party was banned in 1940 after the outbreak of the Second World War. It was re-established as the Labor-Progressive Party in 1943 when its leaders were released from prison. Joining the Labor-Progressive Party effectively meant that one was considered a communist.

be a communist, then life could be difficult, not least because communists in Canada were under surveillance by the RCMP.[12]

Being a communist was even more difficult for Jim because he had to manage his political beliefs and activities in ways that did not undermine his reputation among northern Métis communities that were often religious, politically conservative, and skeptical of collective action. He wrote to Malcolm Norris about one local Métis leader who had been "particularly venomous in anti-communist tirades of an extremely vicious and personal nature."[13] Jim managed his public persona by restricting how much he gave away about his political beliefs. On the topic of communism, he would, outside certain circles, "come out so far and that was it. [Then] he would turn around and talk about something else."[14]

Like a number of people in the North who have several jobs to make ends meet, Jim had two distinct professions, both practical: the first as a community organizer, the second as a prospector. Notwithstanding his propensity toward cynicism, both jobs are for optimists. Community organizers need to have faith that they can unite people and build a better future, but prospectors are the real optimists. "They have something not too many people have. It's a complete faith in the future, an optimism that next year's going to be better. . . . Prospectors, when they make money, often throw it away. They feel 'Oh, well.' The fun to them was the search, the dream."[15]

Jim must have had the dream. It was the only way that he could have kept going for so many decades in his chosen professions. However, the community organizer in him must also have wanted delivery—of change to the system and betterment of Indigenous lives.

Jim's community organizing role had different phases, but the two key ones were establishing and organizing Métis associations in the late 1920s and 1930s and then running various community economic development projects in the late 1940s, 1950s, and early 1960s, funded by the Saskatchewan Department of Natural Resources (DNR).

Many activists go through a phase of thinking that the way to change the world is from inside the system, so it is understandable that Jim accepted work with the government despite previously working to reform it from the outside. The government has such potential to initiate and support systemic change. But it is also where people go for a steady salary, a career, or more power. When these things make them comfortable, their activist aspirations can go the way of birch leaves in a cold October wind.

By the mid-1960s, Jim was disillusioned with the government and its programs. As he told Norris, "after 20 years of monumental blundering the CCF in the North are no longer a political force. The Indians and Metis detest them. After 30 years of association with them it is a rather bitter admission."[16] Turning away from the government, Jim refocused on helping his immediate community in La Ronge and on prospecting. It was a move away from politics and development programs and toward "a new life, new interests, new people."[17] "I liked it," Jim said, "because it is [an] outdoors frontier type of life. You are not actually tied down like a factory slave of punching a clock, and you have considerable initiative and to a great extent you have considerable independence in deciding your program for yourself."[18]

His work as a prospector is key to investigating the disappearance because it connects directly to his outdoor skills and the various theories of what happened out, by, or on Lower Foster Lake the day that they disappeared. Contemporaries say that Jim was a great bushman, though he had little interest in hunting. He had prospected on and off seasonally for many years, and in the mid-1960s with no government-funded employment he went back to prospecting. Scholar that he was, Jim had educated himself about geology and then later completed a prospecting course. Bill Knox described how Jim was interested in "anything to do with the nature of things, so he was naturally interested in rocks and ore structures. Scenery interested him." In a later comment that sounds more like an accusation, Knox added, "I suspect he was a romantic."[19]

I suspect he was too. Jim had a whole creative side about which he rarely seems to have spoken but which is clear from works left behind. He was an artist—a photographer—and a writer of letters, essays, and history. He was a superb wordsmith and an inveterate diary writer; he wrote about class, Métis society, and the North, and he transcribed Indigenous oral histories. The Glenbow Museum holds over 1,000 photographs taken by Jim and over 4,000 paper documents. He could "read equally well in French as in English," noted Knox. "But he was the sort of a chap, you know, one out of a million, that might study Jean Jacques Rousseau on the original which you probably can't find anybody in northern Saskatchewan doing that today."[20]

Despite finding a lot of material about Jim, I found it all a bit disembodied. I was attracted to his intellect, his values, and his motivation to improve the lot of Métis and First Nations people, but I still lacked a physical sense of him. What was his voice like? What did it feel like to be in his company? Looking for something extra from the collection of interviews conducted by Murray

Dobbin with various people who knew Jim, I realized that I had overlooked the interview of Roberta Quandt, the wife of Allan Quandt, a friend, fellow communist, and former colleague of Jim, who lived with the Quandts for about six months in the 1950s.

Roberta was not a fan. "As a woman, I respected Jim's mind and I respected his philosophy about life and his analysis of situations but, as a woman, I disliked him because he was extremely chauvinistic."[21] For one thing, Jim disrupted her household. Cathy Quandt, a daughter, told me that her mother aspired to the 1950s homemaker model and kept their house ship-shape. When Jim stayed with the family, he expected Roberta to make him breakfast and look after him, even while she spent the day doing chores and managing young children. What's more, he wore his boots into her house. In the evenings, when Allan came home, Jim expected Roberta and the children to be quiet and make dinner while he talked to Allan. It was "a monologue. . . . I resented him."[22] Roberta appears to have been the only person with whom Jim did not discuss politics: "In fact, days would go by when he didn't even say good morning."[23] The dislike between them was clearly mutual.

It appealed to me that not everyone liked Jim. It made him more human, less perfect, even though the traits that irritated Roberta would also have irritated me—just as the traits that she did appreciate also appealed to me. Jim was a visionary, but like most of us he was also a product of his era.

His ideas about the roles of women were in keeping with the male chauvinism of the time, but Jim was more complicated than that. He also wanted women to engage in politics, and he chose a partner, Cecilia Dorion, who was fiercely independent and did not live in the shadow of any man. I also heard from a

Jim Brady and Anne Walther, Edmonton, Alberta, May 1948. *Source: Glenbow Archives, PA-2218-298, Archives and Special Collections, University of Calgary.*

La Ronge resident who described how, as a girl, she went along with her mother to Jim's cabin with a group of local Cree women. She recalled that Jim kept a tidy cabin and would serve tea to the women as they discussed politics. Although he could understand some Cree, Jim couldn't really speak it, and one of the women who attended knew only a few words of English. The others would therefore translate back and forth to keep everyone in the conversation. A man who arranged afternoon teas so that he could talk politics with local women would have stood out in either the Indigenous community or the white community in 1960s Canada.

Many people have stories about Jim's everyday kindnesses—lending people money, giving them a meal, sending a rosary to a nun in a convent, taking the time to listen to their personal problems—and his insistence that Indigenous people be treated with respect. Jim asked Allen Sapp, the famous Cree artist from North Battleford, to paint his portrait. Sapp remembers this because he said that Jim was the first person to ever pay him for his art.[24]

Jim Brady leaping from a plane to stake a claim during the July 1957 "uranium rush" in northern Saskatchewan. *Photo credit: Alan Hill.* James Brady and Plane (02). *July 1957.* Source: *Provincial Archives of Saskatchewan Métis Photographs, Regina, call no. R-B6761-2, Gabriel Dumont Institute.*

There are several photos of Jim in a suit in a city, probably attending official meetings with the government. However, my favourite image of Jim is part of a montage and an article in *Saskatchewan Mining News*, which sent a reporter to shadow Jim and Berry Richards during the uranium staking rush that unfolded on July 12, 1957, when the government released aerial surveys to the public.[25] In the photograph, Jim is leaping to shore, axe in hand, from a float plane that has just landed. A real action shot. Jim is focused and skilled: the self-educated activist and Métis political leader who wants to change the world is equally at home as a working man in the bush.

5
THE ENIGMA OF ABBIE HALKETT

The fate of anyone who has not had his or her ideas and actions analyzed, or character described and written down for posterity, is that there is much less available to understand the person. This is even more the case for anyone who lived pre-Internet because the web inevitably offers small insights into an individual's life through Facebook posts or online obituaries. Even if the person does not create such pages, there is often a child or grandchild who does.

This is the fate, it seems, of Absolom Halkett. Although a remarkable man, he ended up in the background in all of the reports made about the disappearance of the two prospectors. In La Ronge, there is a black marble slab erected to the memory of Jim. At the end of the inscription, it says that Jim "disappeared in northern Saskatchewan while on a prospecting trip with a Cree friend in June 1967." The "Cree friend" was Abbie, written into history as an enigma. The *Globe and Mail* obituary of Jim from 2003 doesn't even mention that another person disappeared with him.[1]

Yet Abbie was a Lac La Ronge Indian Band councillor from 1954 to 1965, having become a councillor in his late twenties (a young age to be a councillor), and he was elected to this role because of his leadership qualities and community knowledge. Nevertheless, what exists on the public record is fleeting and contradictory because it captures snapshots at different moments, with no attempt to make sense of the whole person. To someone who never knew him, to a writer, this makes Abbie harder to grasp.

His family members feel differently, of course. For them, he is blood. They can poke themselves in the thigh and know that it is flesh born of his flesh. They have personal and family stories and a deep hunger to know more about him. The woman with whom Abbie lived when he disappeared, Annie, gave testimony in Cree at the coroner's inquest into his disappearance (Annie was fluent in Cree and spoke no English). She still lives in La Ronge but is now very elderly, her mind frail, and we could not meet her.

Before Annie, Abbie was married to Martha Young, with whom he had a daughter, Rema, and he had seven grandchildren, including one granddaughter who carries his name: Amanda Halkett. She put out a plea on Facebook for information and explained how she has suffered because of his disappearance: "I really wish that I can find help to search for his roots and history, so I may be able to piece together the rest of this mystery. . . . I need to find out about him and his family. My family."[2]

We searched through the interviews with Dobbin, and in the interviews that Deanna and I conducted we asked people about Abbie in order to understand the dynamics between him and Jim and how the former might have reacted to being lost in the bush. Abbie is repeatedly described as a follower who would have accepted Jim's lead no matter what, but the more I read, this image of Abbie and his passivity falls away. Jim's star was so bright that it simply outshone others.

In various documents, Abbie is portrayed as Jim's prospecting buddy, but there is much more to their relationship than this. Someone who knew both men told me how Jim used to tease Abbie about wanting to be an Anglican minister, but it is impossible to imagine Jim working closely for weeks on end out in the bush with someone who did not share the same political values, or have similar physical skills, regardless of their religious beliefs. Indeed, though Abbie was less of a political activist than Jim (anyone would be), he was educated, smart, a stalwart of the community, and a motivated organizer. Jim was his good friend.

According to Liora Salter, a left-wing student and activist who met Jim and Abbie in La Ronge in 1966 while working for the Neestow Project,* Abbie was "definitely a political person. . . . I had the feeling that [Jim and Abbie] were in some kind

---

*   The Neestow Project was inspired by the Civil Rights Movement in the United States. It attempted to replicate in Saskatchewan Indigenous communities the same methods of organizing used by African American communities, including through support from outsiders such as white students. Its goal was to mobilize people to fight racism and push for institutional reform. Some of the organizers had direct involvement with the Civil Rights Movement. Malcolm Norris was one of the project directors. See Robert Mahood, interview with Murray Dobbin for the oral history project *Biographies of Two Metis Society Founders, Norris and Brady*, September 10, 1976, PAS, tape IH-394, 2, http://hdl.handle.net/10294/1408; and Ken Mitchell, "The Trouble with Helping the Metis," *Maclean's*, June 18, 1966, 1–2.

of fairly constant contact, that they did have some kind of political vision that they weren't about to spell out, that they saw it as a very long-term effort that they might not live to see the end of."[3] Salter had wanted to interview Indigenous people for the Neestow Project but "had been making absolutely no progress," so she went to Jim to get his advice. He clearly saw Abbie as someone able to engage authoritatively in discussions about Indigenous issues and political possibilities and advised Salter to talk to him: "You go see Abbie Halkett out on the reserve. Why don't you do that?"[4]

Like Jim, Abbie had several jobs. He was a trapper and a prospector—good at both by all accounts—and before that a schoolteacher. His community activism seems to have been done on the side, and these are all good points for starting to understand Abbie. But it is a personal connection, in fact, that provides my first real insight into him.

All through Deanna's childhood was an oft-repeated family story about how her kohkum, her grandmother, a well-known healer, had cured Abbie Halkett from blindness. But it was only in 2002 that Deanna discovered that the man who had disappeared with Jim Brady was the same man who had been healed by her kohkum. This is the story, which took place in the 1940s or 1950s, introduced by Deanna's Uncle Vic: "Abbie Halkett went to school, he was educated. An old man from Stanley Mission came to him, just like you would do in the old days, and told Abbie that he wanted him to marry his daughter. Abbie was going to be a minister; he didn't know what to say, but he didn't want to marry her this way. That upset the old man, who cursed him and told Abbie he was going to become blind." Abbie did start going blind, and here Deanna picks up the story:

In the bush in northern Saskatchewan, going blind makes life terribly difficult. Abbie came to Kohkum because he knew she made medicines and might be able to help him.

Kohkum wasn't sure what to do right away. She told Absolom Halkett to give her some time to think about it. That night she had a dream that a bear was encircled and trapped in the boughs of willows, the leaves of the willow choking him. She woke up and went and collected these leaves and made a poultice. When the young man returned, she gave him instructions to put this paste on his eyes at night and, every morning, go to the lake and wash it off. Three times he would have to do this. If it didn't work, there was nothing more she could do for him.

The ending of the story was always the same, with the same anticlimactic comments: It worked. But Abbie never did become a minister.[5]

There are other stories about Abbie and dreams. After he went missing, Grandpa Halkett had a dream in which he "saw the lost prospectors tied together and at the bottom of the lake."[6] And Abbie himself had had a premonition before he had left that last time. As he told his family members, he had a feeling that he might not come back from his trip with Jim. At the time, they didn't think much about it, but it rang in their ears once the search began. These stories made me want to know more about Abbie's spiritualism: both his Christian faith and his Cree spirituality.

Dobbin's interview with Gwendoline Beck of La Ronge adds to the picture: "Abbie Halkett? Well, he was a young fellow that went out to Indian [r]esidential schools,* was very brilliant, and went on to university. Came back home. But he lived in one of those little log shacks that are tore down now. . . . Went prospecting quite a bit and worked in the bush."[7]

Thanks to oral history, Abbie comes to life: his ambition as a young man to be an Anglican minister; his desire to start a family but not according to the old ways; the blow of blindness but then his seeking out—his faith in—a traditional medicine woman; and the value that he placed on education, not to mention his brilliant mind.

I have found only four photos of Abbie. One is titled "Native Prospectors from La Ronge at Blackstone Lake, circa 1955."[8] There are five men, Abbie in the middle, standing at the entrance of a rough log cabin. It looks like it is early to mid-summer given the foliage on the trees and the fact that they are wearing long sleeves (to fend off mosquitoes). There are tools lying around and a couple of canoes. The men are in typical bush work clothes—Abbie is wearing overalls—and all look a bit awkward. They are not used to being photographed. Abbie is

---

*   Canada's Indian residential school system involved the systematic removal, often by force, of Indigenous children from their families. The system was funded by the federal government and controlled by churches. Its purpose was to isolate children from their communities in order to assimilate them into dominant white culture. About 150,000 children were put into boarding schools, where they were forbidden to speak their languages, contact family members, or practise their cultures. Many were physically, emotionally, and/or sexually abused. The system started around the late 1800s, and the last residential school closed in 1996.

Abbie Halkett in a group of Indigenous prospectors from La Ronge, circa 1955. L TO R: Simon Eninew, George Patterson, Abbie Halkett, James McKay, and Joe Bell. *Photo credit: E.F. Partridge. Reprinted with permission from Saskatchewan Mining Association.*

twenty-seven, tall, straight, slim, with a strong jaw, an open face, and a shock of black hair under a cap set at a jaunty angle.

The second photo of Abbie was found in the collection of Deanna's extended family. It appears to have been taken about the same time as the first because three of the five men—including Abbie—are in it, and they are wearing the same clothes in both photos. This time there are four children in the image, and the group is in a clearing with a white canvas tent and bedding on a clothesline in the background. Abbie is right in the middle, smiling, surrounded by friends and children. It is a wonderful image.

In the third photo, Abbie is thirty. He has aged a lot from the previous photos, no doubt because of all the work outdoors. He is in casual clothes sitting on a stoop outside a shop in the sunshine next to a woman dressed for a party. His weathered

Abbie Halkett at a bush camp, circa 1955. L to R, rear: Joe Bell holding Kathy Bell, Abbie Halkett, George Patterson. Front: Patsy Patterson, David Clinton, Richard Bell. *Reprinted with permission from Patterson family.*

Abbie Halkett and Mary McKenzie Carlson sitting on stoop, 1958. *Source: Lac La Ronge History Group, Facebook. Printed with permission of the Carlson family.*

L to R: Adam Henry Charles, John Morin, and Absolom Halkett, July 25, 1966, at a tree-planting ceremony at La Ronge Hospital, attended by Premier Ross Thatcher and MLA Allan Guy before meeting with members of the Lac La Ronge Indian Band. *Photo credit: Don Neely. Reproduced with permission from Craig Neely.*

face has a big grin—hat again at an angle—and Abbie surely knows how incongruous he looks next to this young woman.

The final photo was taken on July 25, 1966, on the occasion of a tree-planting ceremony at the La Ronge Hospital, attended by Premier Ross Thatcher and MLA Allan Guy. Abbie is standing with two companions, and the three of them are wearing suits and have fresh haircuts because, following the ceremony, the premier and MLA were scheduled to meet with members of the Lac La Ronge Indian Band. Abbie is the very image of the model citizen: straight-backed and proud, waiting patiently as a community representative to meet the visiting dignitaries.

Although a practical-minded bushman, Abbie was also a man who felt things: a calling (to spiritualism), relief and joy (at a second chance to see), ambition (to improve the lot of his community), and happiness at the simple pleasure of sitting in the sun next to a pretty woman. I would like to say that I kept an analytical distance from Abbie and Jim, but that is not the truth. The past came close and pulled me in, and I came to care about them a lot.

6
PRECAMBRIA

Prospectors and geologists are practical, task-focused people thanks to the isolation, extreme weather, tough ground, and occasional tough company, including bears and colleagues. Their famous get-together is the annual conference of the Prospectors and Developers Association of Canada (PDAC) in Toronto, which attracts tens of thousands of people from around the world. The conference was once legendary for its bacchanalia: an orgy of strippers, prostitutes, and alcohol as the men from the bush met with big-city investors and together got drunk. Jim and Abbie most likely would have enjoyed the party but also been alternately fascinated and repulsed by the corporate wealth on display.

Not surprisingly neither the PDAC party crowd nor their sober prospector and geologist colleagues think of themselves as artists. However, like landscape painters, they have an artist's eye for colour (because it discloses mineral content), are sensitive to texture (geological ripples, rifts, and outcrops), and make maps that are an art unto themselves.

Maps are key to shedding light on the events of the disappearance: the coroner's inquest wall map, covered in marks indicating key points in the RCMP's search for Jim and Abbie; Google Maps, which I had pored over again and again checking distances; the poster-size 1:50,000-scale map of the Foster Lakes area that I ordered from the Saskatchewan government and carefully unrolled on my living room table (the map is clean and white, unmarked like fresh snow, but somewhere within its contours are Jim and Abbie); and, in complete contrast, the Saskatchewan Geological Survey map and its riot of colours lying along a northeast-southwest axis mirroring the lakes and rock formations themselves: brushstrokes of teal, pink, grey, mustard, and purple, with daubs of plum, green, red, and gold. Each colour represents specific geological domains crashing into and fracturing each other—quartzite giving way to arkose, slate to fanglomerate, mica schist to psammopelitic gneiss. The words themselves spike and fragment in the mouth. It is a funky representation of rock at least 500 million years old from the Proterozoic era, and among all this colour is the uranium for which Jim and Abbie were looking.

Northern Saskatchewan, compared with southern Saskatchewan, is wrought from different materials. No fertile, rolling wheat fields and native grasslands. Instead, everywhere there is water, muskeg, forest, and the rock that entices prospectors to try their luck and test their knowledge. It is exhilarating, with monumental rivers and granite-like winds. There are parts of the world that feel animated because they literally move, such as the Bay of Fundy or Hawaii's lava flows. Northern Saskatchewan is rock solid on the Canadian Shield—the great ancient swath of Precambrian rock more than 4 billion years old, right at the surface of the Earth, that extends from the Arctic to the Great Lakes—yet it, too, feels alive.

This is where Jim and Abbie made a living. They did contract prospecting, working from season to season for different exploration firms, in turn engaged by mining companies to stake claims, ground-truth claims with surveying equipment following staking, or assay (test the quality of) mineral "showings"— literally spots where minerals "show" through to the surface. Many minerals are found in northern Saskatchewan, and gold is a perennial favourite, but Jim and Abbie were sent in to assess radioactive showings on an old uranium claim that had come open again (a claim has a term limit unless a mine is developed).

In popular culture, a prospector stumbles upon a showing— for example, a thick vein of gold—files his claim, then, presto, starts digging up the riches with a pick and shovel. If only it were so easy. Prospecting involves multiple activities and stages, and an array of factors needs to be right before an actual mine will ever be developed: quantity and concentration of mineral, market demand, price, infrastructure, labour, the ability to get equipment to the site, environmental and social agreements, government permits, and investors with the cash to get the whole process going. Investors—attracted by promoters and developers—are involved along the whole mining chain, but prospecting itself is a specialized business.

Prospectors can be hired on a salary or *grubstaked*, meaning that someone pays for their field and food costs (their "grub") in return for their work staking, sampling, or doing other tasks and a share in any potential future profits. Today mineral exploration often starts with aeromagnetic or electromagnetic surveys and computerized data analysis, and ground-based

Jim Brady writing on a claim post. *Photo credit: Alan Hill.* Jim Brady, a staker for Pre-Cam Explorations and Development Ltd., finishes marking the first claim. *July 1957. Source: Provincial Archives of Saskatchewan, R-A13459-3, Gabriel Dumont Institute.*

prospecting comes later. But until the 1970s the process started with people out in the bush looking for new mineral showings.

Prospectors like Jim and Abbie were dropped off with 1:12,500 claim maps, axes, a compass, a hammer, and a backpack, plus geophysical instruments such as Geiger counters when looking for uranium. They also carried tags for marking claims, bought in advance from the Mining Recorder's Office. When they found something promising, a claim was staked. Staking involves making cut-lines (paths) through the bush and cutting corner posts with initials and dates to establish boundaries. Legally a stake (or post) cannot be a living tree, so prospectors typically cut a tree into a tallish stump, add a tag, and write the date and their initials. For a claim to be valid, it must be registered at the nearest Mining Recorder's Office within thirty days.

After securing the legal right to claim, the prospectors return to dig trenches to obtain fresh samples of mineralized rock from below the surface, map the area in detail, and ground-truth any geological anomalies using surveying equipment. Samples from trenches are tested for mineral content, and if they are positive a diamond drill is used to obtain samples from greater depths to determine if there is an economically viable orebody.

When minerals are discovered, there is a staking rush in which hordes of miners arrive to stake claims. For example, in the 1940s and 1950s, when uranium was discovered in northern Saskatchewan, the bush was crawling with thousands of people. Many of them were new at prospecting, in some cases assisted by the Saskatchewan CCF government's Prospectors' Assistance Plan introduced in 1949 (relaunched as the Prospectors' Incentive Plan in 1972). Others were second- or third-generation European immigrants.

But Indigenous people, including Métis from the late 1700s, had always been in the bush, used minerals, and had knowledge of many deposits.[1] There are many stories of mineral "discoveries" by Europeans that were known to Indigenous people because of their geological shape, texture, or colour (if not the mineral content). Yet, despite their knowledge, Indigenous people were typically given a support role in exploration, such as portaging, constructing buildings, or cutting claim lines—low-paid jobs.

On the whole, the mining industry offered different opportunities to different communities, with some clear racial divisions.[2] Constraints on jobs in Canada were never codified in law as they were under the apartheid regime in South Africa, but social prejudice and a colonial system of education designed to create inequality achieved a similar effect. Visitors to a company office or managers' quarters would find a sea of white faces, and to a mine canteen only a few brown faces, and inevitably the latter workers were in labouring roles, though there were some mechanics and equipment operators. In some mines, Indigenous people occasionally worked underground—positions that carried more responsibility, higher pay, and more status—but this was very unusual before the 1960s.

It was only when the government opened Prospectors' Schools in the North that more Indigenous people had chances to improve their technical skills and get into the industry. Like trapping had done during the fur trade heyday, and before aerial surveys took over, old-style prospecting gave Indigenous people economic independence that also allowed them to continue to hunt and trap seasonally and to stay closer to family members. (The fur season is late fall to early winter, so prospectors who had traplines switched to trapping during this period.)

The government's Prospectors' Assistance Plan was part of an effort to promote and develop the mining sector and the North by providing free food, transportation, and mineral data to prospectors. Prospectors' Schools were introduced to develop a cohort of technically competent people. The earliest version of these schools in 1948 and 1949 provided classes exclusively in Cree, an early initiative by the CCF to promote prospecting among the local Indigenous communities. However, the expanded version of Prospectors' Schools introduced in the 1950s, and the Prospectors' Assistance Plan generally, saw assistance go overwhelmingly to southerners and not to local talent (white or Indigenous). In 1972, the situation changed again with the relaunched Prospectors' Incentive Plan. An annual invitation-only course was held for six weeks in La Ronge that specifically targeted northerners. In this course, according to government records, it was "common for two-thirds of the students to be Indian or Metis and for some individual students to be more fluent in Cree or Chipewyan than in English."[3]

Jim Brady was part of the first intake of the government's revamped Prospectors' School held in La Ronge in 1953. He also earned the second highest mark. He would never settle for being a second-class labourer who did the bidding of a white prospector, for he dedicated his life to overthrowing such a system. Both of his parents had worked in skilled jobs (his Métis mother was a nurse; his Irish father was a land agent, storekeeper, and postmaster), which surely had an impact on his aspirations. As for Abbie, he had studied to be both a teacher and a priest and had ambitions well beyond labouring on a mineral exploration team. In the North, where jobs are scarce, people become

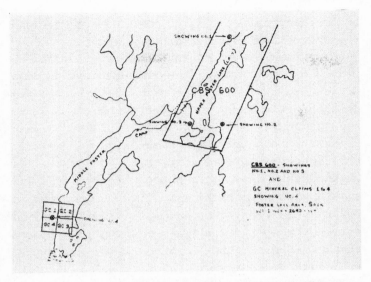

CBS 600: The claim that Jim and Abbie were supposed to explore on Middle Foster Lake. *Source: Saskatchewan Precambrian Geological Laboratory, La Ronge.*

entrepreneurial and do all sorts of things to make a living, including working seasonally at different occupations. Jim and Abbie thus came to work together for at least five summers in a row. Although there were other Indigenous people involved in mineral exploration, as a Métis-Cree team of prospectors Jim and Abbie were nevertheless unusual even in the 1960s.

Local contractors, invariably non-Indigenous, were more open to hiring Indigenous people, probably because of personal relationships, but big companies largely recruited white people from southern areas rather than Indigenous people. This remains a common practice today; however, bolstered by legal interpretations of treaty rights, Indigenous communities are now in a better position to broker agreements with companies to employ people from their own communities.

Jim and Abbie were employed on their last prospecting job by Pre-Cam Exploration and Development, managed by Berry Richards. Richards had no qualms about hiring Indigenous people and first hired Jim in 1957. Pre-Cam was based in La Ronge and did prospecting work across the North. It was contracted to assess radioactive showings in an old claim—property CBS 600 in Saskatchewan Map Reference 74A 11-NW-0026—at the top end of Middle Foster Lake that had come open again and could be restaked. The work involved using a Geiger counter to sample the radioactivity of the showings and collecting physical samples for assaying. Jim and Abbie were engaged to do four specific tasks: completing a radiometric survey, outcrop mapping, trenching, and sampling.

That Jim and Abbie embarked on their trip in early June is significant in that conditions might have been a contributing factor in their deaths. Identifying new showings, staking new claims, or digging trenches for sampling are all difficult when the ground is frozen and there is a lot of snow, though occasionally explosives are used to create trenches and access samples. Because of the enforced break over the winter, prospectors are keen to get into the bush as soon as the snow melts and they are able to see and sample rock. Because they need to travel by float plane and canoe, they must also wait for the breakup of winter ice—which starts about May—and then the melt so that they can travel freely and safely land on water. The prospecting season was therefore well under way when they travelled to the Foster Lakes. However, June is also the month when hungry sow bears and cubs leave dens to forage and aroused males are starting to look aggressively for females with no cubs.

As far as the La Ronge community was concerned, when Jim and Abbie left on their trip to the Foster Lakes in early June 1967, they were seasonal prospectors who did other jobs on the side. But was everything as it seemed? Behind the public façade of prospecting, there are rumours that Jim and Abbie were business partners with three other men in a mining company that will become central to the stories of their disappearance and possible murder.

7
THE DROP-OFF

t is midday at Missinipe on Otter Lake on June 7, 1967. Gerald Mitchinson has almost four hours to collect and load his next passengers. He is a theology student from Manitoba who also has a pilot's licence, and he has come to Saskatchewan for the summer flying season. Mitchinson has been working for Norcanair for four days, flying a float-equipped twin-engine Beech plane. It is his first time flying in the area and his first time transporting a canoe lashed to his plane. Berry Richards has hired Norcanair to transport Jim Brady and Abbie Halkett to the Pre-Cam claim, and Mitchinson is the pilot.

Because flying is expensive, prospectors go as far north as they can by road before hiring a plane to access claims by air. Otter Lake, sixty kilometres northeast of La Ronge, is a popular jumping-off point. Richards drives Jim and Abbie to Missinipe for the rendezvous. Richards has a set of maps necessary for the trip: a four-miles-to-the-inch topographical map for the pilot and half-a-mile-to-the-inch claim maps for Jim and Abbie showing the property location, lakes, and other geographical features.

There are three Foster Lakes: Upper, Middle, and Lower. On the map, they look stacked on top of each other in a cluster in mid-northern Saskatchewan. Each lake is long and skinny, lying along a northeast to southwest axis typical of the Precambrian geology of the area. Richards marks on Mitchinson's map where they need to be put down on Middle Foster Lake and then gives everything else to Jim and Abbie.

A third passenger gets on board. Alec Sarabin is an employee at the nickel-copper-platinum mine at Rottenstone Lake and will be dropped off on the way to Middle Foster Lake. The men load the aircraft, and Richards tells Jim and Abbie that he will visit them in about a week to check on their results and to re-supply them with food.

The weather is patchy, so visibility is not the best. They take off at 3:20 p.m., and Mitchinson's logbook[1] records their arrival at Rottenstone Lake at 3:50 p.m.—the thirty minutes include taxiing to takeoff, flying, and circling to land at the other end. Sarabin is dropped off, and after ten minutes the plane heads to Middle Foster Lake. They fly over the top end of a long, skinny lake. Mitchinson asks Jim if it is Middle Foster Lake, and Jim confirms that it is.

They do a fly-over to check for depth and rocks, then circle around and come in low up the long lake—a rocky ridge rising steeply out of the water to starboard, forested country to port. The logbook records the arrival as 4:55 p.m. They start setting up camp, and it takes two hours to get organized. Mitchinson helps them to unload their canoe, camping gear, tools, and food, and he doesn't take off again until 6:55 p.m. The sky is still cloudy, but there is quite a bit of light since the sun doesn't set until after 9:30 p.m. at that time of year.

Mitchinson returns to Otter Lake and then goes on to La Ronge, getting home at 9 p.m. But all is not well. He feels unsure that he has set Jim and Abbie down in the right place, and this nags at him over the coming days.

Jim records in his diary that on the night of June 7, when they are dropped off, it is close to freezing, and snow starts to fall, continuing heavily into the next day. "Very cold wind in the evening. Had to eat in tent," says his June 8 entry.[2]

Huddling in their tent that night, Jim tries to contact La Ronge by radio but cannot get through, though Alec Sarabin at the Rottenstone Mine hears his radio call. Alec and Jim talk briefly, and Jim mentions that it is snowing heavily and jokes that he needs snowshoes. He says nothing about being on the wrong lake. They set up a schedule of calls at regular times so that Sarabin can pass on any messages to Berry Richards.

On the morning of June 9 around 9:30 a.m., Sarabin waits for Jim's scheduled call, which never comes. He then radioes their camp. Silence.

The first critical date after this point is June 12, when Mitchinson is on a trip to Upper Foster Lake. On his return to La Ronge, he flies directly over Lower Foster Lake, and this possibly triggers his next move. After landing, Mitchinson goes to his boss and tells him about his concerns about the trip on June 7. It is not an easy report to make for a pilot new to the company: after just over a week on the job, he confesses that he thinks he dropped off two men at the wrong location *five days* earlier. But this is as far as Mitchinson's report ever goes.

* * *

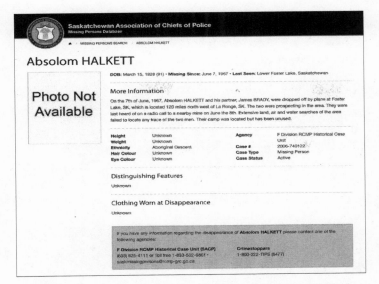

Absolom HALKETT

DOB: March 15, 1928 (91) • **Missing Since:** June 7, 1967 • **Last Seen:** Lower Foster Lake, Saskatchewan

Photo Not Available

More Information

On the 7th of June, 1967, Absolom HALKETT and his partner, James BRADY, were dropped off by plane at Foster Lake, SK, which is located 120 miles north west of La Ronge, SK. The two were prospecting in the area. They were last heard of on a radio call to a nearby mine on June the 8th. Extensive land, air and water searches of the area failed to locate any trace of the two men. Their camp was located but has been unused.

Height	Unknown	**Agency**	F Division RCMP Historical Case Unit
Weight	Unknown		
Ethnicity	Aboriginal Descent	**Case #**	2006-740122
Hair Colour	Unknown	**Case Type**	Missing Person
Eye Colour	Unknown	**Case Status**	Active

Distinguishing Features

Unknown

Clothing Worn at Disappearance

Unknown

If you have any information regarding the disappearance of **Absolom HALKETT** please contact one of the following agencies:

F Division RCMP Historical Case Unit (SACP)
(633) 825-4111 or Toll free 1-833-502-6861 •
sask.missingpersons@rcmp-grc.gc.ca

Crimestoppers
1-800-222-TIPS (8477)

Abbie Halkett missing person notice from Saskatchewan Association of Chiefs of Police Missing Persons database, 2020. *Source: Saskatchewan Association of Chiefs of Police website.*

My mind goes to Lower Foster Lake, and I try to imagine Jim and Abbie's final days and hours. Did they realize that their map did not match the topography, or were they trying, mentally, to make it fit? Did they conclude that they were on the wrong lake or that they had the wrong map? Were they dead by the time Mitchinson told his supervisor that he thought he made a mistake? Did they know that they were about to be murdered? Did they see the murderer and try to reason with him, or did they run, scrambling through the bush, to get away? If they were lost, did they give up hope or panic? It is hard to imagine either Jim or Abbie panicking. Or did calm set in as they awaited their fate? Were they attacked by animals, or did one, or both,

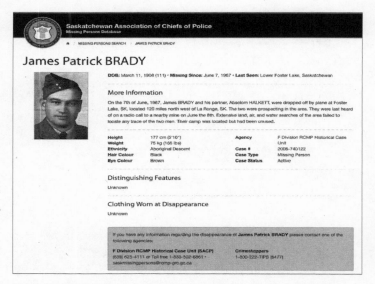

Jim Brady missing person notice from Saskatchewan Association of Chiefs of Police Missing Persons database, 2020. *Source: Saskatchewan Association of Chiefs of Police website.*

somehow become injured? Did they slowly starve or freeze to death, huddled together? Argue with and blame each other? It is hard to imagine this either. Did Abbie call on the spirits and the ancestors, or on the Lord, to give him comfort at the end?

The fact is that, after the final radio call on June 8, 1967, with Sarabin at the Rottenstone Mine, Jim and Abbie vanished. They left almost no clues about what might have happened, and, as I came to discover, what were deemed to be clues in the subsequent police search are open to dispute. There were no signs of an accident, of an animal attack, of an intruder, of murder. There were no bodies or remains of bodies. Deanna's mother might as well be right: "Taken by UFOs!"

8
THE SEARCH

ragedies in small communities have immense impacts. They are heightened when victims are well-known pillars of their society in their prime—Jim Brady was fifty-nine and Abbie Halkett thirty-nine—who have connections to young and old alike, have families, are part of the working population, and help to run their community.

Richards has no inkling when he flies north on June 16, 1967, that what he is about to discover will trigger a series of events to be remembered for generations. After finally locating Jim and Abbie's deserted campsite at the wrong lake, Richards flies back to La Ronge and, at 2:30 p.m., contacts the police. He tells them that Jim and Abbie are missing, probably for a week, and requests a search party. He also informs their families, and word spreads like wildfire throughout La Ronge and the network of people throughout the North who knew them. Uncle Frank's father, Pete Tomkins Jr., goes to the home of Malcolm Norris, Jim's Métis activist colleague and friend, to give him the news. Norris breaks down and cries out: "They killed him! They killed him!"[1]

ASSIST SEARCH PARTIES

...d search for two ...s. Absolum (Abbie) ...d Jim Brady, both ...La Ronge area, who ...been heard from in ...in two weeks, has ...ped up by both ...nd private parties. ...chards, well known ...ert geologist, and a ...e seen strapping a ...a Cessna 180 which

also carries supplies for members of a ground search party who are scouring dense bush in the lower Foster Lake region where the men were last seen. Mr. Richards, who has a working interest in the Rottenstone Mine as well as doing specific surveys for other mining companies, said the missing prospectors had left camp without supplies of

any kind, not even matches, intending to return that night. They must have become lost very quickly for we just have not been able to find a a "they must have become lost very quickly for we just have not been able to find a trace of them." Mr. Richards said. He said, the searchers had been hampered by not finding any trace of cooking

fires. But he pointed out that the cranberry crop is exceptionally good this year and that the men, both experienced northerners, would be able to survive for some time on a berry diet. This picture was taken at Otter Lake, 210 miles north of Prince Albert, as the plane prepared to take off Wednesday.
—Herald Photo.

Local RCMP Seek Direction

Prince Albert RCMP were awaiting word today from headquarters at Regina as to what steps to take next in the search for two prospectors lost in the lower arm of the Lower Foster Lake region.

RCMP Call Off Northern Search

Prince Albert RCMP announced today they have called off the search for two prospectors missing in the Lower Foster Lake area for more than three weeks.

Abbie Halkett and James Brady, both 40 and both from the La Ronge area, were prospecting for the Pre - Cambrian Exploration Company about 310 miles north of Prince Albert.

The area north and south of where the men were thought to have been last working was covered extensively by air and foot and dogs were also utilized in the fruitless search.

A collection of news clippings about the disappearance, 1967. "Assist Search Parties," *Prince Albert Daily Herald*, June 30, 1967, 3, Provincial Archives of Saskatchewan, call no. micro A-1.575; "Local RCMP Seek Direction," *Prince Albert Daily Herald*, July 5, 1967, 3; and "RCMP Call Off Northern Search," *Prince Albert Daily Herald*, July 7, 1967, 2. *Reprinted with permission of Bill Smiley Archives, Prince Albert Historical Society.*

There is a frenzy of mobilization—of planes and ground search parties—and a retracing of their last steps. The same day the police aircraft stationed in Prince Albert is sent north. The commander of the local RCMP detachment, Corporal Clyde Conrad, takes advantage of the long daylight hours and that evening flies to the lake. The *Prince Albert Daily Herald* runs several stories about the disappearance and subsequent searches, capturing the initial flurry of activity in an article titled "Assist Search Parties." The article has an accompanying photo showing Richards kneeling as he and another man strap a canoe to the float of a Cessna 180 being readied for take-off at Otter Lake to fly into the wilderness and join the search.[2]

Lower Foster Lake is 160 kilometres due north of La Ronge. Its main section is forty kilometres long by no more than one kilometre wide, but there is a system of bays and islands poking east through the southern shoreline about a third of the way up its length. Approaching it from the air in a float plane, the lake would have looked like it went on forever.

Corporal Conrad does a preliminary reconnaissance of Jim and Abbie's camp. He walks half a mile along the lakeshore and a short way up the stream that runs into the top end of the lake until he comes to the canoe pulled up on the east bank. Conrad later describes the placement of the canoe in such detail that it puzzles me until I realize his thinking, that the scene might hold clues to what Jim and Abbie were doing when they left the canoe and, more importantly, in what circumstances: "Now this canoe was partly pulled up on the shore line and part of it was still in the water. . . . [It] was a 17-foot canoe and had a three and a half horse power motor on the back of it. And it was tied with half a granny knot to a tree near the shore line. It wasn't a full knot it was just a half a knot. One paddle was thrown up on the shore line; the other paddle was in the canoe itself. . . . There is also a prospector's pick in front of the canoe."[3]

From the air, the police search the area to the east of the canoe but find nothing (because the canoe is on the east bank, they assume that Jim and Abbie set out in that direction). Corporal Conrad requests that a sniffer dog and handler from the RCMP's Saskatoon Dog Section be brought to the campsite, and the next day Constable Baldwin and his dog, Satan, arrive. It is hoped that Satan can track the men or, if they have had a misadventure and died, smell their bodies and lead the police to their location.

Satan finds nothing over the two days that he is in the area. There has been snow and rain, so perhaps the scent has been diluted or covered, making it difficult for Satan to find it. On June 19, the weather closes in with fog and more rain, and there is no visibility from the air. The search is halted temporarily, but back in La Ronge its expansion is being planned.

Indeed, the search for Jim and Abbie becomes one of the biggest of its kind in terms of the number of people involved, the intensity of the search of land and lakes, and the period over which it occurs. A police aircraft, a DNR plane, and a charter aircraft spend about 100 flying hours searching from the air. Other aviation companies—Athabaska Airways, La Ronge Aviation, Norcanair, and Thompson Camps—also join the search. It is not just an RCMP search but also a search by people who have come from far and wide: friends, family members, acquaintances, political colleagues, and people from the DNR, mining community, and Métis and First Nations communities: "We had every native person that could walk on two legs offering to go out at absolutely no pay."[4]

Rapidly the search escalates with multiple teams spreading out across different locations.[5]

JUNE 20:   Ground search parties spread out around the immediate area of the tent and canoe; the creek downstream from the canoe is dragged for bodies. Nothing is found.

JUNE 21:   Berry Richards and Art Sjolander, who form one of the ground search teams, head east from the canoe. They come across two sets of tracks in soft green moss that they are able to follow for about thirty metres, then cigarette butts (Jim and Abbie both smoked), then axe marks in a tree. Sjolander wanders farther, perhaps more than a kilometre, and comes across a single white wooden match lying on the ground. The colour indicates that it is fairly fresh out of the box.

JUNE 22:   More snow; activities are halted.

JUNE 23:   Richards, now in one of the search aircraft, spots a small wooden raft on the west bank of Lapointe Lake, in an uninhabited area about twenty kilometres south-southeast of the campsite. The raft has been partly pulled onto the shore. The theory develops that Jim and Abbie must have realized that they were in the wrong location and were trying to walk out to the Churchill River and made the raft to get across Lapointe Lake. The Mounties shift their focus to the raft and send in a helicopter with divers to search Lapointe Lake.

JUNE 24: The RCMP search the area around the raft and the southern end of Lapointe Lake. It is thought that, after rounding the southern end, Jim and Abbie either headed east toward Rottenstone Mine or continued due south on their way to the Churchill River. Nothing is found.

JUNE 25–26: Aircraft scan possible routes that they might have taken from the raft. A ground party searches around the north end of Lapointe Lake.

JUNE 27: Another ground party—which includes Lloyd Mattson, a friend of Jim's, and several other La Ronge locals—is flown in to Lapointe Lake.

JUNE 28: Searches continue in several locations. Nothing is found.

JUNE 29: An aircraft is redeployed to search the area from Rottenstone Lake all the way to the Foster River (which flows out of the bottom end of Lower Foster Lake in a roughly southward trajectory) since this is where Jim and Abbie would have been if headed to Rottenstone Mine.

JUNE 30: Poor weather halts the air search.

JULY 1:   Having found nothing between Lapointe Lake and Rottenstone Lake, the aerial search is shifted to the area south of Lapointe Lake.

JULY 2:   The police aircraft returns to Prince Albert for an overdue maintenance check; ground searches continue with three canoes.

JULY 3:   The ground search continues.

JULY 4:   Poor weather hampers the aerial search, but activity continues by canoe.

JULY 5–6:   The ground search continues.

JULY 7:   The RCMP pull out "Native searchers," who are flown back to La Ronge.

JULY 8:   The police send their aircraft back to search the north side of the Churchill River. Nothing is found. The official search comes to an end.

The date is unclear, but shortly after the end of the official search "one of the group of Indian searchers found a campfire at the north end of Lapointe Lake." The RCMP "checked this campfire and there was evidence that moss and roots had been eaten by somebody."[6] The police assumed that it must have been Jim or Abbie.

After the official search is called off, the La Ronge community forms a committee to expand the search and raises money

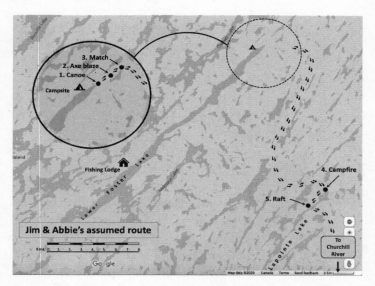

Map of RCMP search area and approximate location of the five "clues." *Source: Created from Google Maps. Adapted by Michael Nest.*

to mobilize men and canoes. A reward of $1,000 is also offered for any information on what has happened to Jim and Abbie.

The search evolves around the five clues found. Mr. D.C. Prefontaine, the lawyer representing the attorney general at the coroner's inquest, sums up the logic: "The area from the canoe, the blaze marks [axe cuts in a tree] and the match, the campfire and the raft would all be pretty well in a line heading south from Lower Foster, eh?"[7] The assumption is that Jim and Abbie realized that they were lost, made a blaze to mark their trail, lit a cigarette (with the match), made a campfire to keep warm, and then built the raft to cross Lapointe Lake—all in an attempt to walk out to the south, as indicated by this trail of clues.

Lloyd Mattson stays on in the area and keeps searching by canoe through the lakes and waterways until mid-August. When available, the police aircraft is also redeployed to fly over the entire area bordered by the Foster River to the west, Churchill River to the south, and Paull River to the east—an area of about 5,000 square kilometres. Over the summer, people occasionally report footprints and other signs to the police, but neither Mattson nor the RCMP ever find any trace. Jim and Abbie truly have vanished from the face of the Earth.

Three details fuel speculation that Jim and Abbie's disappearance is suspicious. First, the fact they used a shack tent, which has a wooden frame and is roomier than a classic triangular tent. Shack tents are used for longer periods in the bush, and locals think its presence suggests Jim and Abbie's planned stay was longer than they, or Berry Richards, had let on (i.e., more than simple staking and sampling).[8] Second, the fact their canoe was tied to a birch stump. Birch is notorious for rotting, so bushmen avoid tying their boat to them out of fear it might pull loose and float away. Locals interpreted this as meaning someone other than Jim and Abbie had tied the canoe to the stump—because Jim and Abbie would never do this.[9] Third, another campsite with mineral cores—tubular rock samples drilled out of showings—is found near Jim and Abbie's campsite. This second campsite is deserted, and the owner is never identified, generating speculation someone else had been there but then left in a hurry when Jim and Abbie arrived.[10]

These details are never definitely resolved. There is no record in the coroner's inquest or Murray Dobbin's interviews that Berry Richards was ever asked about the shack tent, and the birch stump may have less significance than first imagined.

In June, the creek where Jim and Abbie's canoe was found would have been high and fast-running, so the canoe should have been pulled right up onto the bank, not half-sitting in the water—but a temporary tie-up to a birch stump on dry ground should have been fine (although one wouldn't have left it there for a week).[11] As for the second mining camp, it was probably from the first exploration work on the claim before it reopened, allowing for it to be restaked by Jim and Abbie.

Four months later, on November 14, 1967, however, a most perplexing clue appears. James Tough, working for Great Plains Mining Company, which owns a claim beside Lower Foster Lake, is cutting a survey line east of the north end of the lake when he comes across an axe mark in a tree with the following written in the blaze: "J.B., A.H., 9-7-67." *Jim Brady, Abbie Halkett, 9 July 1967*. The blaze is about eight kilometres from Jim and Abbie's camp, and judging by the weathering Tough thinks that it is several months old.

The RCMP never investigate this clue, but there is speculation at the coroner's inquest that the 7 was mistakenly written instead of a 6—for June—because a date of June 9, 1967, would fit with the day on which it was assumed that they left camp for the first time to do some preliminary work. Given that it is a very important part of a prospector's job to mark claims on the specific dates that they are made, it is doubtful that the date is an error. However, why July was indicated instead of June is a mystery.

The RCMP conclude that Jim and Abbie must have gotten lost, and, like thousands of other Indigenous people in Canada, they become officially listed as "missing." Statistics. The jury for the coroner's inquest, however, think that there is more to the story: "We, the Jury, feel that James Brady and Absolom Halkett are missing in the Foster Lake area after June 9, 1967 and due to lack of evidence we can only recommend the verdict be left open."[12] That is, they do not unequivocally accept the RCMP's verdict of misadventure causing them to become lost but keep open the possibility that their disappearance has been caused by other factors.

9
MISGIVINGS

That there was an exhaustive search for Jim Brady and Abbie Halkett is clear, but I have to get *inside* the search to understand its logic and decisions—why it was conducted the way that it was and whether there is anything left off the public record, not necessarily for suspicious reasons, but because it was assumed and therefore not considered sufficiently unusual to be recorded. Our assumptions are silent, but when we examine them they tell us so much about what we think.

There are three main sources of information about the searches that occurred after Jim and Abbie disappeared. First is the transcript from the coroner's inquest, which happened in March 1969, twenty-one months after their disappearance. Second are Dobbin's interviews about the search and the calculations made at the time. These, however, are not contemporaneous accounts of what happened; statements taken during or right after an event are the gold standard for investigations because memories are fresh. Instead, Dobbin's interviews were recorded in the mid-1970s, nine years after the disappearance.

```
C O R O N E R ' S    I N Q U E S T
```

```
La  RONGE,        SASKATCHEWAN
```

I N Q U I R Y:

RE: JAMES   BRADy

- and -

ABSOLUM   HALKETT

(Missing Persons,
⸸Foster Lake District, Saskatchewan.

INQUEST, AS NOTED ABOVE, HELD AT LA RONGE, SASKATCHEWAN,

IN THE ANGLICAN CHURCH HALL, COMMENCING AT 8:00 P.M., THURSDAY,

THE 27th DAY OF MARCH, A.D. 1969.

CORONER: W.C. Chanin.

Mr. D.C. PreFontaine,   Agent for the Attorney General.

Mr. M. Simonot   for Mr. Barry Richards.

Reported by Geo. Symon, Official Crt.Reporter

J U R O R S

Jack McGUNIGAL,   Foreman of the Jury.
Bert VanCOUGHNETT.
Edwin CLARK
Walter K. RIESE
Jean POIRIER.
James BRYCE

Jurors All Sworn by the Coroner.

Constable W.T. Markus, R.C.M.P., Court Officer.

THE CORONER: GENTLEMEN OF THE JURY, you are

Sworn to consider on behalf of the Queen, who the deceased

are and how, when and where James Brady and Absolum Halkett

came to their death. You will endeavour to discover the

cause of death as as to be able to return a true and

just verdict on this occasion. As there are no bodies

to view we shall continue by calling witnesses next.

Coroner's inquest transcript, front page. *Source: Saskatchewan Office of the Chief Coroner. Provincial Archives of Saskatchewan, accession no. R78-132; call no. R-E177: 1–2. Used with permission of the Government of Saskatchewan under the authority of the Queen's Printer, 2019.*

Third are Deanna's and my interviews with people involved in the search. Their memories are fifty years old and make Dobbin's interviews look contemporaneous in comparison.

Over the many months that I scrutinize these documents, curiosity about the logic of the search turns to puzzlement and then to doubt. In turn, the doubts become outright misgivings.

MISGIVING 1: LOST?

If Jim and Abbie thought that they were lost, the conclusion of the RCMP, then why didn't they sit still and signal for help? Everybody who lives in the bush knows that this is what you do. There are two standard ways to attract attention. First, light a fire. June is the start of the fire season, and every pilot in the North would have been on the lookout for smoke, and Jim and Abbie would have known this (Jim even rented his cabin to a smokejumper, Uncle Frank!). Second, chop down several trees so that they fall parallel into a lake. This pattern is unusual and visible from the air. A storm or a beaver might cause one tree to fall, but not two or three in a row, so when they are spotted there is a good chance that humans were involved in felling them.

Numerous people who knew them had no doubt that Jim and Abbie knew what to do in the bush. Special Native Constable Philip Carriere, who participated in the search, said, "I think if a person was lost out there, and two of them especially, they would have made a lot of signs."[1] Art Sjolander, a geologist and prospector involved in the search, noted that "there isn't any way that these two men, even being on the wrong lake, were going to get lost. I don't give a goddamn, they would find their way back to where they came from. Any good bushman can do that.

He'd go back to where he come from. He might have to make a certain different route sometime, or you do get confused at times, . . . [but] . . . you'll get back. . . . And I've always said that there was something unnatural about this whole thing, you know."[2]

What about the fact that Jim and Abbie's map was for the wrong area? That would definitely have confused the two prospectors. Because the topography was "similar" to the map—given the resemblance of the north end of Lower Foster Lake to Middle Foster Lake—it would have added to their confusion. However, being confused is different from being lost. Even without compasses, because of the location of the sun, they would have known north from south and therefore east from west. Lower Foster Lake, from where they set off on their first excursion, was their main point of reference, and—though their map did not match the land—this does not necessarily mean that they could not retrace their steps to their camp. Their situation was very different from being dropped off somewhere totally unknown to them, where they had no idea where they were, with the wrong map—an experience that would totally perplex anyone trying to rely on the map.

I don't know yet what happened to them, but the possibility that they were lost diminishes with everything that I read about the case. Maybe Jim and Abbie were running from someone and didn't want to attract that person's attention by lighting a fire or chopping down a tree. Maybe, because they were running, they didn't have time to light a fire or chop down a tree.

The fact that Jim and Abbie did not signal for help suggests two things to me: either they did not think that they were lost, or—if they thought that they were lost—they were unable to signal for help because something was stopping them: they died quickly, they were incapacitated, or they were worried about creating a signal. Any of these scenarios could involve a third person, a bear, or a calamitous accident.

MISGIVING 2: IRRESPONSIBLE AND INCAPABLE?

In the archival documents and testimony about the disappearance that I scour, Jim and Abbie are routinely portrayed by people who knew them to be patently sensible men. Suddenly, however, a potential bias rears its head in what I'm reading. In Dobbin's interview with Conrad, Dobbin asks him if it were not peculiar that Jim and Abbie decided to walk out of the bush to safety (the RCMP's assumption) instead of staying where they were and waiting to be rescued. Conrad replies,

> I think it was kind of stupid on their part because if they had stayed put when they found they had been lost, they had a radio and they knew somebody would come in if they didn't check in. If they had stayed where they were, well then they would have probably been saved without too much difficulty. . . . But again Brady was a kind of an oddball type. He had a mind of his own. . . . You know, he worked for the DNR [Department of Natural Resources] years ago and whatnot and he was kind of a bullheaded type of individual and it's not too unconsistent [sic] with the way he thinks.[3]

Was Jim an "oddball"? By Canadian standards, I suppose that he was. In the 1960s, Canadians did not much care about Indigenous Peoples, their rights, their treatment, nor were they prepared to stand up for them. Jim did care about these things, and that made him odd.

"Had a mind of his own"? He sure did. The herd had no appeal to Jim Brady.

Was he "bullheaded"? That he was *determined* and knew how to *focus* are evident from his activist work in Alberta and Saskatchewan, but the idea that Jim was so obstinate that he would single-mindedly try to walk out of the bush rather than light a fire is preposterous. Jim thought carefully about *everything*. There was a good reason that he was the backroom strategist rather than the charismatic, talking-off-the-cuff leader for the Métis movement of the 1940s, 1950s, and early 1960s.

Later in the interview, Conrad adds, "You know, for the two people involved, they certainly didn't use their head. It was quite stupid on their part that they didn't stop somewhere, light one hell of a fire because you know, that time of the year is a fire season."[4] Is Conrad actually assuming here that neither Brady nor Halkett, adult men with a ton of experience and knowledge, would not have known any of this? Is he implying that these two Indigenous men were too stupid to know any of this? Is that what he is thinking?

Thirty-three years earlier, in 1934, James Brady and Malcolm Norris gave testimony to the Royal Commission on the Condition of the Halfbreed Population of the Province of Alberta, which considered whether the government should grant land to the Métis. Brady and Norris saw the enemy of the Métis to be Canada's conventional belief that they were "hopeless indigents, irresponsible and incapable of governing their own affairs."[5] Three decades later it appears that this was exactly how Corporal Conrad thought of Jim and Abbie. He concluded that they had decided to walk out, instead of lighting a fire, because they were two hopeless Indigenous men who didn't have the brains to realize that lighting a fire would have saved them. It was a ludicrous proposition.

MISGIVING 3: HOLLERING?

Farther along in Dobbin's interview, Conrad notes that late in the evening on June 25, just before dark, two employees from Rottenstone Mine "heard some yelling. And it sounded like a person yelling. And a pounding noise."[6] The hollering came from the draw that Jim and Abbie were assumed to have been heading through on their way to the Churchill River, yet "neither [of the employees] could be sure if it was a human or animal."[7]

I read and reread this part of the interview. The mine workers heard *what sounded like people yelling*, from a part of the bush where no one lived permanently, a couple of weeks after Jim and Abbie had disappeared, at a distance that they could have reasonably covered in this period from Lower Foster Lake, and at a location that they could have been at if they were headed for the Churchill River. I am dumbfounded.

Conrad, though, dismisses it: "That could have been indicative of them running into a female bear with cubs trying to ward her off."[8] To be fair, an unusual number of bears were reported in the area—Sjolander had counted seven from the air, when one might normally see one in a decade.[9] But waving away this information is flabbergasting. Could these sounds not also have been "indicative" of an altercation between human beings? Of defensive shouts? Cries for help? Might the "pounding" have indicated an attack on Jim and Abbie? Nope. Unbelievably—tragically—it seems that Corporal Conrad was unable to accept that they disappeared for any reason other than character weakness and lack of intelligence.

MISGIVING 4: WAS THE RAFT THEIRS?

The eureka moment of the Mounties' search was finding the raft on the west bank of Lapointe Lake. It gave the search a focal point and was the catalyst for the theory that Jim and Abbie were heading for the Churchill River. The raft was featured in the coroner's inquest, and Conrad was asked about it: "The raft was cut from trees in the immediate area. Examination of the cut marks on the logs used for the raft and also stumps indicated that the axes that were used were dull. The native guides we had with us on examining the chips were of the opinion that they were fresh . . . [w]ithin the last few days. . . . And from all appearances it had to be Brady and Halkett who had attempted to construct this raft and it appeared that they were going to utilize the raft to cross Lapointe Lake."[10]

I've spent hours listening to lawyers examine witnesses and have personal experience of journalists' questioning, and there is a similar style: they ask their questions in a way that gives them the answers they want, in order to validate the conclusions they've already made, in support of the narrative they've already composed. It's a jaundiced view, and I constantly seek evidence to the contrary about these professions. In contrast, the style of investigators—police or otherwise—is typically different because they want to know what *really* happened. Unfortunately there are nuances in Corporal Conrad's testimony that lead me to believe that his mind was made up much earlier about the "narrative" of Jim and Abbie, and by the time of the coroner's inquest Conrad wasn't going to change it.

Here's what I mean. The "native guides" were "of the opinion" that the chips "were fresh." What Conrad does not say is that the guides believed that Jim and Abbie *had made the raft*, and that's because Conrad never asked them this question. I suspect that he "knew" the answer: the freshness of the chips "proved" that the marks were recently made. It seems that in his mind there was nobody else in the area who could have made the raft, and therefore it could only have been built by Jim and Abbie.

"From all appearances it had to be Brady and Halkett who had attempted to construct this raft." Which "all appearances"? This might just be an expression, but it's also important to note that there was nothing else there! The only additional clue was that dull axes had been used, but Jim and Abbie's axes were never found, so we don't know if they were dull or not. There really was nothing else on which Conrad could found this conclusion.

Testimony at the coroner's inquest was given by people directly involved in the search, but they were all white. The testimony of the Indigenous guides was not sought—why would it be when the search commander had been present? Police officers work in a hierarchical organization, and the word of commanding officers is the word of all others. During our research, I met a couple of Cree men who had participated in the search. One told me that "the RCMP just took command and told us what to do."[11] The other said that "we didn't think we were in the right place, but we just did what the police told us to do."[12]

It is the job of the RCMP to manage searches for missing persons, so they cannot be blamed for taking command. The problem is when they don't listen to—or don't even think to ask the opinions of—the people who know the bush, and who know the people who have gone missing, much better than they do.

As it turns out, the Indigenous guides had quite a few opinions about the raft. Jacob McKenzie, a Cree trapper from Cumberland House involved in the search, agreed that the raft had been recently made—in the spring "before the ice went out"—but said that it had been trappers in the area who had made it.[13] Dobbin also asked Philip Carriere for his opinion:

CARRIERE: I'd say it was some trapper. It could have been some trapper made it you know because it didn't look recent to me.

DOBBIN: Because Sergeant[14] Conrad says he remembers it being a recent one.

CARRIERE: Well, yeah, it looked recent alright but it was within the year, yeah.

DOBBIN: Not that recent.

CARRIERE: It was. But I doubt if these guys would just make a raft and not make a big fire so somebody would find them, eh. The raft itself was right alongside the river [lake] and if they went a little ways, they could have crossed the river anywhere because the river was down.[15]

As Carriere says, if Jim and Abbie were trying to cross Lapointe Lake, why would they put the energy into making a raft when they could have crossed the river "anywhere" or made a "big fire"? (People in the bush invariably use matches to light fires to boil water and cook, and both men were smokers, so it is reasonable to assume that they were carrying matches, though it is possible that the matches had become wet or been lost.)

The oddest thing about the raft and its apparent role in Jim and Abbie's attempt to walk out was a tiny detail in its construction. Sjolander examined the raft first-hand. It was made of five or six jackpine logs held together by two cross-pieces kept in place with a rusty nail at each end. There was a "very old, abandoned trapper's cabin on the opposite side" of the lake,[16] and the conclusion at the time was that the four nails must have come from this cabin.

So let's get this straight. Jim and Abbie needed to cross the lake to continue on to the Churchill River, so they decided to build a raft. They wanted some nails to hold it together and spotted the old cabin on the opposite side of the lake, so they *walked around* the lake—"you could walk across the creeks at either end," says Sjolander—to get the nails. They then returned to the first side of the lake, built the raft, but left it on the lakeshore and didn't use it. But they continued on to the Churchill River anyway. It doesn't make sense.

Can we be sure that Jim and Abbie themselves knew they were lost? It might be assumed that, because they were on Lower Foster Lake, the topography they were seeing did not match the map they had of Middle Foster Lake. However, the north ends of both lakes have similarities: the width is roughly the same (narrow); each has a creek emerging from muskeg into the north end; each has a second creek on the western shore with an area to camp not far from the end; and each has a smaller lake of almost identical size to the east. Comparing the lakes on a map at the same time, it is easy to pick out their differences, but if actually walking through the country there are probably sufficient similarities to think that the map in hand is the correct one.

Nevertheless, it is possible that Jim and Abbie figured out they had been put down in the wrong place and realized they were actually on Lower Foster Lake. In this case, they were not lost because they knew where they were. However, they might have feared that others would not be able to find them because they were in the wrong location and decided to head to the Churchill River anyway. But flowing south out of Lower Foster Lake is the Foster River, which directly leads to the Churchill River, and Jim and Abbie would have known this (the Foster is a well-known river). They could have used their canoe to travel this route, a course of action far easier, and quicker, than attempting to walk out.

Together, these misgivings make me doubt the "lost" theory. The fact that yelling was heard near Rottenstone Mine suggests that people in the woods were being confronted with a danger, but this occurrence was never investigated. It was *assumed* that Jim and Abbie were lost but too daft to signal for help; it was *assumed* that they tried to walk to the Churchill River based on a hypothetical trajectory leading from the canoe, to the blaze mark, to the match, to the campfire, and to the raft, but this assumption stemmed from the inability of the people leading the search to think of anyone else who might have left these signs. It appears that Corporal Conrad wanted to defend the RCMP's search at the coroner's inquest, and to do that he had to defend the logic on which it was based.

10
FINDING TRUTH
IN STORIES

The idea that truth can be found in oral history is too often dismissed in settler cultures in which knowledge is thought to be connected to written records, formal education, or professional expertise, a specialized endeavour that only people with certain attributes—such as scientists, historians, and lawyers—are capable of having. An expert has to be able to *see* something, or *document* something, or *prove* something, before it will be accepted as fact.

Indigenous stories about events, especially if the people are poor and lack formal education, and especially if those stories come from culture and country rather than science and modernity, rarely stand a chance. Instead, such knowledge simmers below the surface and is shared in the home and community, away from people whose knee-jerk response is to challenge or doubt or discount it.

An example is the "discovery" by a scientific expedition of the British Polar Exploration ship HMS *Erebus* in the Canadian Arctic in September 2014. The *Erebus* vanished 168 years earlier, in 1845. Its sister ship, HMS *Terror*, which disappeared during the same voyage, was found two years later, in 2016. Both ships were part of the expedition led by Captain Sir John Franklin to find the Northwest Passage. There were repeated searches for the *Erebus* and *Terror* over the centuries, and traces of seventy crewmen had even been found, but experts and historians deemed the disappearance of the two ships a "mystery."

The Guardian reported that the *Erebus* and *Terror* were found "in the same area of eastern Queen Maud Gulf where Inuit oral history had long said a large wooden ship sank" and that the "mystery seems to have been solved by [a] combination of intrepid exploration—and an improbable tip from an Inuk crewmember."[1]

"Inuit oral history had long said. . ."

"An improbable tip from an Inuk crewmember."

That crewman, Sammy Kogvik, had been on the expedition ship for a day when he told the following story to the operations director. Six years earlier Kogvik

> and a hunting buddy were headed on snowmobiles to fish in a lake when they spotted a large piece of wood, which looked like a mast, sticking out of the sea ice covering Terror Bay. [Kogvik] stopped that day to get a few snapshots of himself hugging the wooden object, only to discover when he got home that the camera had fallen out [of] his pocket. Kogvik resolved to keep the encounter secret, fearing the missing camera was an omen of bad spirits, which generations of Inuit have believed began to wander King William Island after

Franklin and his men perished. When [the operations director] heard Kogvik's story, he didn't dismiss it, as Inuit testimony has been so often during the long search for Franklin's ships.[2]

Kogvik's "improbable tip" was the piece of information that led the expedition to the precise location where HMS *Terror* sank. The operations director paid attention because he had learned the value of local Indigenous knowledge from the earlier discovery of HMS *Erebus*. Parks Canada, when announcing that the HMS *Terror* had been found, noted "the ongoing and valuable role of Inuit traditional knowledge in the search."[3]

If Kogvik had decided to talk earlier, five questions basic to any investigator would have solved this centuries-old "mystery."

Who are the spirits in Queen Maud Gulf?

What do they do there?

When did they come?

Where are they?

Why are they there?

His answers would have made clear that the spirits had come with the ships and been lost. Shipwrecked, in fact, but they had stayed close to the *Erebus* and *Terror* in Queen Maud Gulf.

So what do the local people of La Ronge, the Indigenous people there and around the community, think happened to Jim and Abbie? Which "improbable" tips or oral stories exist there regarding the disappearance of Brady and Halkett?

Most think that they were murdered.

Uncle Frank and Lloyd Mattson interviewed local Indigenous people who had been involved in the search, and they all said "oh, they were killed. Murdered." Understandably Frank got angry at this point: "They would listen to a white person who didn't know what they were doing. Everybody knew they were murdered, and no one said anything about it." Frank thought that it was weak of Indigenous people to hold an opinion about something but do a white man's bidding—search for lost persons rather than investigate their murder—when it was at odds with what they believed. "It pisses me off!" Later, in a softer mood, he added that "it's like the residential school system. You never question authority."[4]

For Indigenous people, centuries of hiding—hiding physically, hiding their children, hiding their languages, beliefs, cultures, personalities, and opinions—has had an enduring legacy of pain and distrust of outsiders and authority. I came across a dramatic example of this mistrust and attempt to stay out of sight when researching Abbie and Jim, and it told me something about their lives and influence in La Ronge.

Liora Salter, the activist who worked with Jim on the Neestow Project, described to Dobbin her visit to the La Ronge First Nation after she was sent by Jim to speak to Abbie:

> The reserve was an incredibly cold and hostile place at that point. And as you know, La Ronge, the reserve, is essentially in the middle of town. And the sewer stops on one side [of the reserve] and starts on the other and the power stops on one side and starts on the other. And [band members] have to [have water delivered] by the truck and they have to pay for water by the barrel. And it was the oldest generation of Indian Affairs houses, the one-room cabins papered inside with

newspaper. So I walked down the reserve and I walked real slow. And everybody is out on the door-sill and as soon as I walked by they disappeared into the house, just disappeared. So I got to the house that was supposed to be Abbie's, and I say, "Is Abbie Halkett here?" And there must have been twelve people in the house, you know, and nobody answered. And I said, "Jim Brady sent me." And all of a sudden everybody came out of every house and I was taken into the house and I was given total freedom to talk. . . . There was really an underground of political sentiment going on and it took a long time for trust, but Jim Brady's name was an automatic trust factor. [The community's thinking was that] Jim Brady would not have sent me if I was not okay to talk to.[5]

It is difficult to believe that everyone in those multigenerational households full of children was miserable, so the "cold and hostile place" that Salter first perceived was likely the face that the community chose to show to outsiders for the sake of protection.

Indeed, hiding behind—surviving behind—a wall of silence when faced with authorities from the outside was a theme that preoccupied Uncle Frank, possibly because he spent his life doing the opposite: provoking authority, breaking down walls, stating his mind, and fighting to be included in decision-making. When I finally got to meet Frank and we had our first conversation about Jim and Abbie, out of the blue he told me that their disappearance was "like that Osborne case."[6]

Helen Betty Osborne was a nineteen-year-old Cree woman raped and murdered by four white men in the small town of The Pas, Manitoba, in 1971. According to Manitoba's Aboriginal Justice Implementation Commission, "initial police efforts centred on the possibility that Osborne's murderer was one of her friends or was known to them. RCMP officers rounded up her friends and questioned them. They were all Aboriginal." It was only when an anonymous letter naming suspects was sent to the RCMP in May 1972 that police turned their attention to the white men. Yet, despite numerous comments that the suspects themselves made to people and friends in the community over the years about being involved in the crime, no one ever came forward with information. Charges were not laid until 1986, fifteen years later, after the police had made a public appeal for information and people had finally come forward willing to talk.

At first, at the time of my conversation with Uncle Frank, I'm confused about the link between the murder of Helen Betty Osborne and Jim and Abbie, but as I learn more about Canada and Indigenous people I begin to make the connection: it's another case of people in the community being sure about what happened but not saying anything. It's another story of justice impeded.

No one in the local community thinks that Jim and Abbie got lost. It is too improbable for experienced bushmen. No one thinks that a bear killed them; bear attacks are rare, and it is unlikely that both men were attacked and killed; and, even though it was cubbing season, this part of Saskatchewan has black bears, not the more dangerous grizzlies. An attack by a bull moose is a possibility, but it wasn't the rutting season, and a moose wouldn't have killed both men or made their bodies disappear. Although wolves live in Saskatchewan, no one suggests that they were killed by wolves.[7] Drowning is also a possibility but unlikely for both men.

In the minds of the locals, this leaves one option, drily summed up by Lloyd Mattson: "Death by violence isn't exactly uncommon in the north."[8] Which prompts the question: who wanted them dead?

PART 2
PARALLEL
SWEEP

Parallel sweep: the aircraft procedure used when a search area is large and fairly level, only the approximate location of the target is known, or uniform coverage is desired.

11
UNCLE FRANK'S THEORY

As a Cree-Métis man himself, Uncle Frank kept alive questions and doubts about the disappearance of Jim Brady and Abbie Halkett, and getting his version of events was the priority for determining the direction of our research. Deanna and I decided to rendezvous in Saskatoon in March 2017 so that she could introduce me to him. We all felt more comfortable with this rather than having me simply turn up expecting him to participate in an interview.

Deanna had told me something about northern Saskatchewan, and I had read Maria Campbell's *Halfbreed*, so I knew that it was a place full of woods and lakes and families with varying degrees of happiness and challenges. I had given little thought, however, to the rest of the province. The south. All I knew is that famous artists and writers had come from there or had made it home—Joe Fafard, Yann Martel, Joni Mitchell, Roy Kiyooka—and that it was flat and cold. I figured that the prairie landscape must free the mind and that the cold must be good for focusing, both useful to artists (I was sitting through a

Montreal snowstorm just then, and the blizzard outside made me want to write, write, write). Saskatchewan's wide-open spaces must be a bit like Australia, which I was missing, and it promised a friendly welcome.

I fly via Toronto, and a group of First Nations people get on the plane. They are chatty and look like professionals relaxing for their return flight after a work trip to the big city. I wonder what they could tell me about Jim and Abbie. On the plane, I overhear a conversation about mining a couple of rows in front. One man works for BHP Billiton, the world's largest mining company. His neighbour, an aspiring investor, is full of questions. "I heard cobalt is the next big thing. Do you think that is true? After BHP, what is the second largest mining company in the world?" A fat man with ice-blue eyes sitting farther forward can't contain himself. "Rio Tinto!" he barks through the seats. He is impatient with the naïveté of the conversation. Does *he* know about Jim and Abbie? What can he tell me about the machinations of the mining industry in northern Saskatchewan?

In Saskatoon, I stay at the Holiday Inn. Still on Montreal time, I get up early to a bright prairie morning. *I'm here!* Before Deanna arrives in the evening, my day is about research. My plan is to go to the city library for books about mining in the North and then to the Gabriel Dumont Institute, which promotes Métis culture and runs educational programs. I am looking for reference points, something in books or at the institute about the historical context of this story. Documents, even objects such as the clothes, tools, and furniture in the institute's collection, can be good for that. They lack the immediacy and personal connections of interviews, but they can capture something that transcends time and stretches into the past.

I read the *Saskatoon StarPhoenix* over breakfast: murder, street robbery, stabbing, missing child, pickup trucks on sale. It is a short walk from the hotel to the library. The only other people on the street appear to be Indigenous; everyone else drives. It is early spring, and the city is dirty, concrete, and monochrome brown. There is no warm welcome. Then I go to the Gabriel Dumont Institute and walk into its stunning Christi Belcourt gallery, and finally it's spring. Belcourt's paintings—of prairie flowers, plants, and birds—line the walls, bursting with life and warmth and human stories. *I'm here!*

That evening I pick up Deanna from the airport, and we discuss the project over dinner. The next morning we drive to interview Uncle Frank. There is a lot riding on our meeting, and I have the butterflies of a researcher who wonders what he is about to discover. Frank lives with a daughter in a modest two-bedroom apartment, five miles from the centre of the city. The blinds are down, giving it a closed look, but inside there are comfortable armchairs and family photos and dreamcatchers on the walls.

Uncle Frank is a vision of style in his rocking chair: thick silver hair groomed so that it is almost a quiff, brown horn-rimmed spectacles, a white western shirt with a blue-grey kerchief tied around his neck, black trousers, and blue tartan slippers. Gold glints in his teeth, and his smooth face makes him look sixty. He has dressed up for us and is eager and anxious at the same time. Frank has waited fifty years to have this story taken seriously and acted on.

Two daughters are there to greet us. Connie is chatty, Pat watchful. They have heard their father's stories many times before and must wonder about their cousin and this stranger who have come so far to listen intently and take notes. After introductions, they go out and leave us to interview their father.

Frank has a couple of connections to Jim and Abbie. He was friends with both men when they all lived in La Ronge in the 1960s, and some years Frank and his wife, Irene (Deanna's mom's sister), would invite Jim for Christmas dinner. But Jim was also a figure from Frank's childhood because Jim was a close friend and colleague of Frank's father, Pete Tomkins Jr. Like Jim, Pete was one of the main negotiators with the Alberta government during the Ewing Commission in 1934 into the "Alberta Halfbreed Problem." Also like Jim, in the 1950s Pete worked for the Saskatchewan government to establish cooperatives and government stores across the North. As a child and young man, Frank would have heard Jim spoken about with great respect whenever people got together.

Then, in the mid-1960s, Frank lived in Jim's cabin for four summers in a row when Frank was posted to La Ronge during the firefighting season. It was during this period that he also got to know Abbie. Jim went prospecting during the summer months and wanted someone to look after his cabin, but he travelled back and forth, so Frank had a lot of contact with Jim on his visits back to town. When Jim drew up a will and testament, he asked Frank to be his witness.

Frank has clear memories of being asked to witness the will, and undoubtedly this is because it was the last time that he ever saw Jim. It was in La Ronge in September 1966, when Frank was getting ready to pack up for the year and return south. There was drizzling rain when Jim showed up at Frank's office carrying a typewritten will "at least three pages long."[1] Jim wanted Frank to be a witness, though Frank didn't want to have anything to do with it. "I wouldn't even read it, but Jim insisted, so I read this one part." After reading the will, they went to the house of Allan Quandt, Jim's nominated executor. By the time they arrived, "it had quit raining," Frank notes, and "Jim was outside, and I sat with the door open. I signed it, and then left for Prince Albert. That day was the last time I saw Jim."[2]

Deanna and I had agreed that on this first day we would let Frank take his time and not ask too many questions. But he circles around and around Jim and Abbie's disappearance, going off on tangents about his father and grandfather and the smokejumpers. I assume that he is checking me out: observing, wondering, waiting to talk about the things that have brought us together.

Later Deanna reminds me that Uncle Frank spent a lot of time around communists who shared the particular trait of being cagey around strangers. It was a protective mechanism from the years of surveillance and when the Communist Party was banned in Canada. They had to meet in secret cells, and they feared—rightly so for many—that they were under surveillance or that their group was in danger of being infiltrated. Frank already told us that he was sure he was under surveillance—an issue that I let rest—so his behaviour during the interview makes sense.

When Frank finally gets into his storytelling rhythm, he rocks his chair as steadily as a metronome. Whenever he cannot remember something, or something does not make sense, or he is unhappy with our interruptions, the rocking stops dead until he has collected his thoughts and can continue. Over several hours, all the bits and pieces come out, and gradually his story of what happened takes full shape.

Frank's version of events is tough on everyone: tough on the locals whom Frank implicates and merciless in what he has to say about Bill Knox and Allan Quandt. It is based on things that he heard from reputable people about Jim's business interests, alleged race-based hostility toward Jim and Abbie, known movements of people on Lower Foster Lake right around the time of the disappearance, and what Frank considered suspicious behaviour by Jim's executor.

Here is Uncle Frank's theory as told to Deanna and me that day in Saskatoon:

> Jim Brady formed a company, Foster Lake Mines, with Abbie Halkett, Bill Knox, Berry Richards, and Allan Quandt to explore for minerals. When out prospecting on behalf of the company, Jim made a big uranium find that was going to make them all rich. Bill Knox asked Jim to push Abbie out of the company because Abbie was Cree and Knox was racist, but Jim said, "No way. Abbie deserves his share like anyone else." Knox—and possibly Quandt—then decided to get rid of both Jim and Abbie so they could take over the company and the uranium find. They hired thugs to fly up from the States using the pretense that they were on a fishing trip and put them up at the lodge on Lower Foster Lake. They procured a local man working at the lodge as a fishing guide to lead the killers to Jim and Abbie. It had been prearranged to have Jim and Abbie dropped off at the "wrong" lake as part of the ambush. The hitmen shot Jim and Abbie,

hid their bodies (probably in the lake), and then were flown out of the area almost immediately.[3]

Halfway through telling the story, Connie and Pat return with boxes of KFC. We take a lunch break and leave our research roles. Deanna and the cousins catch up on family news, and I chat with Uncle Frank, who has become more and more relaxed, as signified by his steadily rocking chair.

Deanna has told me some of Frank's theory, but it is only during the interview that I hear it in full. Some might try to dismiss it as the story of an old man, but Uncle Frank is no fool, and there are events that, in the absence of alternative explanations, appear to be odd coincidences.

First, after Jim and Abbie's disappearance, Frank obtained a copy of Jim's will, but he insists that it was not the document that he had signed as a witness: "I got a one-page copy of the will that had my signature, leaving everything to Allan Quandt. It was not the three-page will that I had seen."[4] Uncle Frank says that his signature on this copy was forged, as was the will itself, and he was adamant about this in a statement that he made in 1974: "I have no recollection whatsoever of ever putting my signature on that particular document, but I can positively swear that it is not the Will I have described earlier in this statement."[5]

Second, Quandt, also the executor, rented out Jim's house just weeks after Jim had disappeared. This was a strange move for a friend and business partner of Jim's. If Jim were still alive out in the bush, he might have been found—and therefore would have wanted his cabin back.

Third, and most important, is the explanation of how Frank knew that Jim had made a "big find," because it is what provided a motive for murder according to Frank's theory. In fact, it was unusual that Frank even found out about the big find because secrecy is so important in the mining industry, especially before a claim has been officially lodged:

> No one, except those with whom they were associated in town and their closest relatives (sometimes not even them) knew where they [prospectors] were going. It was essential that if they made a "find" no one else would know about it, at least not until it was staked and safely secured in their name. Soon after the staking, however, the claims appeared on government maps, and it became known that "Joe had made a find."
>
> This brought others into the area, to "tie on" claims to Joe's, in case the original discovery extended beyond Joe's claim boundaries, or that it was a favourable area, and other deposits lay nearby. "Tie on" claims were known as "moose pasture."
>
> The original finder did not then object to disclosure and the arrival of new people in the area. It gave his property publicity and enhanced his chances of interesting mining companies in it.[6]

The need for secrecy about a claim changes abruptly to the need for publicity and excitement about it once the claim has been officially staked. Mining promoters use the "buzz" to entice investors, necessary for the actual development of a mine. During the early stages of exploration, prospectors enquire about which areas have already been claimed—which are on the public record—but do not want anyone to know that their own claims are imminent. Mining Recorder's Office personnel, however, put two and two together based on the enquiries that prospectors make.

In the 1960s, Jim's close friend, Tony Wood, worked in the government Mining Recorder's Office in La Ronge where mining claims were kept. It was a sensitive role because it involved handling confidential information about discoveries and claims. But Frank was also friends with Tony, who (according to Frank) told him that "Jim said 'we're all going to be all right'"[7] because he had made a big find. Frank understood "we" to mean Indigenous people because Wood implied that Jim was going to give away any profits to the Indigenous community. Frank stresses that Wood would have been reliable in his knowledge of this, making the point that, given his access to records through his position in the Mining Recorder's Office, and because of his close friendship with Jim, he would have known what Jim had found—what his big find was exactly.

However, Métis-communist-activist-finds-uranium-mother-load-and-plans-to-donate-profits-to-the-Indigenous-community-and-then-gets-murdered-by-his-partners-who-double-cross-him . . . well, it sounds too good to be true, to be honest. It's not that I don't believe Uncle Frank; I just can't fit together all of the pieces of the puzzle, and after hours of listening I'm tired. We decide to finish for the day—Deanna also has to return to Vancouver that evening—and I make plans to return the next day with follow-up questions, when Lloyd Mattson will also join us. I go to shake Connie's hand, and Connie laughs. "We're huggers!" she says and grabs me in an embrace. Pat says, "Bye."

Back at the hotel, I become obsessed with Frank's idea that Jim might have found a big deposit and that his business partners were behind the disappearance. I stay up late scouring the Internet, freight trains grinding through Saskatoon as midnight approaches. I need to find out something about Knox other than Uncle Frank's low opinion of him. I also need to get some sleep since the next day I'm due back at Uncle Frank's place, where we are to be joined by Lloyd Mattson, who searched for Jim and Abbie over the summer of 1967.

The next morning I arrive early, and Frank greets me with "I slept like a goddamn baby last night!"[8] He was carrying around this story for fifty years and finally got it off his chest.

Twenty minutes later Lloyd arrives. He greets Frank with a broad smile—they haven't seen each other for years—and then turns to me, and we shake hands. Lloyd's body language is simultaneously alert and contained, giving little away, and in conversation Lloyd is taciturn and skeptical. He has done many jobs in his life, and in retirement he is studying filmmaking. I've heard from Uncle Frank and read elsewhere about the personal effort of Lloyd in the search, and I have questions about his involvement and what he thought of the RCMP and, of course, about the murder theory. Most of all, however, I want to ask him about his friendship with Jim.

As he begins to talk, there is no doubt in my mind that Lloyd cared deeply about Jim and that his disappearance created a gap in his life. In 1967, Lloyd used his own money to spend the summer searching for Jim and Abbie; in the early 1970s, with Frank, he tracked down and interviewed people about the disappearance; he wrote letters to mining companies and the Department of Mineral Resources to try to get information about

Jim's mineral claims; he wrote letters to newspapers to publicize the case; and then forty-three years later he started a Facebook page about it.[9] Unlike Uncle Frank, however, Lloyd is not energized by the prospect of someone new giving attention to the disappearance. I go to the bathroom, and as I return I overhear them talking in low voices. Lloyd thinks that the cold case is not going to be resolved. Frank swallows.

Lloyd answers my questions, but he doesn't give much away about his feelings. He and Frank were disappointed that Murray Dobbin had not delved more into the disappearance in his book and that he had rejected the conspiracy theory: that is, that he had rejected *their* theory. Frank explains that, when he phoned Dobbin years later to talk to him about the murder-conspiracy explanation, his comment was "Are you still going on about *that*?"[10]

So what I need to do now is pick *that* apart forensically to get to the bottom of Uncle Frank's theory.

12
PERSONS
OF INTEREST

The world of investigations uses the term "person of interest" to describe someone about whom there are suspicions, but not yet hard evidence, of involvement in a crime or someone who may have important information about a crime. Uncle Frank, in keeping with his take-no-prisoners approach, has a long list:

1. the pilot who dropped Jim and Abbie off at the wrong lake;
2. the Americans (hitmen masquerading as fishing tourists flown up to kill the prospectors);
3. the fishing guide working at the lake (who led the Americans to Jim and Abbie);
4. the business partner (Bill Knox);
5. the boss (Berry Richards); and
6. the friend (Allan Quandt).

In almost everything that I read or hear about the disappearance, these individuals crop up again and again. Four of them are dead, one is in his eighties, and the others—the Americans—are forever nameless. An inauspicious start. Nevertheless, concentrating on them helps to clarify what roles they might have had and helps to have their names crossed off the list if appropriate. Understanding who they are and their relationships to Jim and Abbie is a good place to start unravelling the mystery.

Again I seek the advice of the RCMP's Sergeant Geoff Bennett in Regina, this time on the role of motive when investigating missing persons cases and when these cases become criminal investigations. He advises me that there is a wide range of things that could lead the police to believe that someone's disappearance is suspicious and a potential homicide, such as evidence of a struggle or a witness who saw the missing person with someone who had reason to do him or her harm. The potential motive of a person of interest is part of the equation, but it has to be assessed case by case. The past history of the missing person—such as social networks, associates, patterns of behaviour, prior contact with the police—also comes into play in some instances, but that does not mean the police do not take a disappearance seriously. An attempt should still be made to locate the person. A missing person's history is important because it might suggest a motive for someone to harm that person, but Sergeant Bennett tells me that there is often no single thing that makes police believe that a missing person might have met with foul play. The totality of the circumstances and any evidence recovered must be used to make that determination.[1]

There is an important recurring theme in all of what he says—"the past history of the person," as Sergeant Bennett delicately puts it. Jim's history is extensive, legendary in fact. Jim was famous for organizing opposition to government policies, educating people about colonialism and oppression, being a communist, and building communities. As for Abbie, though he was not a communist, he did what Jim did, just at a more local level.

Were his politics enough to get Jim murdered? Although Uncle Frank is highly political and skeptical of the government—with the exception of Tommy Douglas and his Saskatchewan CCF ("the only good government Canada ever had!"[2])—Frank thinks that Jim's death was business related and never once suggested that it was a political assassination. However, though Frank is preoccupied with motive, he does not do a systematic stitching together of the evidence to see if it supports his theory. Rather, he jumps straight to the why, which, in his mind, is that three white men wanted to take advantage of their Indigenous business partners so that there was more money for them.

Others besides Frank continue to believe that politics is a plausible explanation, and this might have been what Malcolm Norris meant when he cried "They killed him!" after he heard the news that Jim was missing. Having worked with Jim for three decades to reform government attitudes, policies, and programs, Norris knew better than anyone the political forces lined up against them. In the documentary *Jim Brady: In the Footsteps of the Métis Leader*, Maria Campbell also poses the question and provides a similar possible answer: "Why would they want to get rid of [Jim and Abbie]? . . . Well, they were political people."[3]

Norris and Campbell are correct. Jim and Abbie *were* political people, and many other political people had a keen interest in this fact, especially those in institutions who were the targets of their activism: the DNR, the CCF (with which Jim had become disillusioned), other political leaders in Saskatchewan (and Alberta), various churches, and the RCMP, particularly the security and intelligence branches that conducted surveillance on communists and activists. These institutions would have known precisely who James Brady was in 1967, notwithstanding his withdrawal from politics.

In fact, the RCMP likely had up-to-date knowledge of Jim's whereabouts before the disappearance. Until 1984, when the newly established Canadian Security Intelligence Service (CSIS) took over the role, the RCMP routinely carried out surveillance on people considered to be threats to national security. Communists were the primary target.[4] The combination of a Marxist, an ordinary worker, an educator, and a distributor of information was what the Mounties feared the most.[5]

Jim might as well have been dynamite. His activism around the Indigenous and anti-war movements, on top of his communism, guaranteed him a thick RCMP dossier. Indeed, encouraged by Deanna during the course of our research, Uncle Frank made a Freedom of Information request to CSIS for his own file and was taken aback when a much-larger-than-anticipated package arrived in the mail!

Official concern about Jim makes more sense when put into the 1960s context given that, at first glance, La Ronge appears to be an ignorable outpost in global terms. The Cold War was in progress, and communism was considered the enemy. In Africa and Asia, Indigenous Peoples led by clever, charismatic leaders were rising up against white colonial masters, who assumed that they were being manipulated by communists rather than being motivated by a genuine desire for freedom. Across the Americas, governments were convulsing in reaction to the Cuban revolution in 1959 led by that other "practical-visionary," Fidel Castro.[6] Canadian authorities were also worried about the influence of militant Native American organizations heading north from the United States. From this perspective, far from being a *backwater*, La Ronge was a potential *headwater* for a stream of "revolutionary Indians." The "red menace" had a double meaning.

By the time Jim disappeared in 1967, he no longer would have been followed in the streets, undercover style, by the authorities, as he would have been after political meetings in the 1930s, 1940s, and 1950s. This would have been a comical thing to try in small-town La Ronge. Instead, the RCMP used a network of informants, typically members of the same organizations as the people under surveillance.[7] In Jim's case, someone in the local CCF branch or even the Métis Association of Saskatchewan would have provided updates on Jim, possibly on Abbie too, though he would have had a much lower profile. One can only imagine the consternation of the informant and the flurry of communications with Regina and Ottawa that might have followed when word came back that Jim and Abbie had disappeared.

His leftist beliefs and activism were enough to keep Jim under surveillance in Canada in the 1960s and might have been enough to get him killed if he had crossed paths with the wrong crowd at the wrong time in 1937, 1947, or even 1957. However, this is a far stretch from a premeditated political assassination. The aim of surveillance is typically not to kill the suspects but to gather information about their networks. Furthermore, his steady withdrawal during the 1960s from activism and public campaigning makes it hard to believe that *in 1967* politics were enough to get Jim murdered.

Politics, however, might have been enough to reduce the vigour of the official search. While viewing back copies of the *Daily Herald* at the Prince Albert Public Library to see how the disappearance was reported at the time, I find an article titled "Local RCMP Seek Direction." Published on July 5, 1967, three days before the search was called off, it states that the RCMP were "awaiting word today from headquarters at Regina as to what steps to take next" in the search for Jim and Abbie.[8]

Given Jim's politics, would that conversation have gone like this?

> Sir, about the search around the Foster Lakes, it's been four weeks since they were last heard from, and we haven't found anything. How should we proceed?
>
> Who's missing again?
>
> Two prospectors: an Absolom Halkett and a James Brady.
>
> Jim Brady! The Indian? The communist? [long pause] Well . . . a month is a long time. I'm not sure there's much point putting more resources into this one.

Of course, this is speculation; we will never know what transpired in Regina that day at RCMP headquarters, but many people and institutions would have been happy that Jim was no longer around to bother them.

In investigations, there is a proven adage—"follow the money"—to understand potential connections to a crime, so the question is would Jim and Abbie's business partners have been equally as pleased as their political enemies if they weren't found? And what did they stand to gain?

13
THE FLYING PREACHER

f there was one event that determined the course of history in northern Saskatchewan in June 1967, it was the drop-off of Jim and Abbie at the wrong lake. If they were murdered as part of some conspiracy, and it is still *if*, then this act made it possible.

A drop-off at the wrong lake is crucial to the murder plot. In fact, it would be the perfect crime: a pilot puts down two men at what *they* think is the right lake, but is actually the wrong lake, and does not tell anyone, so the deaths seem to be "natural" but accidental caused by animals, exposure to the elements, or eventual starvation. The catch is that Jim and Abbie were expecting a visitor—their boss, Richards—who came looking for them, found their camp in the wrong place, and then raised the alarm. Not such a perfect crime after all. The pilot would also need a motive to participate in it. But whether it was intentional or not, the drop-off at the wrong lake remains the act that set in motion this course of events.

I had no expectation of being able to find the pilot who dropped Jim and Abbie off, but I had some clues from Dobbin's *The One-and-a-Half Men*: his name and that he had been a theology student. I search his name online and find a Catholic newsletter from British Columbia with an article about an interdenominational week of prayer for Christian unity in 2013. It has an accompanying photo in which a Reverend Gerry Mitchinson, of the Evangelical Lutheran Church, is dressed in a white cassock and green stole. *Can this be him? Is he still alive?* I then find another article from 1983 about the life and work of a pilot-priest:

> Gerry Mitchinson is a flying preacher whose parish covers more than 100,000 square kilometres of northern Alberta and British Columbia. That vast space has little room for city preachers who wait for people to visit their studies and it gives short shrift to denominational niceties. An Anglican may have to worship with the Baptist next door. "They say you have to be a misfit, a mercenary or a missionary to live in the North," Mitchinson jokes. "It helps to be a little bit of all three." Mitchinson, an ordained minister of the Lutheran Association of Missionaries and Pilots, will readily admit to being a missionary. But his intention is not to be "just another white person pushing your gospel on [n]ortherners," said his wife. . . . For the northerners he visits, Mitchinson is a vital contact with the outside world, a man who drops out of the sky for a cup of coffee, to share a problem, to marry them and sometimes to bury them.[1]

He must be the pilot I'm after. I contact the church, send a message enquiring whether he is the Gerald Mitchinson who flew in northern Saskatchewan in 1967, and can't believe it when a reply appears in my inbox the next day. It's from *him*. He's alive . . . *and on email.*

> Yes, you have the right person. What has led you into your inquiry? Not able at this immediate time to dig out my files of that event—and my eyesight makes emailing a challenge. . . . On that flight I was using 16 miles to an inch maps for a low altitude flight. Made it difficult to distinguish between Lower Foster, Middle Foster and Upper Foster Lakes. . . . I dropped them off by error on Lower Foster Lake I believe. After that flight I got four-miles to an inch forestry maps which made it easier to navigate where there were small lakes.[2]

It is the first time that I have heard the information that Mitchinson had a sixteen-miles-to-the-inch map, a scale suitable for higher-altitude flying in areas where there are large variations in terrain and the main navigational features are topographical, such as mountains, big lakes and rivers, or large human-made features. However, this scale is wholly unsuitable for low-altitude flying in an area with lots of similar-looking lakes, forests, and rocky outcrops. This information also contradicts what I have read elsewhere.

Berry Richards says in *Gold and Other Stories as Told to Berry Richards: Prospecting and Mining in Northern Saskatchewan* that, when he drove Jim and Abbie to Otter Lake, the departure point on June 7, 1967, he gave Mitchinson the map needed for fly-ing: "I had with me all the necessary maps that they would need to do their jobs. The first one was the four-miles-to-the-inch topographical map which the pilot uses to fly. Then there were claim maps, half-a-mile to the inch, very detailed, showing all the lakes, the locations of the properties, and so on. Before they took off I marked on the pilot's map exactly where they were to be put down—on the north end of Middle Foster Lake."[3]

Although Richards says that the map he gave Mitchinson had a scale of four miles to the inch, Mitchinson has a clear memory of going out and buying four-miles-to-the-inch maps *after* the drop-off because he was concerned that he needed something more reliable than what he had been given. Mitchin-son later writes to me, "For the rest of the summer with those maps, never again was I uncertain of my location."[4]

I cannot reconcile the two accounts, but it would have been irresponsible to give Mitchinson a sixteen-miles-to-the-inch map to use for flying. Unfortunately Richards is no longer alive to defend his own recollection.

It is obvious from my own map of the Foster Lakes area that, if someone standing at Rottenstone Mine (the stop before Jim and Abbie's drop-off) aimed a gun at the top end of Middle Foster Lake, the bullet would pass directly over the top end of Lower Foster Lake. The three points are in precise alignment. When Mitchinson plotted a direct course from Rottenstone Lake to Middle Foster Lake—the natural thing for a pilot to do unless there is bad weather to avoid—he would have looked down and seen a long finger of water pointing to the south-west. With an inadequate map for guidance, and certainly to a pilot unfamiliar with the area and possibly even to someone who knew it, Lower Foster Lake would be hard to distinguish from Middle Foster Lake on a sixteen-miles-to-the-inch map or possibly even a four-miles-to-the-inch map.

Cloudy weather and confusing terrain would have made Mitchinson's navigational task even more difficult. In confusing terrain, especially if using a sixteen-miles-to-the-inch map, it is critical to fly at an accurate speed and heading (compass bearing). Under these conditions, pilots rely on time to tell them when to look for a feature, such as a target lake. However, battling strong winds and avoiding clouds by flying around them can make maintaining a certain speed and specific heading impossible. Assuming that Mitchinson was flying at 125 miles per hour, a typical cruising speed for his type of float-equipped aircraft, the expected air time from Rottenstone Mine to Middle Foster Lake would have been about sixteen minutes (thirty-three miles) but to Lower Foster Lake about twelve minutes (twenty-six miles). If Mitchinson was relying on time to locate Middle Foster Lake, then arriving four minutes early at his expected destination (the wrong lake anyway) would have been a significant navigational error to make over this relatively short distance, but it is not out out of the question given the circumstances.

In the photo that I find online, Mitchinson looks elderly—I estimate that he is in his early eighties—but he stands tall and clearly remains engaged with the community given that the article is about interdenominational prayer. In writing, he comes across as more fragile—with age, with ill health, and with the stress of looking after his wife, who, he tells me, is also unwell. I have a duty of care toward him, but I also want to know what really happened. Mitchinson is the last person to have seen Jim and Abbie alive—well, unless there *was* a murderer—and I feel like I'm close to something.

We correspond further, and Mitchinson tells me that "my brother (an RAF [Royal Air Force] instructor) taught me to fly in 1945 in a J3 Piper Cub when I was 13—No age restriction in that year and at 13 no fear!"[5] Far from being a novice pilot in 1967, as several people reported, it is more accurate to say that Mitchinson was an experienced pilot (he had been flying for twenty-two years by then) but was unfamiliar with the territory of the Foster Lakes. His experience would have reduced his chance of making a navigational error, but it is still feasible given the cloudy weather and topographical similarities between Middle and Lower Foster Lakes.

I ask Mitchinson for copies of any papers that he might still have, and he mails to me a package containing a note titled "Some Memories of My Days of Flying in Northern Saskatchewan in the Summer of 1967," along with three other documents. The note starts thus: "Finally I've had a chance to review my 1967 log book and reflect on it and especially to its relation to the Jim Brady/Abbie Halkett unfinished story. Here are some of my recent thoughts." It concludes by saying that Mitchinson has "the continued memory of wondering if a different decision on my part would have made any difference. I likely will never know."[6]

The three other documents in the parcel are a magazine article titled "Lost . . . Never Found,"[7] appealing for help in finding Jim and Abbie's remains; copies of the two crucial pages of his flying logbook, covering June 2 (when Mitchinson started working for Norcanair) to June 15, 1967; and three photocopies of a map showing the Foster Lakes. His note, maps, and logbook do not reveal much additional information, but they bring me closer to the event. The article, however, is telling. It is a plea for a wrong to be made right, with a sense of hopelessness about whether that is even possible. After posting the package, Mitchinson sends an apologetic follow-up email: "Late in coming, likely not helpful, but good therapy for me."[8]

Several people said that the pilot who dropped off Jim and Abbie must have been paid off, must have known, must have been "in" on the murder plot. But through email, and the letter that he sent, I believe that I've come to know the pilot, now an old man, and I feel that conflict between being the investigator who wants to get information and ask the brutal questions that will get me the truth and being the human being who has compassion for someone who might simply have made an honest mistake and deeply regrets it. Mitchinson has spent fifty years mulling over his role in Jim and Abbie's disappearance, and clearly it has affected him.

When mistakes occur in aviation, and in risk management generally, there is something called the Swiss cheese model used to identify what went wrong.[9] As kids know—because they fashion the cheese slices into sunglasses or poke their tongues through them—what is notable about Swiss cheese is that each slice has random holes in it. According to the model, each slice of cheese represents part of a process, and each hole represents a gap or risk in that part which, if unmanaged, can result in an error. When the random holes (risks) in each slice (part) happen to line up, something is likely to go wrong, resulting in an accident, sometimes a tragedy.

Assuming that Mitchinson intended to put Jim and Abbie down at Middle Foster Lake and that his failure to do so was not part of any murder plot, I can use the Swiss cheese model to illuminate and understand the series of gaps that resulted in the alarm not being raised for nine days after their last radio call. Here are the holes as they appeared.

- The pilot, Mitchinson, was unfamiliar with the territory.
- The map given to Mitchinson had a scale inadequate for identifying the necessary geographical features.
- Mitchinson asked Jim to confirm that it was the right lake, but Jim was also not very familiar with the area.
- Mitchinson waited five days before reporting his misgivings about the drop-off point.
- His boss took no action when Mitchinson reported his concerns about dropping Jim and Abbie off at the wrong lake.
- A likely contributing factor was the culture of secrecy around and occasional deliberate misinformation on prospecting work.
- Berry Richards was not alarmed by the lack of communication from Jim and Abbie because of Jim's habit of sparse communication.

One of the "holes" above—the secret prospecting flights—might sound like an exaggeration, but they are part of the deliberate mystery generated around mining. The desire for secrecy can cause sudden changes in itineraries, with a pilot hiding prospectors in the back of the aircraft so that bystanders won't see them and potentially recognize them as prospectors heading to destination X. When Imperial Oil, for example, was prospecting in central Saskatchewan in the 1950s, it was a cloak-and-dagger operation. Personnel were locked in a motel in Regina, forbidden to communicate with anyone, and loaded onto a plane in the dark before dawn so that no one would see them. The plane took off and headed toward the United States before altering course to fly north once over the horizon and out of sight of anyone at the airport.[10] All of this so that no one knew what and where the company was exploring. Dobbin speculates that this type of secrecy might have been one reason that Mitchinson's supervisor did not forward the concern that the pilot had dropped off Jim and Abbie at the wrong lake: "He was used to prospectors giving false information and even changing flight plans in mid-flight to guard against possible intrusion."[11] The supervisor might have concluded that Jim and Abbie had always intended to go to Lower Foster Lake.

Thus, though the drop-off at the wrong lake is a key factor in the disappearance of Jim and Abbie, at least seven unmanaged risks related to navigation, reporting, industry culture, and communication were contributing factors—those Swiss cheese holes that lined up to make for a terrible mistake and to delay the alarm being raised. Yes, Mitchinson was responsible for recognizing and managing several of them, but different actions by his boss, or Richards, or even Jim likely would have led to a different outcome.

It is important to remember two more things. First, the mere fact of the drop-off at the wrong lake did not cause Jim and Abbie's deaths. The men had supplies to survive comfortably in the bush for at least a couple of weeks regardless of where they were and certainly within the time frame of Richards's scheduled visit (nine days). Second, Mitchinson reported his doubts to his superior about whether he had put Jim and Abbie down at the wrong lake. Even though his superior did not take action—a normal topic of scrutiny at a safety inquest that should have been a major point of inquiry at the coroner's inquest—making the report could hardly have been the action of someone trying to cover up a crime.

14
AMERICANS

Uncle Frank said that it was Americans who had been flown in to murder Jim and Abbie, but this was one lead that I didn't want to follow. How could I possibly track down hitmen who had come from the United States fifty years ago? Making it worse was the fact that they would have pretended to be fishing tourists, and at that time of year there would have been hundreds of fishermen from the United States on any given day on lakes across Saskatchewan.

Then, in a memory flash that I still find hard to believe happened, a scene from Margaret Atwood's classic Canadian novel *Surfacing* came into my head. In the book, a young woman goes to the wilds of northern Quebec to investigate the mysterious disappearance of her father. She comes across two Americans, with guns no less, canoeing on a lake. The "Americans" turn out to be Canadians from Ontario; she assumes that they are Americans because they have shot a heron for sport. I remembered that, when I had asked Uncle Frank about how he knew that Jim and Abbie's killers were Americans, he had replied "I assume they were Americans, but they could have been from Toronto." Meaning that, like Atwood's "Americans," they were not local men, as evidenced by their lack of respect for the land and the ways of the local people, but from that perennial source of money and trouble: a big city to the south.

To understand the logistics of getting hitmen in to kill Jim and Abbie, I started to plan, hypothetically, their murder. I would need contract killers who could be flown into the Foster Lakes area. Not someone from Saskatchewan because, though they might know the terrain, it was too close to home; they would be too likely to talk. But assassins from Winnipeg or Toronto, or somewhere south of the border, Billings or Fargo, would be perfect. They would need a local guide to get into the area, track the men, plan an ambush, and get a couple of clean shots. Flying in outsiders to do the killing would reduce the chance of gossip. It was the tidiest way.

I needed advice on how to arrange such a hit and thought that I might be able to find someone in jail willing to talk. I asked a friend, a criminal defence lawyer in Vancouver, if he knew any murderers, but he had lost contact with his most "suitable" client. The Mafia crossed my mind—there seemed to be no shortage of mob connections in Montreal—but I knew enough about their *omertà*—their vow of silence—to know that their participation was unlikely. Self-consciously, and wondering whether Internet searches for "hitman Montreal" would automatically trigger remote police tracking, I start googling for assassins. Alas, Canada appears to be relatively free of contemporary contract killing—at least if one were unwilling to go the way of the dark web. My innocent search did land a few older cases involving contract killers, but I could not identify anyone suitable. Recognizing that this was all a bit absurd on my part, I admitted defeat—I was at an end in terms of getting any direct counsel from a hitman.

Admittedly there is nothing on the public record about these "Americans" or Torontonians masquerading as fishing tourists, but there is no doubt that, when Jim and Abbie disappeared, there were tourists staying at the lake in a fishing lodge (there was only one). It was June, and the fishing season would have opened just a few weeks earlier on Lower Foster Lake. The lake is famous for its northern pike and trout and attracts sport fishers from around the world. They are mobile, and they and their guides might well have gone to the north end of the lake where Jim and Abbie camped. The owners and staff of the lodge might also have seen or heard something, but unless they were interviewed no one would have known what information they had.

In the early 1970s, when they were trying to solve the disappearance, Uncle Frank and Lloyd Mattson paid a visit to the owner of the fishing lodge. The connection in their minds was not only that the "tourists" stayed there but also that the local fishing guide who helped them was employed there. The lodge owner was friendly until they explained why they were there, and "that's when he got shitty with us."[1] The scene is remarkable as I imagine it: Frank and Lloyd cornering the proprietor and accusing him of conspiracy to commit murder. If the owner was involved in a murder, then he would not have been happy at being exposed. However, if he had no involvement, then I imagine that he was even more upset about their visit and allegation. There is no reason to doubt Frank and Lloyd's account of their visit, but the owner's anger at their approach is certainly not proof of any kind of involvement.

The confrontation did not resolve anything in that Frank and Lloyd did not obtain information either to implicate or to exonerate the visiting "tourists." As it turns out, the central figure in the hitman angle to Uncle Frank's theory might also not have been from the United States or Toronto but closer to home...

15
ZOMBIES
IN TORONTO

Uncle Frank's explanation of the motive behind the disappearance of Jim Brady and Abbie Halkett centres on business interests linking them to Bill Knox, Allan Quandt, and Berry Richards through their co-ownership of the company Foster Lake Mines. The company only ever registered five claims in Saskatchewan, all for uranium, including the one at the top end of Middle Foster Lake. From Dobbin's interview with Knox, we know that Foster Lake Mines had at least one owner (Knox), so Frank was right that Knox was involved. The question is were there other co-owners, and, if so, who were they?

I spend days looking online for information about Foster Lake Mines, a long shot given that it wound down a good twenty-five years before the web became a repository for documents. Eventually I find a prospectus dating from 1979 for another company, Manitou Lake Gold Mines. The purpose of a prospectus is to pitch a new company or project to investors, so it is important to include information about the founders' and managers' backgrounds and credentials.

Buried in a description of the managers' profiles at the back of the document are two minor references to Foster Lake Mines. In a long paragraph detailing previous positions of a Mr. Murphy is the following: "Foster Lake Mines Limited, cc (May 31/67–Feb. 2/70), d&o," and then the same for a Mr. Kehler: "Foster Lake Mines Limited, cc, May 31/67–Feb. 2/70), d&o." What this means is that from May 31, 1967, to February 2, 1970, men named Murphy and Kehler were directors and officers of Foster Lake Mines.[1]

Jim was out in the bush when these appointments occurred. He had been staking a claim for Knox immediately before the Foster Lakes trip and was back in La Ronge only for two or three days before flying out again on his final trip.[2] Is there any significance that the appointments occurred while Jim was absent and one week before his disappearance? I search for references to Kehler and Murphy and find that Kehler, an accountant by trade, went on to have a long career in business and was on the boards of numerous companies, including in the mining industry. What's more, he's alive. He is ninety-one, and I find a phone number with a Toronto prefix. (I give up searching for Murphy. The name is simply too common.)

Toronto, where the money is. It's the same everywhere in the mining world: investment funds are raised in big cities far away from the mines. No giant pits, dust, monster trucks, or communities dispossessed by mining in Toronto, London, Sydney, or New York. I pick up the phone and take a deep breath. Am I calling someone who helped to take over Foster Lake Mines back in 1967?

There's no answer and no personalized recording, but I can leave a message. A few days later I try again and get through to a woman who turns out to be Kehler's wife. She has a quavering voice and tells me to speak slowly since she's a bit deaf. I hear her loudly relay my request to her husband: "Have you ever heard of James Brady?" "Have you ever heard of Berry Richards?" "Have you heard of Foster Lake Mines?" "No" comes the answer each time.

Once again I'm at a dead end, but there is a whole Canadian story in the "dead" of this term. And it relates to zombies.

After I phone Kehler, I go to an anti-corruption conference in Toronto and attend a session on "beneficial ownership." The session is presented by Robert Cribb, an investigative journalist for the *Toronto Star* who wrote about extensive corruption uncovered in 2015 by the Panama Papers, the largest leak in the history of confidential corporate and banking data. The data came from Mossack Fonseca, a law firm based in Panama, whose clients were rich, famous, and powerful people from around the world. These folks had shell companies established for them by Mossack Fonseca, often with zombie directors—better known as nominee directors—appointed to run them, at least on paper.

The release of the Panama Papers was an earthquake in the corporate and political world. They contained 11.5 million files on 214,000 corporate entities, including over 3,000 Canadian individuals and firms. Among the thousands of people named were 140 politicians in fifty countries, a dozen of them current or former presidents or prime ministers. Elites who had espoused transparency but hid their money, or advocated the rule of law but evaded taxes, were exposed for their hypocrisy.

Nominee directors of these companies were typically employees of Mossack Fonseca. The most famous was Leticia Montoya, a sixty-three-year-old administrative officer paid

$900 a month who, over several decades, was the director of, or on the boards of, no fewer than 10,696 companies. I find a picture of Montoya looking glum, not surprising given that she was photographed by one of the journalists who descended on Panama to find out more about Mossack Fonseca and its clients.

"Directors" such as Montoya are zombies, the walking dead. They appear to be alive—okay, they really are alive because they are real people—but they perform no corporate function other than to fill the role of director and to sign documents for company owners about whom they know nothing. Just as zombies are controlled by supernatural forces—hidden, secret, malevolent—so too zombie directors can be controlled by malevolent forces in the corporate world.

Setting up shell companies and appointing nominee directors offshore are not illegal, but these arrangements can be used to hide something, and this attracts certain kinds of owners. The Panama Papers showed that many owners used their companies to hide income and assets, avoid taxes, launder money, pay bribes, channel money to terrorist organizations, and even fund secret arms deals. What's more, Mossack Fonseca knew about this and facilitated it, also illegal. Company owners hid their actual ownership behind zombie directors and laws that did not require them to state their beneficial interests.

Which brings us back to Canada. Neither federal nor provincial law requires all legal and registered owners, or beneficial owners, to be named. (In contrast, in the United Kingdom, full ownership information is publicly available on a single website.) Company directors—including nominee directors appointed by shareholders to represent them on the company's board—also do not need to be reported. Owners can remain anonymous, and company directors who are nominees do not need to disclose whom they represent.

No wonder finding information about Foster Lake Mines and its ownership was so difficult!

In 2016, the anti-corruption organization Transparency International published a special investigation of beneficial ownership. It found that, in Canada, "more rigorous identity checks are done for individuals getting library cards than for those setting up companies. Corporate registries do not verify identification and most do not require information on shareholders, let alone beneficial owners. Most provinces also allow nominee directors and shareholders, who do not need to disclose that they are acting on someone else's behalf. . . . The lack of available information on private companies and trusts, and who owns them, is a huge obstacle for law enforcement and tax authorities."[3] *And researchers*, I think.

At the conference, as Cribb describes Montoya and her role as a zombie director, I sit up. Can this role help to explain someone like Murphy or Kehler? There was no reason to think that Foster Lake Mines was a shell company; it is the question of nominee directors that grabs my attention. Could Kehler have been acting like Montoya had? That is, not a criminal, not at all, but someone who fulfilled a legal requirement for a company to have a director so that the owners could remain private, hidden from public view?

Uncle Frank and Lloyd Mattson recollected that Foster Lake Mines was co-owned by Jim, Abbie, Richards, Knox, and Quandt and that there were no other owners, so this meant that Kehler (and Murphy) were directors only and not shareholders. Depending on whether there were intermediaries, it is likely that the directors had no idea who really owned Foster Lake Mines. So, when Kehler answered, via his wife, that he had never heard of James Brady, Berry Richards, or Foster Lake Mines, I had no good reason to doubt him.

But I could ask other questions. Why were two directors appointed to Foster Lake Mines one week before the disappearance of Jim and Abbie? Was the timing a coincidence? Did the two prospectors even know that these appointments had been made?

There is more. I find online a letter to the advice column of the February 2004 issue of *The Explorationist*, the newsletter of the Ontario Prospectors Association, about new shares for Foster Lake Mines being issued two weeks after Jim and Abbie were dropped off. The letter writer notes, "I was going through some papers of my parents the other day and ran across two mining share certificates. They are from a company called Foster Lake Mines Limited. They are dated April 19, 1967 and June 21, 1967. Would you be able to give me any information on this matter?"[4]

The Explorationist never published a reply to this enquiry. However, there was no other Foster Lake Mines, so the share certificates that the letter writer had found had to be for the company that, according to Uncle Frank, Jim and Abbie co-owned. So I had another question. Why were shares being issued on June 21 for this company when two of the co-owners had just gone missing and the search was in progress? Companies routinely issue shares to raise funds to continue activities, so it is not the act but the timing that is in question. And who authorized the new issue?

16
THE CAPITALIST

I n a story of larger-than-life characters, Bill Knox looms over the rest. The descriptions that I hear are not flattering, but he is certainly remembered by everyone: "Foxy Knoxy," "looked like a Trump," a "shady character," a "shyster," a "wheeler-and-dealer," and from Uncle Frank, who doesn't beat around the bush, "a notorious mining promoter and crook!"[1] Another man told me that Knox would rap on the door and when asked "Who's there?" would cheerfully reply "Opportunity Knox!"

Knox was such a character that he made it into the history books. Al Scarfe, a mining recorder in La Ronge who would have seen hundreds of promoters, described Knox as "the most interesting promoter-person I've ever met." Scarfe also said that Knox "could sell mining properties like nobody else, particularly in combination with his wife Gigi. If a mining representative came to town and went to the Knox's for a drink or an evening they would be entertained royally. And Bill could sell them anything."[2]

I find documents for a proposed new mine that Knox sent to Ontario's Ministry of Northern Development and Mines. His cover letter is titled "Boulder Mine: The Long Lost Gold Mine" and talks of a motherlode first identified ninety years earlier that numerous prospectors, mining companies, and geologists failed to relocate . . . until now. Found by Knox, of course. It is vintage promoter spin.[3]

Knox was the personification of the Prospectors and Developers Annual Convention. In his fedora, he would tell investors about imminent riches to get them to part with their money. Knox's wife, Gigi, was French and sophisticated, wore short skirts, and had an immaculate 1960s beehive hairdo. One person told me that she danced on the table when Knox was entertaining investors. No wonder all those down-to-earth people in La Ronge remembered the Knoxes so well!

Always keen to promote himself, Knox wrote an autobiography, *Tit in the Wringer*,[4] an idiom meaning "in a tenuous situation" or "hanging by a thread." It's a title that captures the life of a mining promoter. Whatever else can be said about him, Knox, who died in 1991 after a career in the mining industry, was obviously good at raising capital.

His method was to find a promising claim and attract investors into a syndicate, retaining a portion of the shares for himself. It is difficult to piece together his personal business interests, but over the years Knox was probably involved in dozens of small companies established to explore and develop specific claims. These companies would have become defunct if their claims were not viable or sold to larger mining companies if something valuable were found, and Knox couldn't raise money to finance the projects themselves. All of this is normal practice in the mining industry.

Ironically the only person who seems to have been unequivocally well disposed toward Knox was Jim. Malcolm Norris introduced Jim to Knox in May 1958 when the latter wanted to hire a couple of prospectors. Jim and Norris had a lifelong correspondence, and some letters mention Knox. The tone of these letters is a bit difficult to judge, but in general Jim had a particular sense of humour that comes through in other documents, such as titling a wedding photo "Hymeneal Atmosphere" and one of his own cabin "Jim Crow Quarters." In a letter from January 1967, Jim writes how Knox tried to secure the nomination of a certain candidate at the Liberal Party convention in Uranium City, only to be almost thrown out of the congress. "Poor friend Bill," Jim writes. "I'm afraid that entree to the Liberal plunderbund [political corruption] is irrevocably and forever closed to Brother Knox."[5]

Making gentle fun of Knox and calling him "friend" and "brother" hardly suggest animosity (in correspondence, Jim was not one for sarcasm). In a subsequent letter, he writes that "Bill Knox came back crestfallen from the Liberal convention."[6] Unless Jim heard this from someone else, it seems that he and Knox talked politics. They would have had diametrically opposed views, but the fact that they engaged in a political dialogue suggests a certain mutual respect. What I cannot imagine is that someone as sensible and cynical about capitalists as Jim was would go into business with one. Work for one, talk with one, yes, but business partner with one?

What brought them (and Abbie) together was uranium, a strange glue if ever there was one. Abbie's attitude toward uranium is not known, though Abbie was prospecting for it, so presumably he had no objections. Jim's views were contradictory. By prospecting for uranium, Jim was contributing to the nuclear industry. Yet there is a photo of him with Norris at an anti-nuclear rally in Regina standing in front of a banner proclaiming "Education not Annihilation." This apparent contradiction might be explained by the era: the protest took place in 1961 and was against nuclear *weapons*. It was well before serious nuclear accidents at Three-Mile Island in Pennsylvania, Chernobyl in the Soviet Union, or Fukushima in Japan, which turned later generations against nuclear *power*. Jim might well have been in favour of nuclear energy but likely was against nuclear bombs.

He also regularly visited Knox and his wife. "I had him up to my house after every trip," said Knox. "I'd feed him a big home-cooked meal and my wife was very fond of Jim."[7] Gigi and Jim probably relished the opportunity to converse in French in what was an otherwise anglophone town.

There is information on the Jim Brady–Abbie Halkett Disappearance Public Group Facebook page suggesting that Jim might have held or been promised by Knox a 10 percent share in the value of the claims that he staked for him or that Knox had agreed to let Jim keep some of the claims as his 10 percent share.[8] However, to be legally binding, this 10 percent share should have been declared on the form transferring the claim from Jim (the staker) to Knox (the owner)—and there is no evidence that it was—or any claim(s) promised to Jim should have been recorded in his name. Otherwise, any such promise was a "gentleman's agreement," which has an uncertain status when one of the parties disappears.

Knox might have been a showboating entrepreneur, but that does not make him a murderer. He and Jim worked on and off together for nine years, and Jim would have known that it was Knox who hired Pre-Cam Exploration and Development to do the uranium staking work at Middle Foster Lake. In his interview with Dobbin, Knox also makes it clear that, immediately prior to this ill-fated trip, he had employed Jim on another job.[9] So Jim the communist was happy, it seems, to work for Knox the capitalist.

"So what!" Uncle Frank might say. In his mind, it was Knox who betrayed the friendship with Jim by conspiring against him to take control of his big find and not the other way around. But it was also Knox who headed the private search committee for Jim and Abbie when the RCMP and DNR pulled out. Uncle Frank dismisses this as a ruse—an effort by Knox to get the police off his tail. Given that the RCMP and other searchers might have found Jim and Abbie—Knox couldn't predict which lakes the police would drag for bodies or control the movements of the different search parties or what they might find—publicly heading up a search effort doesn't seem like a good way to cover up involvement in a murder. Knox's involvement in the search doesn't make sense—unless Knox was trying to manipulate the search to implicate someone else.

17
THE BOSS

As in life—in which he was a significant businessman and personality across the North—Berry Richards is everywhere in this story. He was the one who employed Jim and Abbie as prospectors to fulfill Pre-Cam Exploration and Development's contract with Foster Lake Mines, he was the one who discovered their abandoned camp, he was the one who helped to organize the private search, and he was a witness at the coroner's inquest.

Politically Richards was a socialist and reformer. He was elected to Manitoba's legislature at twenty-eight in 1943 as the CCF representative from The Pas—the first CCF candidate ever to win the seat. A CCF leader described him as "clever, quick in debate, young and handsome, attractive to both men and women; if he had been able to adhere to CCF policy he undoubtedly would have become provincial leader. With his ruthless philosophy, acid tongue and uncompromising attitude, it is my firm opinion that Richards would have been a disaster as leader."[1]

I met a geologist who knew both Richards and Knox and put them into the same category in terms of being wheeling-and-dealing entrepreneurs, but no one else had a bad word to say about Richards. Even Uncle Frank was reluctant to be explicitly critical of him.

Richards was an indefatigable community member who routinely aligned himself with the collective interest. After leaving politics, he moved to Saskatchewan, where he focused on business and taught at Prospectors' Schools in La Ronge and Uranium City (he was a qualified mining engineer), and he helped to establish a community health clinic in Prince Albert. He took it upon himself to collect oral history stories about mining, which became the basis for the book *Gold and Other Stories as Told to Berry Richards*. In an era when the contributions of Indigenous people to the mining industry were ignored, Richards dedicated the book to "the Indian and Métis trappers of northern Saskatchewan who brought many important mineral occurrences to the attention of the White Man."[2]

Richards first met Jim when they lived in Cumberland House in northern Saskatchewan. He later became the geologist in charge of field operations for Pre-Cam, overseeing core drilling, monitoring mapping work, and hiring prospectors. At the coroner's inquest, Richards stated that he was the manager of Pre-Cam—not an owner—and I have found no evidence that he was a co-owner of Foster Lake Mines.

Richards hired Jim to do seasonal work for Pre-Cam for much of the decade between 1957 and 1967. The two men were friends. Given their similar political views, it is not surprising that they got along well, though this did not happen straightaway. Richards, a warm-hearted and communicative extrovert, took a while to feel comfortable with Jim, whom he found hard to read and was never entirely sure what he was thinking.

The disappearance of Jim and Abbie put Richards's reputation on the line. First, Richards was their boss and had a duty of care for them. He had recruited Jim and Abbie for the job, kitted them out, and hired Norcanair to drop them off. Second, though prospectors getting lost in the bush is not that unusual, companies are judged by their responses in terms of their efforts to find them, especially when the missing persons are so well known in the community. Third, there is the scale of the map that Richards said at the coroner's inquest he gave to the pilot. The scale did not come up as a contentious issue at the inquiry but should have.

In his interview with Dobbin, Richards says that he thought Jim and Abbie probably got lost, and then some calamity occurred, such as one of them drowning and the other subsequently also having an accident. Richards is convinced that the raft found at Lapointe Lake was made by Jim and Abbie, but he is also positive that it could never have supported two adult men.[3] Since they could not have pushed the raft back across the lake for the second person to use, this brings us back to the question why, if lost, Jim and Abbie would have spent precious energy making a raft that could be used by only one person. Of course, it is possible that only one of them was alive at this point, but the raft theory remains improbable regardless of this possibility.

Twice booted out of the CCF's caucus and enamoured of life and people, Richards is the least likely murderer whom I've ever come across. This is not because he was so respected, at least outside the CCF (there is a legion of respectable people who do devious things in secret), but because of the absence of a compelling motive. Richards had little interest in money and was a maverick motivated by principles and dreams rather than anything material. He clearly had a long and happy working relationship with Jim and Abbie since he kept employing them and they kept agreeing to be employed by him. It is difficult to imagine that Richards would care enough about what he could gain from the deaths of Jim and Abbie to motivate him to conspire against them. I suspect that Uncle Frank simply couldn't figure out how to leave Richards out of the plot and therefore implicated him by default. I had to keep digging.

18
TOUGH OLD
NORTHERNERS

After months of trying to find information on possible persons of interest on Uncle Frank's list, in August 2017 Deanna and I decide to go to La Ronge to do more interviews. We arrange to meet a couple of people with first-hand knowledge of the search, and we know that it's important to meet with Jim Brady's daughter.

Checking the news while changing planes in Toronto, I notice a BBC headline: "My Partner Vanished without Warning. I Had to Find Him."[1] It's about a man who disappeared from the lives of his wife and two children and the devastating impact that this had on them. I had spent a lot of time thinking about how and why Jim and Abbie disappeared but had thought less about the consequences for those left behind— wives, girlfriends, children, grandchildren, brothers, sisters, parents, cousins, friends—and reading the article hit me like a brick. It is the sudden absence—the vanishing and the uncertainty—that causes such grief and ongoing pain. No closure, as they say.

The Northerner newspaper, published in La Ronge, printed an article in 1977 in which Lloyd Mattson writes about how the ten-year anniversary of the disappearance of Brady and Halkett "re-kindles painful memories" and how "they still haven't been declared dead. There have been no memorial services. Relatives can't even erect tombstones. The living cannot rest."[2] An old Cree man who participated in the search and was convinced that Jim and Abbie were dumped in Lower Foster Lake told me, simply, "Buried in a lake. That's no burial."[3] In emails that I exchange with Abbie's granddaughter, Amanda, she explains how her grandpa's disappearance had an impact through the generations of her family: "I know [Mom] suffered tremendously without her father. I know all too well how that feels. It's a cycle that I'm praying ends with my one and only daughter."[4]

The generational impacts of such disappearances are writ large across Indigenous communities, most notably and tragically with mothers, daughters, and sisters. This injustice has finally been brought to public attention by Canada's National Inquiry into Missing and Murdered Indigenous Women and Girls. The RCMP by their own tally estimate that, between 1980 and 2012, 1,181 Indigenous women and girls were murdered or disappeared. (The equivalent number of non-Indigenous women and girls for the Canadian population would be 24,000). Of the number for Indigenous women and girls, 1,017 were homicide victims, and 164 are unresolved missing persons cases. Of the homicide cases, 120 murders—12 percent—were unsolved as of 2014.[5] These are astounding, shameful facts.

Jim's disappearance in particular had a fundamental impact on the Métis political movement. Long-time researcher and historian Darren Préfontaine told me, "After Jim Brady disappeared it all kind of broke apart. The Famous Five were the last generation that worked together for the development of a particular kind of Indigenous self-sufficiency and self-governance, and his disappearance really tore the community apart."[6] Préfontaine explained that Brady had wanted the Métis to be economically independent, but Indigenous organizations are now reliant on government funding, so they are more careful about what they say and do. The Métis movement continued, but Jim's death dealt the final blow to the dream of a particular kind of autonomy based on Indigenous-owned cooperatives like those that Jim established across the North.

When I land in Saskatoon, it is a hot summer day. It feels wonderful to be back and to see the horizon all around after the density of Montreal. Deanna arrives from Vancouver, and we head to Prince Albert, where we have an interview scheduled with Vern Studer. He employed Jim to do mining work in the 1950s, was involved in the search, and has his own theory about the disappearance of the two men.

On the drive north, Deanna calls her cousin, Eric Bell, who lives in La Ronge and is to become the third member of our research team. The phone is on speaker: "Vern is keen to talk to you," says Eric. "He kept a diary about events around the time of their disappearance, including some things that weren't in the official reports." I can sense Deanna thinking the same thing: *What things weren't put into the official reports? What does Vern know?* She then calls Vern, and he invites us to visit him first thing the next morning. He tells us that he has his own room in the senior citizens village where he lives where we can go to "talk privately." We both register this. *What doesn't Vern want other people to hear?*

We overnight at the Prince Albert Inn. It's connected to the Northern Lights Casino, between the prison and the cemetery and across the road from the Optimist Tourist Park. I go for an early morning walk, and the air is clean and fresh. A man walking in the middle of the road next to the prison passes me, looking intently, anxiously, around. "Have you seen a guy?" he asks. "No," I say. *Is he trying to rendezvous with an escapee?* After passing him, I turn around to take a second look, and he has vanished.

We pull into the parking lot of Vern's residence and notice a rangy older man pacing around outside. Sure enough it is Vern waiting for our arrival and keen to talk. He is ninety-two, dressed in practical, comfortable clothes, and is sharp as a tack. The epitome of the tough old northerner. Vern tells us that he went into the bush at eleven years old and heard the "Call of the North" and its life of trapping and prospecting.[7] He later became a smokejumper with Uncle Frank.

Vern knows or has met just about everyone involved in this story, including Jim and Abbie, Clyde Conrad, Bill Knox, Berry Richards, and Allan Quandt. It was Vern who flew Lloyd Mattson into the area when Lloyd started his own search. I remember Sergeant Geoff Bennett's words about trying to speak to people with contemporaneous knowledge of the events and feel as if I've struck gold.

Vern tells us that Jim was "very capable in the bush. He was a strong, powerful man but had diabetes and high blood pressure." It is this information about ill health that never got into any official report. Vern is sure about Jim's health problems because in the late 1950s he hired Jim on a drilling job but had to have him flown out because his legs swelled up and he couldn't walk.

Without prompting, Vern also tells us about Jim's politics. He tells us that Jim was a "very strong Communist Party member" and how once, on a prospecting trip, he had read aloud from Marx's *Communist Manifesto* to the crew. We erupt in laughter and picture the scene: a group of rugged outdoorsmen sitting around a smoking red campfire in the middle of the bush listening to smoking red words.

I ask about Abbie, and all Vern says is "He would have followed Jim to the ends of the Earth."

Back in June 1967, Vern was on another drilling job at Reef Lake when he noticed a plane flying around in circles. He knew that something was up; it was the first aircraft sent up to look for Jim and Abbie. He joined the search using his own plane and followed from the air their presumed trail, then participated in the ground search and saw where it was thought that they had made a fire at Lapointe Lake.

Vern's theory of what happened hinges on Jim's health, especially his diabetes, and can be summarized as follows:

> Because Jim and Abbie thought that they were only going out of camp for a short time, Jim left his medication at the tent and didn't take it with him. Because they were on the wrong lake, they didn't find the mineral showing that they were looking for, but when they tried to correct themselves they got lost and wandered away in the wrong direction. They headed southeast, trying to walk their way out. There are narrows, shallow water, and they found tiny jackpines to make the raft to cross Lapointe Lake, and this was the raft found during

the search. Vern was at the raft site when a police helicopter landed to investigate it. He heard the pilot radio through to the base saying "Send divers to search the lake," and they were flown in and trawled the lake later that day, though nothing was ever found.

The only reason that Jim and Abbie didn't make a fire when they were lost must have been because their matches were wet. There simply could be no other reason why they didn't light a fire. By this time, they would have been getting tired and hungry, and Jim didn't have his medication. Bad weather then closed in. Because of the poor weather, Jim and Abbie would have left Lapointe Lake to shelter in nearby bluffs or the forest. Eventually they died from hunger and cold. Thus, they were close to where the raft was but not actually at the lake, and the RCMP should have searched a wider area around the raft's location. As for Abbie, "Abbie wouldn't leave Jim. He would have stayed with him until the end." And thus they both died. Also, Abbie had tuberculosis, and this might have weakened him.[8]

It is true that Jim had suffered ill health. He had a bad fall just before Christmas 1966 and then heavy colds over the winter. In February 1967, he wrote that he had not "fully recovered from various ailments, dislocations, rheums and indispositions."[9] If he and Abbie had been far from their camp, or trying to walk to the Churchill River, then there is no doubt that weakened health would have been a major factor in their survival.

I ask Vern how he felt when he heard that Jim was missing, but he doesn't answer the question. Part and parcel of being a northerner, it seems, is an inability to talk much about feelings. To avoid more awkwardness, I change the subject and ask Vern what he would have done had he been in Jim's shoes. Vern is clear: head west back the way that Jim and Abbie had come to Lower Foster Lake and, after reaching the shoreline, head north back to their camp. Vern emphasizes that Jim was an intelligent man with good bush skills and that, though they were lost—according to Vern's theory—they had a compass and should have been able to retrace their steps. The only reason that they would not have retraced their steps or lit a fire was because they were too ill to do so, probably made worse by bad weather, they did not have matches, or their matches were wet.

Vern dismisses the likelihood of a bear attack. Although he admits that it is possible, it is unlikely that a bear, or bears, would have attacked and killed both men. "Although," he adds, "the only good bear is a dead bear."

Deanna asks about the theory that Jim and Abbie were murdered as part of a plot to seize secret business interests linked to a mining claim. Vern does not give a direct response at first. I wonder whether he does not believe it or is reluctant to say bad things about these other men, whom he describes as having been "close" to Jim. Finally Vern says, "I don't think anyone murdered them."

We now have a clear picture of Vern's theory and how details about diabetes and medication possibly being left behind were not considered by the RCMP or mentioned in the coroner's report. Vern is dismissive of the Mounties' search because it did not include the wider area around the raft (other than the lake itself), the Mounties instead assuming that Jim and Abbie had headed to the Churchill River. We say our goodbyes and head to La Ronge.

We stock up on coffee for the drive north. Deanna says that Prince Albert has a good Tim Hortons and a bad one, but the good one is being renovated and is closed. Australians like their coffee strong, so having tried Tim Hortons before and been unimpressed I'm pleased to discover that Prince Albert also has a Starbucks, and we end up there. The route is long and the day hot, and I take in the scenery: golden wheat and hay fields gradually giving way to forest and lakes. The fattest, glossiest ravens that I've ever seen stride along the road shoulder, flapping off as our car approaches. Deanna and I go over our interview with Vern, discussing his theory about Jim's diabetes and seeing if we can connect other bits of information that we've accumulated. We have many questions, but no answers, and fall into a reverie as the tires hum their song.

An hour before La Ronge we pass a group of young Indigenous men walking along the highway with a couple of support cars following. I slow right down, and Deanna calls out to ask "What are you walking for?" "Suicide awareness," comes the reply. They are not trying to raise funds but simply want to draw people's attention to the crisis. Deanna gives them twenty dollars for cool drinks.

After a long straight stretch, we see buildings in rapid succession. We cross a bridge over the Montreal River, take a final curve, then drive into town. La Ronge is so key to the story that I feel like we're entering Jerusalem. Deanna grits her teeth.

19
LA RONGE,
LATE SUMMER

La Ronge unwinds beside a bay on the western shore of Lac La Ronge, 380 kilometres north of Saskatoon. The town-site was established in 1898 when a sawmill and an Indian residential school were established, but it was only in 1947 that it was connected by road to the rest of the province. The town is now the largest centre in northern Saskatchewan and the jumping-off point for miners, loggers, truckers, government officials, and tourists going north. It is also the regional hub for government and for people to stock up on supplies, and its educational facilities are the destinations for students from small communities across the North.

Stores, government buildings, a handful of hotels and bars, and a few restaurants cluster along the main street, with some newer housing and industrial developments inland. Burgers are a menu staple, though the best are actually found at Cravings restaurant in Air Ronge, across the river from La Ronge. Buildings in La Ronge are designed to keep the heat in and the long freezing winter out, so money is spent on insulation rather than looks. This means that they are sturdy, with few windows, and every entrance is covered or raised to cope with drifting snow. In contrast, the lake is open and beautiful, and in late summer its shoreline is green with parks, trees, and reeds.

The combined population of La Ronge, Air Ronge, and other nearby communities is 5,800. Seventy-five percent of the residents have Indigenous ancestry, mostly Cree, but there are Métis and Dené people too. It is a community that allows some people to prosper and thrive, but it also remains a small town, four hours by road from the nearest big city, Saskatoon. And though it might be the biggest town in northern Saskatchewan, jobs and opportunities are limited, and many young people want to leave.

I try to picture La Ronge in 1967 and quickly discover that there are outsider and insider perspectives. Murray Dobbin wrote that "La Ronge would defeat almost anyone."[1] Art Davis, a sociologist, described it as "a small community with great distances inside it."[2] Liora Salter, the activist who met Jim in 1966, said that it had "all the sharp contrast between the tourists and the wealth and the poverty."[3] Jim himself said that social distinctions and differences were "definitely polarized at opposite ends in that community. . . . The natives, you see, are not acceptable to the whites socially."[4]

But La Ronge has also always been full of families, a place where babies are born and children raised. Deanna had dozens of aunts, uncles, and cousins there and used to visit in the summer, so for her it was a place of school holidays and family memories. It also became home for both Jim and Abbie. Abbie lived on the reserve, and Jim moved there in 1951, eventually building a cabin behind the credit union.

Although Deanna has many relatives in La Ronge, she is especially keen for me to meet her cousin Eric. He was a child at the time of the disappearance, but like Vern Studer he personally knows many of the people involved or their families. Eric and his wife, Wanda, have invited us to stay. They are warm, funny, generous, and wonderful hosts. Wanda serves tea and muffins, and we all talk at once. Deanna and I have discussed our research over the past six months, but we've done a lot of the thinking solo. I relish the opportunity to bounce ideas around with Eric, who knows the people and the country and has loads of practical bush skills, and with Wanda, who can spot a flaw in an argument a mile off.

The first person we call on is Anne Dorion, a teacher, writer, activist, and community organizer—and Jim Brady's daughter. We are anxious to explain our project, and as we walk to her house in the warm evening I feel tense because this will be the clincher. Up to this point, we have used publicly available materials to identify lines of inquiry. Now we want to start talking to people in the community, to get into the messy human details. We've put in a lot of effort so far, and it's true that Jim is a public figure, but if Anne does not want us to go ahead we would need a lot of persuading to continue. We want her to say that it's okay.

Anne invites us around to her backyard because the house is hot from baking. There is a planter box of red, blue, and dark purple flowers on a tangle of long green stems—poppies and bachelor's buttons, with pansies pushing up from below—and raised garden beds full of summer vegetables. Anne wears jeans and a white cotton blouse and sits in a swing seat, one leg folded yoga-style in front of the other hanging down, with a ram-rod posture. We chit-chat, and she offers cigarettes. I've read so much about Jim Brady, I'm so aware of his historical stature, that it feels like meeting Nelson Mandela's daughter. I immediately wonder if this is how people have always approached Anne and whether that has been a burden.

We explain what we hope to do, and Anne asks about us and our work; she wants to know who we are. Deanna has some connections to Anne through family members, friends, and colleagues, including Uncle Frank, but I'm conscious of being the outsider, of my accent. Deanna explains, "Michael does work on corruption and mining," and it sounds so blunt—a crude signal of what we think might be behind the disappearance.

Gradually the conversation evolves. We know that Anne is Jim's daughter, and she must know that this is why we are here, though none of us is saying this. The potential for pain hangs in the air, and I am reminded yet again of the sensitivities around researching human lives. Anne takes a deep breath and finally says that "Jim Brady was my dad—but it was such a long time ago,"[5] and there is some kind of release. She explains that she doesn't know much, that she has a child's memory of her dad and the disappearance, and that many people ask her about what she thinks happened. Anne isn't interested in the stories or discussions. She simply does not know and will not spend energy on them. It is clear that she is proud of her parents and family, but she is her own woman and will not be defined by them. Anne wishes us well and gives us two huge slices of freshly baked chocolate and zucchini cake. We have her permission to continue.

The next morning we explore La Ronge. Deanna revisits memories from her childhood summers spent here and points out various stores, landmarks, and homes of family members and other people she knows. I visit the Anglican Parish Hall, where the coroner's inquest was held in 1969. It is a long squat building, with white wooden walls and a red roof, and I peek through the windows. The interior and furniture look little changed from the 1960s, with Formica tables and metal-framed chairs with yellow wooden seats and backs.

I picture the drama that unfolded the day of the inquest: the coroner presiding; the lawyers in suits; the jury of local white men; Corporal Conrad accounting for and defending his search; Allan Quandt, present as a witness; and a sombre public gallery packed with friends and relatives of Jim and Abbie. The inquest starts at 8 p.m., and two hours later the government lawyer, Mr. D.C. Prefontaine, tells the coroner that he has no more questions. Almost immediately, though, he remembers that there is still someone and announces that he has "neglected to mention to you gentlemen" a Mrs. Annie Halkett.

Annie is seated in the witness box, and the coroner asks, "You understand English perfectly, do you?" To which she replies, "No." An interpreter is called, and the coroner instructs her to "kiss the Bible." Speaking fluently in Cree, Annie explains that she is not actually married to Absolom, agrees that she has not seen him since he flew off that day in June 1967, and admits that she does not know where he is. She is not asked if she knows any reason why someone would want to kill Abbie or Jim. I picture Annie, an almost forgotten afterthought; one of the last people to see Abbie and one of the closest to him at that time; the only family member of Jim or

Abbie called to give testimony and not understanding a thing because nothing has been interpreted, except her own brief testimony into English.

After the Anglican Parish Hall, we stop by Robertson's Trading Store. Deanna scans the shelf for books by Indigenous writers while I stare at the furs and Indigenous carvings that line the walls. I have a foreigner's enthusiasm for squirrels and am taken aback by the pelts hanging on the walls. Empty of flesh, they seem to be small and pathetic; then I remember that Canadians might well view kangaroo hides with the same dismay when they visit Australia.

Anne told us about the memorial erected to her dad by the local Métis Society, the Jim Brady Métis Local 19. It is at the site of his cabin, which she donated to the local fire department for practice after it fell into disrepair. The site is behind the credit union, and we have instructions to walk through the carpark and then a copse of trees behind it. I go poking around in the bushes looking for the memorial. I cannot find anything but notice five or six men sitting quietly in a circle under the trees.

"Hi," I say.

They look surprised and a bit suspicious.

"Do you know where the Jim Brady memorial is?"

"Jim Brady!" says one.

"No," says another.

As I start to walk off, one of them calls out, "Are you Australian?"

"Yeah, how did you know?"

"The way you sound," comes the answer.

His friend asks if I've got a couple of bucks.

"No," I say.

We go to Kosta's Restaurant for lunch and have chicken quesadillas, mesmerized by the beautiful view to the east across Lac La Ronge. A well-groomed older man with silver hair and a couple of younger people in tow head past the restaurant toward the shore. Deanna exclaims, "That's Tom Jackson!" The famous actor and singer, who is also Métis. Everyone here knows him from his starring role in the classic 1990s TV series *North of 60,* set in the Northwest Territories. He is now also known for his annual pre-Christmas "The Huron Carole," which raises money for the hungry. We wonder what he is doing in La Ronge.

20
THE GUIDE

On our last day in La Ronge, we interview a man who does not want to be named but who has information about one of the persons of interest who quickly becomes central to this story: the fishing guide working at the lodge on Lower Foster Lake.

Joseph Mason. Number three on my persons of interest list developed from Uncle Frank's theory.

Mason is everywhere but nowhere. In *The One-and-a-Half Men*, Dobbin calls him X. Mason would have been alive when Dobbin's book came out in 1981, and Dobbin was probably worried about a defamation lawsuit. In his interviews, various people talk about Mason's alleged involvement, and several people Deanna and I speak to name him as the murderer. Uncle Frank also thinks that Mason is connected, though simply as the guide who led the American hitmen to their target. Mason is dead, so legally I am free to name him, but an ethical briar looms.

The Masons are a large, respected, traditional family of the North, renowned for their hardworking sons and daughters and for contributing to the community. I met some Masons myself, and they were straight talking and kind.

Joe Mason veered from this path. Very little information is available about him, and people in the community speak cautiously. What can be gleaned is that Joe grew up on a trapline in northern Saskatchewan and was treated badly as a child. His mother was the one reliable source of love in his life, but she was unable to protect him. His mom was his centre of gravity, and Joe clung to her.

Somewhere, somehow, he became violent. There are stories that Mason murdered other people, but the RCMP never investigated these deaths as murders, and he was never charged. Then, in the early 1980s, he was convicted of a series of horrific violent offences and jailed in the Prince Albert Correctional Centre. In the 2000s, Mason was convicted of more of the same offences and went back to jail, where he died in 2009 at the age of eighty-two.

The man we speak to in La Ronge and who wants to remain anonymous had a connection to Mason's trial in the early 1980s. He describes Mason for us: "Kinda squat with green eyes. He looked happy! He was good in the bush. Walked straight lines in the bush."[1] Then we get a description of Mason's character. "I was leery of him. . . . He had a deranged mind and was not a sane man. . . . He was a lay reader in his church, and he would play with the hands of women in the congregation when they greeted him, as custom dictates, at the start or end of services." What he meant was that Mason would apparently stick his finger into women's palms in a sexually suggestive way. I heard from others that Mason had a maniacal laugh, that he slept with an axe in his bed for protection, that he was an excellent marksman, that he was evil. People disliked Mason and were afraid of him.

He worked as a fishing guide and prospector, and I ask why he got hired if he was such a creep. Stated simply, demand for labour in the North is seasonal, and when it is needed it is *really* needed. Businesses will hire anyone that they can get, and Mason was a competent bushman good at many jobs.

In the car on the way back to Saskatoon, Deanna and I mull over what we have found out about Mason, in particular the need to find a motive and any evidence connecting him to the other people implicated by Uncle Frank; otherwise, the whole conspiracy theory does not work. As more and more fingers point in the direction of Mason, I feel energized that we might be getting clarity about a possible murder suspect, and my mind goes into full investigation mode. But in the middle of our conversation, Deanna says in a quiet voice, "You know, I don't really want it to be Joe Mason. It just feeds stereotypes of the brutal savage."

I suddenly feel naive and out of my depth. Why didn't I anticipate this? Learning about stereotypes is a difficult—but essential—part of understanding another culture, but it is like walking on muskeg: the ground is firm one minute but then gives way, and you plunge into a muddy hole.

Maya Angelou writes in *All God's Children Need Travelling Shoes* that prejudice "confuses the past, threatens the future, and renders the present inaccessible."[2] But being naive about prejudice also runs the risk of confusing history and misunderstanding what is going on in the present.

Rumours of his involvement in Jim and Abbie's murders followed Mason until his death, causing him to be assaulted and resulting in threats to his life—hence the axe in his bed. Looking for a connection between Mason and Knox, Quandt, or Richards, I go back over Dobbin's interview with Knox, which establishes two things: (1) Knox also thinks that Jim and Abbie were murdered; (2) he identifies Mason as the killer. "[I] had every Indian coming to me with any clue and several of them independently came to me and said that [Mason] had been drunk and had boasted that he'd shot two men coming down the side of a steep cliff onto Foster Lake."[3]

Wait a minute! Mason actually said that he had murdered two men on Lower Foster Lake? This was never mentioned in the coroner's inquest. Had no one thought to tell the police?

The story goes that Mason was coming up the lake from the south when he saw Jim and Abbie climbing down the cliff toward the shoreline at the northeast end of the lake. Mason was an expert shot and killed them both. Just like that.

Knox decided at some point to set a trap to get Mason to confess: "We got him a job with a drill crew and I gave the drillers instructions to try and get this chap drunk. And they said they got him drunk but they never could get him to talk." Later a man even broke Mason's arm over it; people were "so sure that he was the chap [who had killed Brady and Halkett] . . . that they put him in Coventry."[4]

My instinct after hearing all of this news was to be skeptical. Mason was reportedly drunk when he said that he'd murdered two men, and Knox hadn't heard it directly from him, so it's hearsay. There are two facts, however, that can be checked. Is there a cliff on the northeast end of Lower Foster Lake? And was Mason on that part of Lower Foster Lake at the time? An affirmative answer to either question does not make Mason guilty, but negative answers would weaken the credibility of the story or even rule it out as a possibility.

The first question is easy to resolve: topographical maps show that, for about two kilometres along the eastern shore of the top end of Lower Foster Lake, the ground slopes steeply upward about thirty metres from the water to create a ridge. Not exactly a cliff but close enough. In time, I will travel to Lower Foster Lake and verify the geography for myself, but thanks to Air Canada I have an unexpected opportunity to view the lake. On a subsequent flight to Saskatchewan, I'm on a plane with seatback screens connected to Google Earth's 3D satellite representation. What's more, the system lets me navigate using a finger, just like on an iPad or tablet. Why didn't I think of this before? As soon as I realize this, I "fly" to northern Saskatchewan, and there it is: Lower Foster Lake with a ridge extending along the northeastern shore.

Regarding Mason's whereabouts, it is a fact that Mason was on the lake at the time of the disappearance, and there was a group of fishing tourists on the lake, a key element of Uncle Frank's theory that the hitmen were disguised as fishermen. At the coroner's inquest, Corporal Conrad testified that he had spoken to both Mason and a second guide, Noah Charles (who had arrived at the lodge to start work the day before the RCMP came in, so he was not actually there during the critical period). As Conrad stated, "We asked [Mason and Charles] if they had known of the camp at the north end of the lake. They stated they hadn't and they hadn't heard or seen anything."[5] This is a wholly unsatisfactory style of questioning and clearly not part of a potential murder inquiry: asking a person of interest if he knows anything and believing him immediately when he says no without trying to get other information so as to determine whether or not he is telling the truth?

There is a final piece of information about Mason's presence on the lake that overshadows everything else. It is a contemporaneous account of a conversation that Lloyd Mattson had with Berry Richards, as recorded by Mattson in a two-page summary of his and two others' efforts during the initial days of the search: "We beach on the east shore about halfway down the lake, directly across from Gary Thompson's fly-in tourist camp.[6] There had been a group of American tourists there, along with two guides, when the prospectors had been dropped off. Berry Richards, one of the men's two employers, told me that the tourists had informed the outfitter by radio that the guide had gone missing for three days and left them alone."[7]

Wait a minute! *The tourists complained that their guide had abandoned them for three days precisely when Jim and Abbie went missing?*

In the fishing tourism business, nothing is worse than a guide abandoning the clients and not taking them fishing. Having met Mattson, who comes across as utterly level-headed, I have no doubt that this conversation with Richards occurred and that Mattson's note is an accurate recollection. But Richards never mentioned this in either his interview with Dobbin or his account of the disappearance in his book *Gold and Other Stories as told to Berry Richards*. Did the police ask Mason where he had been during those days? Most likely not because Conrad had already "established" that Mason knew nothing about Jim and Abbie's camp.

The lodge owner should have been a critical witness for the Mounties. The RCMP should have had him confirm that he had hired Mason; the term of employment; what he knew about Mason's background and previous behaviour (had there ever been previous complaints or violence?); whether he knew of any connection that Mason had to Jim or Abbie; whether tourists had complained about being abandoned; and how Mason explained his absence during those three days. Surely it was a sackable offence to abandon clients. The owner should also have been asked who else was at the lodge at the time and their whereabouts and behaviour during the critical period. There is no record that the lodge owner was ever asked any of these questions. It's hard to understand why this was the case.

During a later visit to Saskatchewan, I telephone the lodge owner and put some basic questions to him. He confirms that Mason was a guide at the lodge at the time of the disappearance but says that he cannot recall anything about the police search, whether or not Mason disappeared for three days, or being cornered by Uncle Frank and Lloyd Mattson several years later. The owner is sure, however, that he personally wasn't on the lake at the time. The owner is now in his mid-eighties, and, as with others in this story, it is only fair to allow for memory lapses.

How, you might ask, would Mason have known that Jim and Abbie were on Lower Foster Lake given that they were dropped off there by accident? Uncle Frank's expansive version of events would say that it was all part of the plot: the pilot was in on it; the lodge owner was in on it; the fishing tourists were in on it; the guide was in on it.

Yet the radio call between Jim and Rottenstone Mine might have been how Mason became alerted to their presence on the lake, because people in the North listen in on each other's calls.

Eric Bell, with his local knowledge, helped me out here: "Oh, it was DNR's 'XLJ51 La Ronge.' That's the frequency everyone listened to."[8] However, because Jim probably thought that he was on Middle Foster Lake and had no reason to think that he was on Lower Foster Lake, he would not have said that he was on the latter lake, so eavesdropping alone can be discounted. Furthermore, if Jim had asked to be put down on Lower Foster Lake as part of a deliberate secret plan to disguise what he and Abbie were actually doing—in keeping with a secret prospecting flight—then he also would not have said where they were.

A simpler explanation is likely: Mason heard, or saw, the float plane land at the northern end of the lake and went to investigate. Sound travels over water for many kilometres, especially if there is little wind and especially in northern Saskatchewan, where it is eerily quiet. This means that, even if Mason was halfway down the lake close to the lodge, he likely would have heard the plane (if he didn't see it). Alternatively he might have overheard the radio call and seen the float plane land and put two and two together.

Missing from all of the above is an outstanding piece of information: motivation. Why would Mason want to murder Jim and Abbie? Was he someone else's instrument or an independent assassin? Was there any connection to Jim or Abbie that might have been a motive for murder?

As Deanna and I drive back to Saskatoon pondering these questions, we have a final task at the Prince Albert Courthouse, an imposing heritage building with manicured grounds, a traffic circle in front, and a view over the downtown core. Wills of deceased persons are lodged in a court and available to the public, and Jim's was in Prince Albert. I had submitted a request in writing, emphasizing that Jim was a public figure, and telephoned saying that I would be in Saskatchewan and would stop by to collect a copy of the document.

We arrive, park, and after the drive find ourselves springing up the long flight of stairs to the entrance in great anticipation of reading the will. On our minds is what will the document reveal about Jim's business interests and connections to the persons of interest?

Unfortunately the magistrate has not yet signed off on the release of the will. The clerk holds the file two feet away but can't even show it to us, and I feel like snatching it and running out of the building. I must have looked disappointed—or desperate—and the clerk offers to ask her superior. The manager, a no-nonsense woman, crisply states that the magistrate has to sign its release first; then she asks whose will it is. "A Métis activist from the 1960s called James Brady," I reply. "Jim Brady!" she exclaims, eyes wide. Still, there is nothing to be done, and we leave.

It was an anxious week before a long manila envelope with a "Court of Queen's Bench, Judicial Centre of Prince Albert" sticker on it turned up in my mailbox.

21
RIVER ICE

For six months after our visit to La Ronge, I'm preoccupied with establishing life in Quebec: getting my driver's licence; organizing a new permanent apartment, which mostly involves colour (forewarned about the dark of winter, I paint the walls glowing orange and verdant green); resisting *The Globe and Mail* and forcing myself into the world of francophone media; and undertaking work.

Wanting to engage in the life of Montreal and inspired by Canada's Tessa Virtue and Scott Moir's gold-medal performance at the PyeongChang Winter Olympics in 2018, I take up skating at the outdoor rink in Vieux-Port. I go mid-morning when the retirees go for their workout. Their skates whisper and slice, and they never fall. I clip-clop like one of the Percheron carriage horses pulling tourists around the Old City and tumble like a bowling pin. The rink has artificial ice kept in shape by a Zamboni, but there is a track outside the rink on water pumped from the St. Lawrence River into a former dock. River ice,

I discover, is rough and cracked. I also learn the two skills for a beginning skater to master: momentum and balance.

Equally good advice for writing a book. Every day I think about Jim and Abbie and plot a return to La Ronge as well as continue to accumulate more information. I need the momentum to follow leads and close off others, but what I'm really wrestling with is balance.

Momentum comes in the form of articles of incorporation and business licence registration documents for Foster Lake Mines Incorporated from the Saskatchewan Corporate Registry. Not surprisingly these documents do not give a full picture of who owned the company, but they confirm some information. The company was incorporated in Ontario on October 13, 1966, and had three founding directors (who were also shareholders), yet their names are completely new to this story. There is no mention of the usual suspects: Brady, Halkett, Knox, Richards, and Quandt. The number of shares issued initially was 40,000, valued at one dollar each, but the documents do not list all of the shareholders, so it is still not possible to know for sure whether Jim, Abbie, or their alleged business partners were co-owners. More than a month later, on November 22, three new directors were appointed, and this time the list includes Kehler, but again the other two names are completely new.

The appointment of Kehler on November 22, 1966, contradicts information from the prospectus that I found online, which states that he was appointed a director of Foster Lake Mines six months later, on May 31, 1967. The latter date suddenly looks less significant in relation to the disappearance and is possibly the result of careless fact-checking for a prospectus.

What I am left with is Knox's recollection to Dobbin that Knox personally sold Foster Lake Mines claims around Middle Foster Lake: "I'd sold these claim blocks to a promoter in Toronto and he'd put up the money and I'd got Berry [Richards] in, not only on the writing [of] the original report but got Berry to start the prospecting."[1] Clearly Knox was at least one of the owners of Foster Lake Mines, possibly right from the start, though we'll never know because this information is contained nowhere in the corporate registry documents.

With hindsight, it is obvious that Foster Lake Mines never claimed anything valuable, though this would not have been known when the claims were actually made. But this also means that there was no good business reason for co-owners to murder each other, though the possibility of assassination for other interests remains on the table. The last chance to obtain definitive information about business interests as a possible motive linking Jim, Abbie, Knox, Richards, and/or Quandt was shaping up to be the local repository of mining documents: the La Ronge Mining Recorder's Office.

It is not just ownership of mining companies that I am chasing now. I am also on a mission to find out more about Joe Mason, including the crimes for which he was convicted and any possible motive for killing Jim and Abbie. If I had precise information about his court trials, then I could request the transcripts, on the public record, and this information would free me to describe him in more detail.

I search various websites, googling "Joseph Mason Obituary," hoping that something might turn up. There are dozens of Masons, many of them Indigenous, possibly related to Joe, and many of them young. I'm impressed by the sizes of the families.

Everyone seems to have dozens of brothers, sisters, aunts, uncles, cousins, children, grandchildren, and great-grandchildren. The Internet has their photos and heartfelt messages posted by families for his passing.

But this search is also difficult to undertake. Whereas some men and women live to a grand old age, many Indigenous people die young. There is a formula for obituaries that starts with immediate surviving family members and then moves to "predeceased by. . . " Many Elders, I find during my search, are predeceased by their great-grandchildren, grandchildren, and children or by nieces and nephews. My own (alive and healthy) nieces and nephews appear in my head. Online I'm looking at the human face of the life expectancy gap between different communities in Canada. The early deaths in the Indigenous populations do not surprise me, but the lack of surprise does not make them less depressing.

I then come across a photo in the Glenbow Archives of Joseph. He is outside, staring straight into the camera. The photographer is Jim Brady. It has to be him: his age looks about right, and given their work they might well have come together at different times, giving Jim the opportunity to photograph Joe. Eric shows the photo to some people who knew Mason, and they confirm that it is him. Did Jim come across Joe working outdoors and ask to take his photo?

In the photo, Joe's eyes are narrowed, I assume because of light reflecting off the snow, and his face looks youthful. With a different expression, his face might be described as "open," but I find it inscrutable. In contrast, his stance seems to be relaxed, yet with an air of impatience, as if he is waiting for Jim to be done. And, far from Jim being the detached observer of the photographic subject, Joe stares right back. Who is observing whom?

While searching for more information about Mason, I hear of a documentary about Jim produced by the Missinipi Broadcasting Corporation in La Ronge in 2011—*Jim Brady: In the Footsteps of the Métis Leader*—and I finally manage to track it down. The film focuses on Jim's legacy and what it means to people today. The people interviewed—scholars, family members, contemporaries of Jim—talk about the disappearance and allude to reasons why someone might have wanted him dead. However, like the *One-and-a-Half Men* book, there is silence around one of those five Ws that guide investigators: *who*? A potential killer is never named. The producer of the documentary is Deborah Charles, and I call her to ask about the theory that Joe Mason was somehow involved. Deborah is friendly and helpful: "If you want to speak to people who knew him, I can introduce you," she says.[2] My planned return visit to La Ronge has regained momentum and focus.

I call Eric to ask him if he will be around and run over my plans to meet Mason's relatives. "You know," Eric counsels me, "Indigenous people don't like to speak badly about the dead."[3] My first reaction is to think "What a mannered culture. The world could learn something!" My second is to clutch my head and ask, "So what am I doing rummaging around in memories of Joe Mason?"

With whom am I hoping to speak? His family members? Can I bring myself to ask them, "About your relative, who went to jail for violent offences, do you think he was a murderer too?" For different jobs, I have done scores of interviews, including with murderers and terrorists and someone who lived through a mass killing, but I cannot think of anything more sensitive than speaking to one of Mason's family members.

Which goes to the question of balance. I want justice for Jim and Abbie, and I want to find out if they were murdered. This line of inquiry is propelling me toward Mason, and I want to know his role, if he had one. At the same time, if the rumours are true, then what authority do I have to write about this, to speak ill of the dead, because in what other direction could this possibly go? I need to be honest about my objective, but I don't want to interview Mason's family members for salacious details and then have the information published if it will traumatize or shame them.

Encouraging me is something that Louise Penny wrote in her crime fiction set in Quebec: "No man is as bad as the worst thing he's done."[4] From interviews that I've done in jails, I agree with this. But I have to be frank: *this* story isn't about finding the good in Joe Mason, and it isn't about understanding why he became the person he did, though I would like to know more about that. My hoped-for interviews are about understanding more fully why Joe might have killed Jim and Abbie and the consequences of this act for the community today.

Keeping the dictum "no man is as bad as the worst thing he's done" in my head ensures that I don't demonize Mason as a brutal man, which I have no interest, or business, in doing. Having detached myself from Mason's possible acts, I can focus on what is more important: the community's collective memory of Jim and Abbie.

Ultimately I conclude that publicly exposing the link between Jim and Abbie's disappearance and Joe Mason has to be negotiated with Mason's family members. Mindful of the people who want to know what happened to Jim and Abbie, I'm reluctant to keep Mason's name out of the manuscript that I'm writing about our research. However, I'll give his family members the power to decide how far this story will go.

It is in this spirit that I plan a return trip to Saskatchewan, but I'm anticipating river ice.

PART 3
DEAD
RECKONING

Dead reckoning: a mariner's term referring to finding one's location by the distance and speed travelled from the departure point rather than by landmarks or the stars.

22
IN PLAIN
SIGHT

n preparation for the return to La Ronge, I go over documents to check which gaps I need to fill through more interviews. I reread the article in *The Northerner* from August 4, 1977, "Disappearance in 1967 Still Causing Controversy," written by Lloyd Mattson, and there it is, hiding in plain sight in a newspaper, a forgotten clue about where Jim and Abbie might have ended up.

As his money started to run out after two months of searching in 1967, Mattson organized in August a final effort back around Lower Foster Lake. He managed to get McIvor Eninew of Sucker River involved, who "had the reputation of being one of the best bushmen in the La Ronge district."[1] Most Indigenous trackers learned their skills from childhood and can read the country like other people read books. What they see, which others do not, is detail. For example, when a tree is cut with an axe, the texture and "look" of the sap in the cut show how long ago the cut was made. Cut a tree in fall and it will freeze, but its sap will run in spring just as in a live tree, so you can tell

if the cut occurred before fall or not. The height of axe cuts
and broken twigs along a trail indicate how tall the person was.
Cuts and broken twigs on the left or right side of a trail indicate
whether the person favours the left or right hand (which might
help to narrow down the identity of the person who made the
trail). Step on a certain kind of moss and it will stay depressed
in a whitish footprint for a long time; even if it's raining the
footprint will remain.[2]

After walking the eastern shore of Lower Foster Lake,
Eninew told Mattson that he became suspicious of something
that shouldn't have been there:

> [There was] quite a bundle of white moss and
> straw (reeds) with stems as wide as a man's thumb.
> This was under shallow water, less than a foot deep,
> near the shore. It didn't belong there, because
> there wasn't any moss or grass like that growing
> anywhere near that spot. On the rock there was
> still the mark, almost an inch wide, where a boat
> had docked. I don't think it was a canoe.
>
> There was a sand beach some two hundred
> feet away where it would have been natural for a
> boat to land, not on the rock where the mark was.
> I looked over the straw and moss to see if there
> were any traces of blood, but couldn't see any.[3]

As he was trying to make sense of what he found, Eninew
noticed a plane circling their camp farther south. The plane had
come to take him back to Otter Lake. Tragically Eninew's son
had drowned, and his family had sent for him to help with the

recovery of the body. Eninew left the search for Jim and Abbie and never went back. No one ever pursued his clues.

So one of the best trackers in the area found suspicious signs that someone might have carried bloody cargo in his boat, requiring a bunch of moss and reeds to clean it out. What's more, the driver of the boat avoided a perfectly convenient landing spot just 200 feet (sixty metres) away and landed at a point on the shore where the boat could not be properly docked—unlike at the nearby beach, where the boat would have left a record in the sand. It seemed to be improbable that these faintest of clues could still be tenable weeks after the disappearance, especially when there was no sign of blood or human remains, but then I remember Kogvik and the HMS *Terror*. It's worth a leap of faith. But, then again, perhaps no leap is required, just confidence in traditional Indigenous skills.

The course of action seems to be simple for someone ignorant of lakes: find the spot identified by Eninew and use equipment that can search underwater. I don't expect the bundle of moss and reeds to be there, but the sand beach is likely to be. If Lower Foster Lake were a river, then its banks would have changed with flooding over the years, but the shoreline of a large lake would have remained more stable, especially if there were no great fluctuations in water levels (as is the case for Lower Foster Lake). Energized, but having no idea how feasible it is, I google "searching for bodies underwater in lakes" and come across the website of Gene and Sandy Ralston, who live in Idaho.

The Ralstons have made it their mission to help families locate the bodies of loved ones who have drowned. In thirty-five years, they have found over 120 people,[4] the key to their success being equipment called side scan sonar, towed underwater behind their boat and sensitive to unusual shapes on the lakebed. The Ralstons don't ask for payment, merely that costs be covered.

On one of their expeditions, the Ralstons searched for two American fishermen who disappeared on a lake in Nunavut in 2013. This piqued my interest because surely the logistics and costs would be similar to those of a search at Lower Foster Lake if we tried to do one there. The Ralstons had driven to Flin Flon, Manitoba, and had their equipment flown to the lake, about 800 kilometres farther north and even more remote than Lower Foster Lake. My mind starts racing, and I wonder if we could organize such a search.

I contact Gene and explain what I'm trying to do and that I've found clues about the possible location of the bodies of Jim and Abbie in the lake, though the precise location isn't really necessary for his search technique. Gene just needs to know which lake to search, get his equipment in place, and then go back and forth. One concern that I have is the depth of Lower Foster Lake and whether his equipment will work at its depth.

I ask Gene if he rents out his side scan sonar, if it is expensive, if it can be towed behind an ordinary boat, and whether an untrained (or quickly trained) person could operate it effectively. Alas, no. "The system we use primarily weighs about 150 pounds, so it requires the use of a powered hoist and boom to deploy. It would be very difficult to deploy from a small boat." He goes on to note, "We do have a lightweight starfish, but it is limited in the depth it can be used. In a situation like yours, it would be necessary to have a very well trained and experienced operator to be able to recognize what you were looking for."[5]

And, as it turns out, the search of the lake in Nunavut was unsuccessful. It was at the end of the season, the weather turned bad, and the Ralstons had to retreat. There was the possibility of returning the following summer to try again, but the lodge owner had quoted $20,000 for air transport of personnel and equipment, accommodations, meals, and support (the owner would have had to forgo clients to accommodate the team). I gulp at the cost, and my heart goes out to the family who could not afford it. There is also no way that any funds Deanna has available at this point could cover that amount. The one piece of good news is that side scan sonar can work at great depths, though the lightweight starfish has limitations. What I now need to find out is the depth of Lower Foster Lake at the point where the bodies might be.

I need to speak to Eric Bell. In addition to running a successful company that provides ambulance and paramedic services to the local community, he is a former parks ranger, a hunter, a boatman, and a fisherman. I know nothing about lakes, boats, or fishing, so Eric is the man to ask about how we could organize a lake search. Given that we are not capable of operating the equipment, could we raise the money for Gene himself to come to Lower Foster Lake? Would the local band council put up any cash? Is crowdfunding a possibility? Is there a La Ronge company that might sponsor us?

23
JIGGING
FOR TROUT

I n mid-March 2018, I arrive back in La Ronge, reaching the town at lunchtime and heading straight for the Saskatchewan Precambrian Geological Laboratory (the Mining Recorder's Office) which everybody simply calls the Mines Office. Although I am keen to help find the bodies of Jim and Abbie, I am equally keen to identify a motive for their possible murders perhaps linking them through a business interest to Knox, Richards, or Quandt. This connection is critical for Uncle Frank's theory to work. I know that Knox had some stake in Foster Lake Mines and that it had made at least five uranium claims, and I know that it had directors appointed in 1967 and ceased to exist in 1973, but I know almost nothing else. I am hoping that hard-copy claims files kept at the Mines Office might tell me something not available from corporate registry documents and arranged a visit with the woman running the office, Natalie Thompson.

In a town full of capable people, Natalie rubs shoulders with the best of them. Through managing the Mines Office over the years, she has accumulated knowledge of local history, geology, minerals, prospecting, mining, the bureaucracy around it, and the records that support it all. Like Eric, she knows the families of almost everyone involved in the events of the disappearance. Amazingly she also has an interest in unsolved missing persons cases and has tried to find out what happened to Jim and Abbie. As I walk in and introduce myself, she reaches out to shake hands. I've found a kindred spirit.

Our conversation is like a fire igniting. We follow tangents, explain ideas, interrupt each other, and propose hypotheses about what might account for different events. Natalie puts her long legs up on the desk; I lean forward on my elbows. I had emailed her in advance, and she has prepared a bundle of papers related to Foster Lake Mines. She also has at her fingertips various computer databases and knows how to use them at lightning speed. Even before I finish asking some of my questions, she has found the answers.

I explain about Gene Ralston and how he uses special equipment to locate bodies under water. "Oh, you mean side scan sonar," Natalie says matter-of-factly.[1] While I am expounding on the possibility of having Gene come to Lower Foster Lake—but also noting my uncertainty about its depths and whether his equipment might work (I read somewhere that it is almost 100 metres deep)—Natalie swivels to her computer, clicks a few times, and without a word walks out of the room while I am mid-sentence, mouth open. She comes back seconds later. "Here's a bathymetric chart of the lake," she deadpans and hands me a 38 × 107 centimetre poster that she has just printed out. I have never heard the word before—bath-uh-me-trik—but there it is: a map of the entire lake and its depths. Its deepest point is about forty metres, definitely within range.

I spend all afternoon at the Mines Office. I get a small thrill from the fact that it is the very building where Jim used to file his claims. It is also 100 metres down the hill from where his cabin used to stand. Documents and glittering rock specimens cover every surface. There are geological maps in drawers, on rails, and hanging all over the office; files, ledgers, and diaries (resident geologists used to keep diaries of daily comings and goings in the office) are kept in cabinets and pigeonholes lining the walls.

Natalie solves another puzzle, this one concerning the claim post found by James Tough four months after Jim and Abbie disappeared that had their initials on it but a date of July 9, 1967, one month after they most likely died. When I raise the "mystery" of the post, she immediately notes, "That's a practice prospectors used if they thought they could not get out of the bush in time to register the claim within the required thirty-day period or simply to buy more time. They put a date beyond the actual date of staking. It's illegal, but it happened." Natalie's explanation makes me laugh about the coroner's inquest and the cluelessness about prospectors' trickery, because the officials at the inquest had assumed that Jim and Abbie must have "quite possibly mistook June as the 7th month instead of the 6th."[2] It's what Deanna has been telling me about—this continued assumption that Indigenous people aren't competent enough— that those *damn Indians can't even get the date right!*

I'm secretly pleased that Jim and Abbie were likely just gaming the system. If it is true, though, then Richards is also implicated. At the inquest, his testimony shaped the official conclusion that

Jim and Abbie put the wrong date on the stake in error, because it was Richards who told Conrad that the date must have been a mistake.[3] Richards surely would have known that prospectors put incorrect dates on claim stakes, and it could have been Richards himself who suggested that Jim and Abbie do so. This would have made Richards like so many others in the mining industry, but he would not have wanted this to go on the public record—both to protect Jim and Abbie from allegations of illegal behaviour and to safeguard his own reputation. We can't know for certain, but it is within the realm of possibility.

After a long afternoon in the Mines Office with Natalie, I head back to Eric and Wanda's house, where I am staying again. The next morning, within thirty seconds of Eric walking downstairs in his pyjamas, even before the coffee is poured, he and I plunge deep into conversation. He too has been thinking about Jim and Abbie all night.

Having never used bathymetric charts before, I ask Eric about the chart from Natalie, which wasn't made until the 1970s. I wonder how Joe Mason would have known where the deeper parts of Lower Foster Lake were to dump the bodies of Jim and Abbie. "Oh, he'd know all right!" says Eric. "That's his job as a fishing guide. He'd know all the deep parts of the lake where he'd take clients to jig for trout."[4] Trout school in deep holes in rivers and lakes, and those who fish for them use landmarks to remember where those holes are—knowledge passed down through the generations and between fishing guides. It's a metaphor for this whole project: the outsider (me) trying to make sense of an apparently undifferentiated lake surface and shoreline and the locals with generations of knowledge about what is going on beneath the surface.

Eric and I study Natalie's chart and ascertain that there are two deep areas in the northern section where McIvor Eninew found the clues. One of these areas—the deepest part of the lake—is not far from the top end, just off the ridge on the eastern shore where, according to some stories that I heard, Mason allegedly shot Jim and Abbie. The priority search areas are looking right back at us from the chart.

Later that morning I return to the Mines Office to look through some documents in detail. I also have follow-up questions for Natalie, who has also been thinking about the disappearance and has some theories of her own.

Complete information about the ownership of Foster Lake Mines remains elusive, but what does become apparent is Knox's connection to the companies involved. From available documents and Internet sleuthing, I find that Knox likely had a stake in Pre-Cam Exploration and Development as well as Foster Lake Mines. This part of the story illuminates the skullduggery that often is a theme of Canada's mining history.

Both Pre-Cam and Foster Lake Mines did prospecting work and made mineral claims, but Pre-Cam also supplied services to other firms, such as staking, line cutting, prospecting, trenching, and assaying. Pre-Cam was registered in Saskatchewan in 1955 and was wound up in 1989, but it did little work after the 1960s.

To understand Knox's connection to Pre-Cam, it is necessary to go back a step. Knox previously fully or partly owned another company, Sico Mining Limited. Registered in Ontario in 1955, it appears to have been a less-than-ethical company in several respects. First, it had problems with American authorities when it illegally sold securities in the United States. It was put on the Securities and Exchange Commission's Canadian Restricted List in November 1959, and its charter was cancelled in 1964 (though a Toronto brokerage firm was still trying to sell its stock illegally in 1960 after it was blacklisted). Second, also in 1960, Sico sold certificates of ownership to an orange grove in British Honduras, now Belize. A man whose father owned one of those certificates, as well as Sico shares, wrote to an investment advice column in 2007 wondering whether his orange grove certificate was worth anything and explaining that he had correspondence from William Knox in 1962 saying that Sico's headquarters had been moved to Belize. According to the columnist, "it does not smell right. I doubt that there is any value in the land, or even if the one to two hectares of oranges are real. Deeds to nonexistent land was a common equity promotion technique. They would put dummy figures on a sheet of paper to hook suckers into buying stock, but the ownership of the ground was not real. It was more common in Florida before the Second World War."[5] I wince on behalf of the man's father, whom the columnist labelled a "sucker." I also wonder about Knox.

Being put on the restricted list in 1959 would have scared investors away from Sico Mining, making it difficult for the company to raise capital. What happened next is not entirely clear, but there is a record of Sico being amalgamated into or merged in some way with Pre-Cam. A merger could have allowed Knox to retain an interest in Sico's mining claims through a new legitimate business: Pre-Cam. So Knox was a part owner of Foster Lake Mines, which hired Pre-Cam—which Knox might also have partly owned—to do the uranium assay work carried out by Jim and Abbie.

Trying to trace ownership of mining interests is like a game of mirrors and sliding doors, and this is just the way that the industry seems to like it. The case of Pre-Cam adds to the challenge. The Saskatchewan Corporate Registry has no document on file for Pre-Cam—the official who answered my call was apologetic but didn't sound surprised. For a company registered in 1955, you might think that this is not unusual, for perhaps the documents were thrown out or got lost in a relocation of the archives. The difference is that Pre-Cam is actually well known in certain legal circles because of a court case between it and a former employee called Douglas McTavish. It was a case of "master versus servant" and centred on intellectual property regarding knowledge of mineral deposits. The case went all the way to the Supreme Court of Canada, and Pre-Cam has a profile in legal circles because of the precedent set by the court's judgment.

In brief, a man called Maurice Murtack staked some claims and wanted further exploration work done. Murtack hired Pre-Cam, which hired McTavish, to do the work. McTavish found evidence of mineral deposits in adjoining areas during his contract with Pre-Cam. He quit Pre-Cam and then staked these neighbouring claims for himself. Normally an employee would have to tell Pre-Cam about these deposits, and the company would have staked them for its client (Murtack). Pre-Cam took McTavish to court saying that he had illegally used knowledge gained in the course of employment with Pre-Cam to benefit himself. Murtack and Pre-Cam won the case; the Appeals Court overturned the decision, finding in McTavish's favour; Murtack and Pre-Cam then took the case to the Supreme Court, which ruled in their favour on June 21, 1966. There are scores of subsequent judgments that quote *Pre-Cam v McTavish*. Ironically, though, for such a prominent case, it is a challenge to identify the actual owners of Pre-Cam.

With the help of 411.ca, I track down one of the lawyers for Pre-Cam during the case, still living in Saskatchewan. He was young at the time, not long out of law school. Now in retirement, he has memories of working on his first big, exciting Supreme Court case but, alas, cannot remember who actually owned the company.

One thing is certain about Foster Lake Mines: it is the only entity that would have benefited from an incorrect date on the claim stake discovered by James Tough after the disappearance because the work was done in its name. Given that Jim and Abbie would not have benefited personally from this false date unless they were owners, and that was becoming less and less clear anyway, they must have done it because they were told to do so. The direct instruction likely would have come from Richards at Pre-Cam, but Pre-Cam would not have benefited either since it was simply doing the work for its client. Therefore, Richards likely would have been asked to do this by whoever represented Foster Lake Mines on the ground in La Ronge.

And that person would have been Knox.

24
DREAMS

At lunchtime I finally take my leave from Natalie; although I try, no thanks can suffice for her assistance. For the rest of my time in La Ronge, a booth at Kosta's Restaurant becomes my office; indulged by staff who let me sit there for hours, I hold my interviews there, meeting person after person. The spring equinox has almost arrived, and the dark northern winter has turned brilliant: sunshine and blue sky with a wind chill of minus a million. I can see twenty kilometres clear across the frozen lake: an ice fisherman in the foreground, a long low line of smokey hills in the far distance, a white void in between. A black skidoo zooms around the lakeshore, then a blue one takes off across the ice.

That evening Wanda goes out, and Eric and I catch up. In addition to everything else that he does, he coaches a local hockey team. After hearing of my skating travails in Montreal, he gets up and demonstrates in his socks on the living room floor how to do parallel hockey stops and forward crossovers for corners. In my socks, I imitate his movements.

After the day's events and conversations, I go to bed early. Around 2 a.m., I'm woken by a dream. One of Joe Mason's daughters is trying to telephone me. She cannot reach me, but in the dream I know that it is important, and frustration that I cannot speak to her wakes me up. It is an hour before I can get back to sleep.

The dream heralds a series of conversations over the next twenty-four hours that resolves one issue: *why* does everyone think that Mason murdered Jim and Abbie? Knox said that he had heard his confession from a couple of people, but Mason was reportedly drunk when he told one or two of them. I need to hear it from someone else, preferably someone alive, who will admit that Mason said it when he was sober.

What I discover asking around La Ronge is that Mason repeatedly told several people in and around the town—and a couple of these people are still alive—that he had murdered Jim and Abbie and disposed of their bodies. One local man says that he heard first-hand that Mason had killed them, wrapped their bodies with some wire, and dropped them overboard in the centre of the lake. People believed Mason when he said these things because of his reputation.

Declarations of guilt by killers are not new in either fiction or fact. In Fyodor Dostoevsky's classic novels *Crime and Punishment* and *The Brothers Karamazov*, a murderer seeks people to whom he can confess his crime. Real-life murderers regularly do the same: they confess to friends and family members, to fellow inmates, to nuns and priests, on their deathbeds, and occasionally to police officers.

In investigations there are three basic questions to ask about murder suspects. Is it likely that he or she could kill someone?

Is there a motive? Was there an opportunity to do it? Taken as a whole, the stories about Mason suggest that he was capable of killing, and the RCMP should have pursued this angle through a more thorough and careful investigation. Interviews with witnesses, friends, family members, colleagues, and employers would have enabled the police to assess Mason's background, including behavioural patterns, criminal history, personality, and any confidential intelligence about him held by authorities. Normally an assessment would also be done of the crime scene, if there is one, and any connections between the victim(s) and the murderer looked into thoroughly. The Mounties neglected to do any of this. Why? Because it appears that they didn't believe the disappearance of Jim and Abbie involved murder. They decided that the men simply had gotten lost and died. But let's review the other two questions. In regard to opportunity, Mason was on the same lake and disappeared for three days when Jim and Abbie disappeared. And now motive: *why* would Mason kill them?

The explanation that I hear in La Ronge is blunt and unexpected but in some ways all too predictable: Jim was having an affair with Mason's mother. This was well known at the time within the family and community, and Mason didn't like it one bit. Jim had a reputation as a ladies' man, and when Mason found out about the affair he became enraged by the idea that his mom might be just another affair for Jim. We don't know how Mason's mother, or Jim, viewed the relationship, but their views wouldn't have mattered to a protective and controlling son.

The story that I find most disturbing is about a different sort of killing. Mason told a couple of people that he had shot two deer at Lower Foster Lake around the time of the disappearance.

Locals scoff when they hear this because there are no deer around the Foster Lakes. (Saskatchewan's two species of deer, whitetail and mule, are found farther south.) But I picture these imaginary deer—in actuality Jim and Abbie—lying dead in the snow. It's gruesome, and possibly this is the effect that Mason intended.

Surprisingly the only person I meet who has a decent word to say about Mason is Uncle Frank. "I didn't think he was so bad!" he tells me.[1] This is puzzling because Frank also thinks that Mason was involved in Jim and Abbie's disappearance, albeit as the guide for American hitmen rather than as the assassin. I never get to the bottom of this, but maybe it's because Mason is the only Indigenous person in Frank's version of events, and Mason is an instrument of the white architects of the crime. If you were Indigenous and participated in "the system"—did the bidding of white people—then you needed your eyes opened. Meaning that Mason went along with the white man's plot not because he was bad but because he was not enlightened. Jim Brady would have called it false consciousness about one's real interests, which to Frank meant supporting your own people and not conspiring against them.

Uncle Frank also thinks that Mason's participation took a terrible personal toll on him. Frank says that Mason was so ridden with guilt at what he'd done that he "basically turned into a vegetable and a drunk" and then—in a sure sign of guilt in Frank's opinion—"to religion." I'm not totally persuaded by Frank's account; for one thing, Mason's violence went on long after 1967. It actually says more about Uncle Frank, who cannot believe that an Indigenous man who murdered Jim and Abbie would be able to live with himself.

What I discover after all of this is that stories of Mason's involvement in Brady and Halkett's disappearance percolated in Saskatchewan for fifty years. I find it hard to believe that the RCMP officers based in La Ronge, including Corporal Conrad, would not have heard these stories before the coroner's inquest, which took place twenty-one months after the men disappeared. Yet the possibility of their murder was never raised at the inquest, and no witnesses were called who might have ventured to talk about it—well, no one except Abbie's partner, Annie, and how difficult would it have been for her to challenge the narrative of all those white men speaking English back then?

While the search was under way in 1967, Lloyd Mattson tried to speak to the police about the possibility of murder, but it appears that Conrad just wrote it off. In the 1970s, Dobbin also asked Conrad if he had been aware of rumours about a murder.

CONRAD: Yeah, well, see anytime anything happens up there, (chuckles) from my experience in working in La Ronge, you get millions of stories. . . .

DOBBIN: Right. So, you treated that story basically as the kind of thing that naturally comes out of a disappearance in the north?

CONRAD: Yeah, right.

DOBBIN: Was there ever any consideration of investigating that at all?

CONRAD: No, it was discounted when we found the evidence
that they had been at Lapointe.[2]

The problem is that the raft was not evidence that Jim and Abbie were at Lapointe Lake.

On my final morning in La Ronge, I meet with Deborah Charles, CEO of Missinipi Broadcasting Corporation (MBC), who produced the documentary *Jim Brady: In the Footsteps of the Métis Leader*. Although it is Sunday, Deborah has agreed to come into the office so that we can have coffee and visit. She is that rare combination of a capable executive who is also genuine and warm. MBC is one of the foundational partners of the Aboriginal Peoples Television Network, which I've now watched quite a few times, and on the drive to La Ronge I listened to MBC's news in Cree—mainly, I admit, because it was the only station that I could get in the car.

Deborah asks me about my project, and I ask her about MBC's documentary and its conclusions about the disappearance. I recognize that she went through the same struggle to create a compelling text about the disappearance half a century ago of two men whom everyone in the community knew and about whom everyone has an opinion and wants answers. When I compliment Deborah on what her film says about Jim's impact and legacy, I inadvertently hit a sensitive point regarding the documentary's silence about a possible murder suspect. She tells me that after the documentary came out a number of people complained, accusingly noting, "You didn't name the murderer!" She retorted, "I'm not an investigator, I'm a producer."[3]

My original plan for this meeting with Deborah included meeting some of Mason's relatives, to whom she was to introduce me. But for various reasons this arrangement did not work out. To be honest, I'm relieved, though I would like to meet them eventually. I tell Deborah that I would like to name Mason as a possible suspect if the family agrees. I feel compelled to do this given my commitment to all those who want and need to know what happened to Jim and Abbie. Deborah advises me, "Our traditional way is that you are to ask the family member for permission" to use the name of a person who has passed away. We agree that she will contact the family for permission to pass on a phone number to me, and then I will call to ask for their permission to name Mason.

25
THE FRIEND

My stay in La Ronge becomes the quintessential research trip in that nothing goes as planned and is thus full of anticlimaxes. I accomplish few of the big things that I hoped to do, namely obtaining definitive answers to key questions. However, I find a host of details and clues that fill out more and more of the overall picture. In particular, I narrow in on one of Jim Brady's best friends and political comrades and, according to Uncle Frank, a key conspirator: Allan Quandt.

Quandt joined the Saskatchewan Department of Natural Resources in 1946. In 1949, he was posted to Cumberland House, where he quickly became friends with Jim. The following year Quandt recruited Jim to be a field officer for the Fish Board. They spent much of the next two decades together: in the CCF, in the Communist Party, working for the government. In fact, Jim lived with the Quandts for several months in the 1950s, and he remained a frequent visitor until 1967. Jim said that he and Quandt were good friends, "except for once in a while when we get in a critical mood. One thing that I like about Quandt is I can criticize him. In other words, he can hand it out but he can take it too."[1] At the coroner's inquest, Quandt also described himself as "a very close friend" of Jim's,[2] and he named his youngest child James Malcolm Quandt after both Jim and Malcolm Norris (whom he also knew).

Quandt ran as a CCF candidate in the 1960 provincial election (he didn't win). The Pahkisimon Nuye?áh Library in La Ronge has his campaign brochure, in Cree syllabics and English. Quandt is on the cover in a buzz cut, tweed jacket, and open-necked shirt, wedding ring visible and pen in hand with papers in front of him—ready to sign progressive legislation into law! He has a striking, almost gaunt face with intense eyes looking straight at the voter and a boxer's jaw. The haircut, prominent wedding ring, and suit jacket hint of conservative gestures, calculated to soothe fears that he wanted to revolutionize society (which of course he did).

Quandt was Jim's "closest political confidant."[3] Jim regularly sent letters to Quandt in which they addressed each other as "Comrade," though this was probably partly tongue-in-cheek given Jim's sense of humour. Like Jim, Quandt had a wry sense of humour. In 1960, he did some redecorating as part of his political campaign: he painted his house from communist red to colonial grey.[4]

Quandt also knew Abbie well and had a lot of respect for him. They had worked together on a couple of different prospecting contracts.

Just about the first person Berry Richards told about Jim and Abbie going missing after he found their abandoned camp was Quandt, working at Otter Lake that day in June 1967. Unlike

Richards, Quandt always suspected foul play and criticized the RCMP investigation: "There was never an adequate investigation on the spot . . . only rudimentary questions by young inexperienced officers that did no follow-up, didn't know the bush, and got eaten by bugs."[5]

At the coroner's inquest, concerned that it was treating the case as a search for lost persons rather than potential murders, Quandt prompted the lawyer representing Jim's estate, Marcel Simonot from Prince Albert, to ask whether anyone else was on Lower Foster Lake at the time of the disappearance since the issue had not been raised and the police had not thought it important enough to mention. Corporal Conrad's reply that there were other people present—Joe Mason and his wife—and that he'd spoken to them ensured that these facts became part of the public record and not otherwise forgotten. Quandt believed that Mason was the murderer, but he also thought it unfair that he was named publicly without a proper inquiry.

It was the connection to Jim in death that put Quandt squarely in Uncle Frank's sights. As the executor of Jim's will—a sign of trust by Jim—Quandt took control of his estate. Once probate was issued, he arranged for most of Jim's papers to go to the Glenbow Archives in Calgary, though he retained a few documents that went to his daughter, Cathy, when he died.

Eric Bell went to school with Cathy, who grew up in La Ronge and now lives in Saskatoon. He discovers that she has come to town the very weekend that I am there, and we arrange to meet at Kosta's Restaurant. Unlike everyone else in La Ronge, dressed in baggy casual clothing and dirty snow boots on this chilly winter's day, Cathy is a breath of city chic. She has a stylish haircut, wears a classy grey jacket with a row of black buttons down the front, and asks me about my travels, suggesting that I keep aside a few hours in Saskatoon for its new art museum, the Remai Modern. I like her straight away.

I explain our project. Cathy knew Jim well having seen him constantly as a child, and she is intrigued. She has brought a friend, and when I mention that Jim and Abbie disappeared at a lake and there are rumours of murder, the friend chimes in: "A group of seven artists were murdered on a lake in Ontario." I'm dumbstruck. What a violent country I've come to! In fact I've misheard her friend, who has actually said, "One of the Group of Seven artists was murdered on a lake." At home I research this episode. The Group of Seven painted the landscape in a new way, laying the basis for a distinctive Canadian art movement. The artist who disappeared was Tom Thomson, not officially a member of the group, which formed after his death, but he greatly influenced it. Thomson disappeared on a lake in 1917, and 100 years later rumours persist that he was murdered, though some say that it was a case of suicide or drowning. I'm not too sure about art movements, but this mix of fact and dark mystery, connected to an isolated lake, is starting to feel very Canadian.

Cathy has only good memories of Jim but says that he "wasn't like a typical dad who would ruffle your hair."[6] Unlike some adults who ignore children, Jim talked to her, "and he called me Raggedy Anne because I was a tomboy." She also remembers intense conversations about politics between her father and Jim.

Cathy asks me what Uncle Frank says about her dad, and in that instant I realize that she is not aware of what he thinks. I try to be gentle: "Frank's murder theory is expansive and encompasses a lot of people, including your dad." Cathy flushes, pauses for a couple of breaths, then recalls Frank coming to their home and "having a rip-roaring argument" with her father. "It was the first time I ever heard Dad say *fuck*." Quandt told Frank, "Get the hell out of my house!"

When I hear this, I am sure that the argument was about Jim's will. Months later I find Roberta Quandt's summary of this moment: "[Lloyd] Mattson and [Frank] Tomkins walked into our home and accused Allan of killing Brady."[7] Normally I admire Frank's uncompromising style, but I cringe to think of its impact on those who might be targeted unfairly.

Cathy promised Eric that she would bring along the documents related to Jim that she had inherited from her dad, and during a lull in the conversation she pulls out from under the table a sheaf of material in a blue manila folder and passes it to me. I'm intrigued by what has just come into my hands but, remembering my manners, resist the temptation to ignore everyone and start looking through the papers.

Examining them that evening, I find Quandt's copy of Jim's will (the same as what I obtained from the Prince Albert courthouse); probate papers prepared for Quandt by Simonot & Hansen, the legal firm in Prince Albert; statements from 1974 by Berry Richards, Lloyd Mattson, and Leonard Isbister that they did not find evidence that Jim and Abbie were still alive; a letter from a Dr. Ken Hatt, a sociology professor, whom Quandt asked to prepare an inventory of Jim's documents; and an 8 × 10 inch photo portrait of Jim looking clean-cut in a suit and tie. The gem in the folder is a seventy-five-page typewritten list—I assume made by Jim because it is on the back pages of old fisheries cooperative reports—of what appears to be every book that he ever owned or read (about 4,500 titles). It is an extraordinary historical document that offers insight into Jim's reading habits. Other people would have thrown the list out, but the fact that Quandt kept it shows that he understood its value. I call Deanna, knowing that this document will interest her since she is a professor of English and Indigenous Studies. She responds, "If someone wants to know what a Métis was reading in the 1960s, show them this list!"

Two things set Uncle Frank against Quandt, leading to the angry confrontation that Cathy remembers. First was the fact that a "couple of days" after the disappearance Quandt went to Jim's cabin and cleared out all his books and papers and then rented the cabin to someone else. Quandt, as executor, had authority over Jim's estate, but the search was still in progress, which makes the timing of this act so odd. For all Quandt knew, Jim and Abbie might still have been alive, shortly to be rescued. Frank's theory is that Quandt and Knox wanted to get their hands on certain papers of Jim's.

This is so strange that I need "triangulation": that is, confirmation by a third person that it is true. It's not that I don't believe Uncle Frank, it's just that taking Jim's possessions out of his home before Jim was pronounced dead is extraordinary. Fortunately, not only is the man who rented Jim's cabin still alive, but also Eric knows him and tells me that he will verify this story (and I thank God for small communities).

The man who rented the cabin when Jim went on his last prospecting trip was John Beatty, who tells Eric that he did so *before* the disappearance, not after it. During the prospecting season, Jim was constantly in the bush, so renting out his cabin was a way to earn money and ensure that someone kept an eye on it. Beatty was actually supposed to go with Jim and Abbie on their prospecting trip to Middle Foster Lake, but he got a job at the pulp mill in Prince Albert. It was Beatty's wife who was living in the cabin when Quandt and Knox came to take Jim's things. However, this was a few weeks—not days—after the alarm went out.

Uncle Frank seems to have confused the timing, but the basic issue remains: not so long after Jim and Abbie disappeared, possibly after the RCMP search had concluded but certainly many months before the coroner's inquest made any official pronouncement regarding their disappearance, Knox and Quandt went to Jim's cabin and removed his things. Jim was not officially dead, so why did they do this?

There are a couple of possible reasons. Executors have a legal responsibility to keep assets and not to reduce their value until they can be disposed of according to the person's wishes, and Quandt might have worried about Jim's things being removed by others. Quandt later said that "a lot of stuff [was] stolen, but I secured the cabin and boxes. . . . We had all the records in our attic. We had to wait seven years. [Frank] Tomkins was angry because I wouldn't give up records."[8] From his perspective as executor, Quandt needed to secure the estate. Even family members were not allowed to take anything until it was formally settled.

But there is a complication here. Executors of wills cannot "execute" their duties unless the person is deceased. Under Saskatchewan law regarding what was described as an "absentee person" at the time, Quandt became the executor only after a judge had declared that Jim had disappeared, and his whereabouts were unknown, or there was no knowledge about whether he was dead or alive. When his possessions were removed from his cabin, no one knew for sure if he was dead. Legally, therefore, Quandt was not yet the executor, and entering Jim's cabin might well have been trespass and removing items from it theft. Perhaps Quandt was not aware of this legal complication. Alternatively he might have known about it but been motivated by something that outweighed breaking the law: securing certain things of value.

Jim had one of the largest private libraries in Saskatchewan. Quandt—an educated man who would have appreciated the collection—might have wanted to ensure that the books were not thrown out. He also would have understood the historical value of Jim's correspondence with the likes of Malcolm Norris and Pete Tomkins Jr. (Uncle Frank's father) and other documents about the organization of Métis associations and wanted to preserve them.

There is a more intriguing possibility. As a member of the Communist Party, Quandt might have been concerned that Jim's papers contained compromising information about party business and members. Taking Jim's possessions was the easiest way to ensure that they did not fall into the hands of the RCMP.

Quandt had good reason to be worried about the police, for he himself was under surveillance. He discovered this through a botched postal delivery and an ensuing small-town comedy. The RCMP had retained a local resident to keep tabs on Quandt and then post reports to a handler—a routine method. Somehow, though, one of those reports was sent to the wrong address. The recipient returned the package to Canada Post, which dutifully opened it to look for information on who should get it. Canada Post found Quandt's name and sent the package to Quandt, thus alerting him to the fact that he was being watched.[9]

Deanna and I spent three days poring through Jim's papers at the Glenbow Archives in Calgary looking for anything about communists or the Communist Party or his mining and business interests. There was a noticeable lack of materials about either, other than a few items from the 1930s, including Jim's Communist Party membership card. In addition, though the archives contained information about thirty-five mineral claims and a few other prospecting-related papers, including hand-drawn maps and directions on how to get to remote mineral showings, there was not a single scrap of paper that mentioned Foster Lake Mines. This does not mean that such documents were not once part of the collection in Jim's cabin. However, even if mineral claims had been removed, legal ownership could not have been transferred to someone else without the involvement of the original claim recorder (i.e., Jim himself), though the information could have been.

We'll never know for sure whether Quandt or Knox removed documents from Jim's possessions or, if that is what happened, did so with the intention of destroying some of them (e.g., Communist Party documents) or benefiting from them (e.g., mining-related documents with transferable value). However, if they did remove documents, there is no evidence that Quandt gained any material advantage by doing so.

There is one more potential legal complication related to wills. If someone has a reasonable claim to access the property of a deceased person, such as wanting to view documents, then the executor should allow access to it. Uncle Frank wanted access to Jim's papers because he was sure that Jim and Abbie had been murdered and wanted an investigation. Should Quandt have permitted this? Legally no. If Frank thought that Jim's papers contained evidence of a motive for assassination, he should have gone to the police, who could have gotten a warrant to seize the documents. The problem is that the RCMP would have paid no attention to Frank. Jim and Abbie were listed as missing persons who got lost while prospecting, and, as far as the police were concerned, that was that. It was a catch-22: without access to the documents, Frank couldn't prove a motive for murder, but without evidence of a motive the police wouldn't investigate. No wonder Frank was frustrated.

Frank's second criticism of Quandt is about the will itself. Frank swears that the will shown to him by Quandt (a one-page document) was different from the one that he signed (at least three pages) and that his signature was forged. Serious allegations.

Frank is sure that the probated will is a forgery because, according to him, the original version that he witnessed and signed bequeathed Jim's cabin in La Ronge to Frank's parents. Naturally this stuck in Frank's mind because it gave his parents a personal connection to the estate. The probated will left everything to Quandt except for a parcel of land in Lac La Biche, Alberta, which went to Jim's brother, John.

If Frank's account of the will is true, then the normally careful Jim made a basic mistake. Ideally witnesses for wills should be totally disinterested. That is, they should receive no benefit from an estate. Asking Frank to be a witness, when leaving the cabin to his parents, gave him an interest. If a lawyer drew up the will, then this was an egregious error for a lawyer to make. If Jim wrote it, then it was an error of judgment because it would create complications down the track for probate. Of course, the will that Frank recalls never got probated.

In the Name of God, Amen: This is the Last Will and Testament of I, James Patrick Brady, Prospector, ordinarily resident in the Village of La Ronge, in the Village of La Ronge, in the Province of Saskatchewan, Canada. Made this 3rd day of July, 1963 in the said Village of La Ronge, Saskatchewan, Canada.

I do hereby appoint Allan K. Quandt, Buisness Agent, in the Village of La Ronge, Saskatchewan, as the Executor of my Estate.

I do hereby devise and bequeath unto my brother, John Redmond Brady, Railway Employee, of the Town of Lac La Biche, in the Province of Alberta, Canada, the following described parcel of Land: All that portion of the North West Quarter of Section Thirty Six (36) Township Sixty Six (66) Range Fourteen (14) West of the Fourth (4th) Meridian in the Province of Alberta, the land herien described containing twenty-eight and sixty-eight hubdredths (28.68) acres more or less. Ref. Certificate No.81-V.58. Seal 140-M-103 North Alberta Lands Registration District.

I hereby devise and bequeath unto Allan K. Quandt all the remainder of my real and personal property. Given under my hand and signature this 3rd day of July, 1963. A.D.

Witness: *Malcolm F Norris.*   J.P. Brady
Witness: *Frank Land*   A.K. Quandt

Jim's Last Will and Testament. *Source: Judicial Centre of Prince Albert. Reprinted with permission from Anne Dorion.*

The date of Jim's will is also different from what Frank remembers. He says that he signed it as a witness in September 1966, a date connected in his mind with his packing up from firefighting that summer and returning south. The will from the Prince Albert Courthouse is dated July 3, 1963, three years before Frank says that he signed it, another reason that he says his signature is a fake. It has his signature as well as that of Malcolm Norris as a second witness.

Could there have been two wills? It wouldn't be the first time that this happened, but we simply don't know, and Frank insists that he signed only one will. Hypothetically, if Quandt manufactured the will dating from 1963, what would he have gained from it? The Alberta land went to Jim's brother, and Jim's other assets were $651.14 in the Canadian Imperial Bank of Commerce, personal effects valued at $100, papers valued at $1, and his cabin on leased land and valued at $500. The total value of the estate was estimated at $1,252.14 (about $10,800 in today's money).

Quandt did not benefit from the cabin. When Jim's daughter, Anne Dorion, legally became an adult, she inherited it from her father's estate. Anne told us that over time the cabin was abandoned, and when it fell into disrepair she donated it to the local fire service to practise putting out fires. Quandt donated Jim's papers to the Glenbow Archives (but they had historical rather than monetary value anyway), and he paid himself five dollars (about forty-three dollars in today's money) for expenses associated with his duties as executor—a proper and normal thing for an executor to do. I don't know what happened to the $651.14 in the bank, worth about $5,600 today, but Jim would have had income tax and some bills to pay,[10] and Quandt would have used some of these funds for this purpose—again entirely appropriate for an executor to do. In 1967, and even more so in 1978 when Jim's will was probated, Quandt was financially comfortable, so the idea that he might have manipulated the will to get the equivalent of perhaps $5,000 is extremely unlikely. In fact, Quandt's application for probate made on June 9, 1978— granted on June 15—explicitly renounces his right to receive any proceeds from Jim's estate, with the exception of expenses and fees that Quandt could legitimately claim as executor.[11]

Overall, his fulfillment of executor duties seems to have been capable and just. Certainly the public should be forever grateful that Quandt arranged for Jim's papers to go to the Glenbow Archives. He did not make this decision unilaterally. Quandt asked Anne Dorion if she was happy to have the papers deposited there, and she was. He also gave her a trunk full of Jim's personal items.

There is a remaining question about the letters probate process, which relates to Quandt as the witness used by the court to authenticate the will. At first glance, this is odd given that he was the executor, because normally a court would use a disinterested witness to authenticate a will. But the answer to this is simple. There were two witnesses to Jim's will: Norris, who was dead, and Frank, who had accused Quandt of forgery and conspiracy to commit murder. Frank would hardly have authenticated the will, and Quandt wouldn't have asked him. When there are no witnesses available, and if the executor was present when the witnesses signed the will, then the court will accept a statement from the executor that he or she saw the will being witnessed. This was the case for Jim's will: Quandt was present when Norris and Frank witnessed it, and he made an affidavit to this effect and included it in his probate application.[12] The court accepted the affidavit as ground for authentication.

At the start of the project, knowing nothing about Quandt or Knox or Richards, I was open to the idea that they could have been diabolical enough to plan Jim and Abbie's murders. This would have been the greatest of ironies because Jim once said that only three white people in La Ronge ever invited him into their homes: Quandt, Richards, and "another family," who surely must have been Knox given that we know Jim stayed with him.[13] The fact is that I simply couldn't find corroborating evidence of their involvement in the disappearance. For heaven's sake, if they wanted to kill Jim, then why didn't they just send an assassin at night to his cabin to shoot him? Jim was up at all hours reading and opened his door to anyone, ready to lend the person a book. What's more, why would Richards and Knox become so involved in the search? Uncle Frank thinks that this was a ruse to make sure suspicion did not fall on them, but this would have required considerable effort for an already complicated plot.

Mentally exhausted by the twists and turns of my stay in La Ronge, I pack my things, say goodbye to Eric and Wanda, and get on the road to Saskatoon. I am on the lookout for hitchhikers with whom to chat and keep me alert while I drive. It is -8 degrees Celsius, and I pass an older Indigenous man walking along the side of the road in the middle of nowhere, but he is headed north. I wave; he waves back. At the airport, wanting to reflect on everything that I've heard and jot down a few more notes before boarding, I stop at Timmies for an apple fritter and a coffee.

26
THE BIG FIND

On my return home, I am confronted by an outstanding issue about Uncle Frank's theory. Did Jim make a big find? His discovery of a valuable mineral deposit is what allegedly drove Jim and Abbie's white business partners to take over the company in whose name the deposit was registered. Without a big find, Knox, Quandt, and Richards don't appear to have had a motive, so I must complete this part of my investigation.

I was doubtful about the big find. It seemed too . . . Hollywood. Yet Knox corroborates precisely this in his interview with Dobbin. According to Knox, Jim went up a river and found a rusty scarp, and "anything rusty you look at" because that colour in rock indicates mineral content. Knox offered to grubstake Jim, on the basis of a fifty-fifty partnership, to return to explore the deposit more in 1967: "[Jim] had the sketch maps and everything but I never did get a chance to make the applications out before he was gone on his last and fatal trip and I never got his signature." Knox continues: "I applied to the government for the claims to be recorded for part of [Jim's] estate because he thought he'd found something pretty valuable. And the strange thing is it was right in the middle of what later became Gulf permit #1 not far from Wollaston Lake and if we had been allowed to stake, to record the claims, I think Jim would have made a lot of money out of them because that's where the first big uranium discovery was. Up at that Rabbit Lake area near Wollaston Lake."[1] Several uranium deposits were found and mined around Rabbit Lake and Wollaston Lake, the first in 1968, with production starting in 1975. Production at the last mine ceased in 2016.

Jim's big find preoccupied Uncle Frank, though he says that it was the Key Lake uranium deposit that Jim found (Key Lake is about 150 kilometres from Wollaston Lake) in 1966. In 2013, Frank wrote to a Queen's Counsel lawyer in Saskatoon in a last-ditch effort to get someone to investigate Jim and Abbie's disappearance. Among the information that Frank provided to the barrister is the following: "In the Fall of 66 Jim showed me a map of Key Lake and where he had staked out claims saying we are going to be all right since the property was going to be worth a lot of money."[2] The problem is that a staked claim becomes *property* only once it is recorded at the Mining Recorder's Office and if it remains in Jim's name. So what we need to know to understand his mining interests is which mineral claims did Jim own?

In 1974 Lloyd Mattson wrote to the Saskatchewan Department of Mineral Resources (DMR) asking this question. The DMR reported that Jim had recorded (claimed) ten properties in total (it had no record of any claim in Abbie's name).[3] Seven of them were transferred subsequently to companies. Transfers are standard industry practice: the claim is recorded in the name of the person who staked it and later transferred to the company that engaged the person to do the staking. Six of the seven transferred claims were transferred prior to the disappearance. The seventh claim was for a property that Jim recorded on February 2, 1966, transferred on February 15, 1968—two years after being recorded and eight months after the disappearance—to Selco Mining Corporation. Selco's manager explained to Lloyd that the delay had probably been caused by the company's possession of a transfer form signed by Jim, who apparently had done the staking as a Selco employee, and this form had been submitted to the DMR only after the disappearance to avoid confusion regarding ownership.[4] This is a reasonable explanation suggesting that Selco thought the property had little potential and was thus not in a hurry to do further work on it. All seven transferred claims eventually lapsed, meaning that they became open to others to explore and claim.

Of the three claims that Jim recorded but never transferred, two lapsed on June 1, 1967, just before he disappeared. At first glance, this timing appears to be significant because someone else could then have moved in and made claims. However, no third party can cause such claims to lapse. Under the law, they lapse *automatically* after a defined period when no work is done on them—and usually no work is done because no one thinks that they are worth further exploration.

The third claim never transferred was for a property at Brabant Lake, 175 kilometres northeast of La Ronge, which lapsed on July 1, 1967, while the search was under way. Under Saskatchewan law, there was a period of grace for claims recorded by persons who died or became "insane" (presumably to allow family members or the authorities to sort out the situation), but even such claims lapse eventually, as did Jim's Brabant Lake claim. Given that Jim had disappeared, it seems to be odd that this claim did not stay in his name until he was officially declared deceased and his estate was probated. However, this step would have required knowledge that Jim actually owned the claim and then quick thinking and a lawyer to request a court action or to appeal to the DMR to halt the automatic lapse—surely the last thing on anyone's mind while the search was in full swing. The bottom line is that, in the absence of information that Jim co-owned a company, such as Foster Lake Mines, all we know for sure is that when he disappeared he owned a single mineral property in his name in Saskatchewan.

In the early 1970s, Uncle Frank and Lloyd Mattson managed to see some of Jim's documents kept by Quandt. In a note about this, Frank says that anything pertaining to Key Lake was missing from the papers. I'm not exactly sure when Frank got the chance to look through these documents, but he is adamant that the missing documents were those that Jim showed him earlier "saying we were going to be all right—meaning that there was big money involved."[5]

A geologist I met who worked in La Ronge and knew Jim dismissed the whole story about Key Lake. "I don't believe it," he said. "Four or five different people told me they found Key Lake."[6] I wonder, however, whether it was possible for several people to have discovered Key Lake in that they all identified uranium deposits in different concessions, but it was only the concession over the main ore body that was commercially viable and brought into full production. At Rabbit Lake, the same situation might have applied, and the deposits there did eventually become five different mines.

Several things are muddled about the alleged big find: its location, the date, and whether Jim actually recorded a claim. Amid all of this confusion, there is more. Isabelle Impey, Anne Dorion's sister and Jim's stepdaughter, tells me that a short time before the disappearance (she cannot remember whether it was a week, a month, or longer) there was a burglary at the Hudson's Bay Company store in Cumberland House. Her mother kept some papers in the store's safe, including certificates in her name to claims around Wollaston Lake, and these certificates were stolen. Two hundred and forty kilometres away in La Ronge, there was a burglary at a shop where Jim kept documents in a safe, and they were stolen *the same night*. Two burglaries, the same night, both times documents stolen, and, according to Isabelle, no one was ever arrested. Were the valuable documents in the safe in La Ronge Jim's mineral claims? No one could steal the titles, but the thief could steal information such as the coordinates of any finds.

Attempting to verify the details, I contact the Cumberland House RCMP detachment and speak to a polite officer surely perplexed by this query about a burglary that happened so long ago. Her response is what I expect: they no longer keep records that old (assuming that there was even a report by Hudson's Bay Company staff and a subsequent RCMP investigation). In regard to the burglary in La Ronge, I know neither the name of the store nor the date of the robbery, giving me no lead to go on, and there appears to have been no local paper at the time that might have had a weekly crime column and reported on the matter.

It is another dead end. I am glum at the lack of progress on this business angle and wondering where to turn next when we get a tip that changes everything.

27
A TIP-OFF

Late one evening, ten days after returning from La Ronge, I miss a call and then minutes later get a text. Both are from Eric Bell, and I'm curious why he is trying to contact me at such an hour. I open the message and read the following: "Just found out that a guide and an American tourist snagged a body on Lower Foster Lake a few years back. The American told the guide to cut the line as he did not want to get involved with a murder case. I will get the name of the guide. I think I know who it might be."

What?!

I immediately call Eric, who goes over the story again. Slowly, slowly, I exhale. Eric is silent. "We've got to go to the lake," I tell him. "I'll call Deanna."

During our conversation, Eric explained the circumstances in which he had heard the information. A month before our phone call, Deanna, Eric, and I had concluded that the cost of getting Gene Ralston and his sonar to search Lower Foster Lake was beyond any funds that we could muster. Then

Eric remembered that the previous year some locals had hired two high-powered underwater cameras, normally used for fishing, to locate a boat that had sunk in Lac La Ronge, which has depths like those of Lower Foster Lake. Eric himself uses a similar AquaVu camera to locate trout when fishing. He contacted the people to see how much their cameras cost and explained what we were trying to do. This prompted one of them to recollect hearing about the guide whose tourist client had snagged the body. There was one more detail: the body had its wrists tied.

The body must have been that of Jim or Abbie. How many deceased persons could there possibly be in Lower Foster Lake, an isolated lake with no permanent inhabitants around it? The fishing lodge has perhaps a couple hundred visitors per year, but hopefully the proprietor would notice if a guest didn't return from a fishing trip. Furthermore, no documents about Jim and Abbie's disappearance mention a third person vanishing on the lake.

There were important facts to establish about the snagged body. Who was the guide, where did his client snag the body, when did it happen, what was the deceased person wearing (was there a match with clothing known to belong to Jim or Abbie?), and who was the tourist? Eric knew the guide's father, who had several sons, so it was just a matter of identifying which son guided the tourist. If we knew *where* on the lake the body had been snagged, then we could focus on a particular area in any search. If we knew *when* it occurred, then we could determine two things: first, we could anticipate how intact the body was likely to be now (if it was intact four to five years earlier—after some forty-five years of being in the lake—then that augured well, assuming that it sank back into similarly deep, cold water); second, if we could get the name of the tourist and which American state he is from, I might be able to match it with a name in one of the lodge's old guestbooks and track him down to get his account of what he found that day.

On this last point, I feel grim. Generalizing about Americans is one of Canada's (and Australia's) favourite pastimes, but I have American cousins, lived in New York City for seven years, and have loads of American friends. The truth is that it is a complicated country full of diverse people. Yet I am angry that this tourist was more concerned about an interruption to his fishing vacation than regard for a murder victim, whom he wanted to throw back in the lake like a fish the wrong size. He feeds the stereotype of Americans who use foreign countries as their playground with no care for situations that unfold, even when they are directly implicated.

I wonder too about the guide and his decision to cut the body loose. I also wonder whether he has broken the law by not reporting the body or keeping it at the surface. I call Eric and tell him, "If you identify the guide, don't tell me who he is." I'm sure that the guide wouldn't want to be identified anyway, but I want to protect him by maintaining my own ignorance.

Imagining that it can only be a crime to find a body, get rid of it, and not report it, I decide to talk this over with my friend, the criminal defence lawyer in Vancouver, and ask for confirmation that the guide committed a crime. Much to my surprise, the answer is no. Section 182 of the Criminal Code of Canada makes it illegal for someone with a *duty* to the dead—such as a paramedic, a doctor, or an undertaker—to neglect this legal obligation, whatever it might be. It is also a crime to interfere or tamper with a body. *Tamper*—such a mild word, almost like *tickle*—but it belies what Section 182 can really mean. The full horror of tampering was illuminated by the 2019 trial of Toronto serial killer Bruce McArthur, a gardener, who cut up his eight victims and buried the parts of their bodies in his clients' potted plants.

People who have no legal duty to a body, such as an ordinary member of the public, have no obligation; as long as they don't tamper with it, the law doesn't require them to do anything proactively, including reporting that they found it. Because all the fishing guide did was cut the line after the tourist snagged the body on Lower Foster Lake, in all likelihood neither he nor the tourist committed a crime.

I call Deanna, who has already heard Eric's news. She is doubtful about the story because she can't believe that someone would cut the line. In contrast, I think that the story must be true because I can't believe that anyone could make up such a tale. I say to Deanna that, if she can cobble together the funds, we need to go to the lake. "We are the only people who are ever going to do this!" I plead. "Fifty-one years have passed, and if we don't do it now, no one ever will."

Aside from shielding the guide from legal ramifications, is it right to bring up the bodies of Jim and Abbie? If I thought that they were resting in peace, then it would be a definite no. But they cannot be in peace. As the old Cree man told me in La Ronge, "Buried in a lake. That's no burial." *Dumped* in a lake is a more appropriate description. I tell myself that our intention is not to snag them; we'll use cameras to locate where they are, and then it will be up to the coroner to arrange to have the bodies retrieved with respect.

A couple of weeks after Eric received the tip, Deanna confirms that she can get the money together for us to go to the lake. Staying at Jim and Abbie's actual campsite has some appeal to me—I think that it would somehow bring us closer to them—but it isn't the most practical or cheapest option. We'd have to rent equipment (including a boat), buy food, and organize a float plane to get us there. "You know, it'd be a bush camp—birch, and poplar, and muskeg," Deanna reminds me ("Hooray!" thinks the Australian). The alternative is to stay at a fishing lodge, which offers four-day packages that include air transportation, accommodation, boat hire, and all meals.

But, before we do anything, we need to check what family members think about this next step. Deanna contacts Jim's daughter Anne and explains our plans. She has no objection. I email Amanda, Abbie's granddaughter, and ask, "How do you feel about us doing this?" She replies,

> I am truly grateful for this. I knew I could not do that part on my own. I did everything that I could do with the tools I was given in life. I believe I have angels watching over me, and I believe my Grampa is one of the angels. I hope to be able to meet all of you in person, so I can express my gratitude. I am just happy knowing that lake will be swept. It will be searched and I have 100% faith in you and the team you work alongside with. . . . I cried happy tears that morning I read that email in regards to this underwater search. It made me feel like I am not alone. . . . Hiy hiy! Thank you.[1]

A weight of expectations plants itself onto my shoulders, but this is what I signed up for. The challenge of writing about real people and traumatic events brings with it a duty of care, and I know that I have to see it through.

At the start of this project, solving a murder mystery was part of my motivation for wanting to find Jim and Abbie. "How cool!" I thought. "Solving a murder!" But soon I realized that I had no interest in finding a body just for the cool heck of it. It seems macabre to me now, and we all care too much about these men. We want to find their remains in Lower Foster Lake so that we can go to the RCMP and ask them to do their job, *their duty*, to investigate, to make up for their failure back in 1967. So often in life we cannot undo mistakes, but in this case there is an opportunity for the police to have a second chance to solve this missing persons case and to do better by these men.

28
"MY ANSWER
IS NO"

Returning to La Ronge and going to Lower Foster Lake is not just about looking for the bodies of Jim and Abbie. We will have a few days in town, and I want to make the most of our time there. At the top of my list is speaking to Joe Mason's daughter, Vivian.

She owes me nothing, has no obligation to me, and perhaps I have none to her. Mason is dead, so I have no legal obligation to care about his reputation. However, though I've never met his family members, I think it would be unethical to name him without permission to do so, given the potential to hurt them.

Jotting down notes of all the things that I want to ask Vivian, and summoning up the courage to call her, I get through to a woman with a firm, clear voice. I explain who I am and that Deborah Charles from Missinipi Broadcasting Corporation has put me in touch with her. I still don't know if I am being cowardly, or respectful, or sensitive to Vivian's feelings, but I can't bring myself to say, "I am calling because I wonder if your dad murdered Jim Brady and Abbie Halkett." In the end, I ask, "Did Deborah mention why I might call?"

Vivian is to the point. "If you're calling about what I think you are, then unless there is any concrete evidence, my answer is no."

I am equally direct: "The short answer is there is no concrete evidence, and there never will be. The alleged murders happened on an isolated lake without witnesses. If bodies are found, and if they have a bullet in them, we'd still need the gun to do ballistics testing—and none of this is likely." I explain that there is, however, circumstantial evidence: people have said that "Joe" himself told them that he murdered Jim and Abbie, and ostensibly he disappeared on the lake for three days right around the time that Jim and Abbie had vanished.

We talk for about another twenty minutes. Vivian asks me questions, and I explain to her what I know and what information I have or don't have. Her words that strike me the most are, "The man above will be the one to judge my dad and probably already has."

I later email Vivian to thank her for being so gracious and candid. I ask her if we could meet when Deanna and I are next in La Ronge, and Vivian invites us to her home. That is an incredibly generous thing to do given the circumstances: two strangers walking through her door to talk to her about something bad that we suspected her dad had done. In the end, Vivian decided not to go through with the meeting, saying that she couldn't do anything about something that happened fifty years ago and that she wanted to leave the past behind. I can't say that I blame her. I'm not in her shoes. I appreciate and respect her perspective.

* * *

And now, reader, you know: the real name of the alleged murderer I have been writing about is not "Joe Mason."

The convention of true crime writing is to identify murderers and expose them. To name them. That is what "solving the crime" means, and at the start of the project, that was our intention. With the passage of time, however, we've concluded that there is little to be gained from using Mason's—or his daughter's—real name. This decision not to name publicly an alleged murderer from a small community where many people are sure about his identity brings with it a certain irony. I had visions of attending a book launch in La Ronge and looking out at a sea of local faces knowing that perhaps a third of them— especially anyone over sixty—would know exactly who "Joe Mason" was. But even Jim's daughter Anne commented, "Nothing is served by naming him."[1] Using Mason's real name, however, has the potential to rip open old wounds. Naming and revealing more about the alleged murderer would also weaken the focus on Jim and Abbie. So why do it?

Not meeting a member of Mason's family makes our return trip to Saskatchewan clearer, in terms of its focus, but not easier. Lower Foster Lake is not the Arctic, but it is remote. Access is by float plane, but finding the bodies of Jim and Abbie is not as simple as catching a plane to a lake and getting on a boat.

29
OMENS

I n 1974, Jacques Cousteau, the famous French marine scientist and explorer, made a documentary about beavers. He wanted to film them in the wild, and of all the two million lakes in Canada that he could choose he selected Lower Foster Lake. The lodge that the crew built to shelter them during the months of filming is now the only place to stay: Beaver Lodge Fly-Inn.[1] It is where Deanna reserves rooms for us in August 2018.

It is the height of summer on the prairies when Deanna and I rendezvous back in Saskatoon. We will drive to La Ronge, where we'll board a float plane to take us to the lake, but our first stop is to see Uncle Frank. Deanna has become acutely conscious of his age (now ninety-one) and recent frailty. She wants to say hello, let him know what we are doing, and that we are going to try our best to locate the bodies of Jim and Abbie. This is our last effort—anyone's last effort?—to find them. I already decided that the lake trip will be the end of any book that I might write about this story, whatever the outcome, because

I can't see how I can continue contributing. I just hope that the end is finding the bodies of Jim and Abbie.

Thick smoke from forest fires in British Columbia and Alberta wreathes the city, catching in our throats and reducing visibility to a few hundred metres. The sun is blood orange and low in the sky. "Looks like a bad omen," Deanna says.

On the way north, we stop in at the cabin of Harold Johnson, a Woodland Cree writer and lawyer and a former miner, logger, and navy seaman. Harold lives on a bucolic patch of land, sitting above the surrounding muskeg, where the Montreal River starts its journey to Lac La Ronge. He collects us in his boat from the dock where we park the rental car. In keeping with his eclectic professional life, Harold also has an interest in Jim Brady and once looked into what happened. We wonder if he has any new information.

Harold is the eighth person we have met who tried to investigate the disappearance. It is encouraging that so many people attempted to do what we are doing, and Deanna and I feel supported knowing that there has been a desire for the mystery to be solved. His personal connection to the story is through Allan Quandt, whom Harold got to know during the last years of Quandt's life.

Harold interviewed Quandt about his relationship with Brady, the disappearance, and what Quandt had heard about a possible motive for murder. We knew that Quandt was aware of the allegations regarding his involvement in the disappearance because of his argument with Uncle Frank, who effectively accused him of murder. What we didn't know was how Quandt felt about this, but Harold does. "I asked Allan why he wanted me to investigate, and he said, 'So you can clear my name.'"[2]

In an incredible act of generosity for a writer—for we are very possessive of our notebooks—Harold gives us his original notes from the Quandt interviews and an unpublished story that he drafted about his research.

I have with me some loose papers, and Harold goes upstairs to get me something to put them in. He returns—in another act of generosity—with nothing less than Jim's own document portfolio. It is worn and slightly damaged but was once an elegant, slim, brown-card portfolio. It closes with a strong zipper and is of a length to carry legal documents (eighteen by twelve inches). Quandt kept it when he took possession of Jim's estate and passed it on to Harold. It is a personal memento that evokes Jim's intellect and work, and it takes me back to a time when Jim tucked it under his arm and strode off to political meetings with Malcolm Norris.[3]

After two hours of visiting with Harold, we clamber back into his boat for the ride back to the car, the afternoon light shining gold on the river. Deanna and I hold the portfolio and notebooks close to our bodies as we pass reeds and loons, the air crisp and clear of smoke, blowing fresh in our faces.

30
"A LOT OF WATER OUT THERE"

At 7 a.m. on August 17, we arrive at the Osprey Wings water-side airbase in La Ronge, its cream and red Twin Otter plane at the dock waiting to take us to Beaver Lodge. We greet Eric Bell and meet the search team from Grandmother's Bay Reserve, a small community that is part of the Lac La Ronge Indian Band: Thompson McKenzie, older and jovial, and Stanley Roberts, younger with a wickedly dry sense of humour. They are carrying briefcases containing the sonar equipment we will use to scan the lakebed. Also waiting are Mike and Jim from Texas, a father-son duo coming to fish for Lower Foster Lake's famous northern pike and lake trout.

Our group is not exactly undercover, but we think that we have to be cagey about what we are planning to do. We don't want to raise expectations—on the dock, I actively trample on mine in order to prepare myself for disappointment—and La Ronge is a small town where gossip travels as fast as a Facebook post. Jim from Texas asks Deanna if she is planning to fish, and she says that she isn't but that Eric is a fisherman. Jim then asks me, and I say, "No, but Eric knows how to fish." "Oh, so *you're* fishing?" he says to Eric. "Well, sort of," comes the reply. In fact, Eric hasn't even brought his rod. Jim from Texas looks perplexed, and I wonder what he makes of this group of five that includes two big men carrying black briefcases, an Australian, an English professor, and her cousin, our reported leader, and not a single fishing rod among us. Too late to have this thought, I realize, but we really should have brought a rod or two as cover.

It takes a little over an hour to fly the 160 kilometres to Beaver Lodge. Water splashes up against the windows on take-off, and a drone sets in, vibrating the plane and passengers. I can hardly believe that we have got to this point. *We're doing it.* We're going to the lake to try to locate the bodies of Jim and Abbie. The chance that we will find them is slim, but at least we can return to Uncle Frank with our heads held high and say that we tried our best.

The first thing that becomes clear from the air is the idea that Jim and Abbie tried to walk out is absurd. Rock, water, and vegetation—muskeg, forest, and the occasional meadow—stretch for hundreds of kilometres in every direction. The scope for getting lost is enormous, not because everything looks the same, but because the visual composition of every square metre is different from the next. The variation is bewildering. Of course people do walk this country but only if they know it in great detail or have the technology to help them. If you are already lost, then choosing to walk out would be folly, especially if you could return to your camp and wait to be rescued or even light a fire to attract attention. The second thing that becomes clear is how my original lake search strategy had been the ambitious plan of a clueless novice. I really had packed a snorkel, goggles, and swimming trunks, and I had asked Eric to borrow a wetsuit for me so that I could duck-dive down to the lake floor in case we spotted anything with his fishing camera. I'm not sure if he deliberately omitted it from his luggage, but just before our departure Eric told me that he "forgot" to pack the wetsuit. Possibly this was a lucky lapse that saved me from cardiac arrest in icy-cold water six feet under. We later had a belly laugh at the absurdity of my original plan, Deanna and Eric relieved that they didn't have to pull out a half-drowned Australian from Lower Foster Lake.

But my plan has fallen apart primarily because we realize that the lake is too deep for fishing cameras. That is when Eric finds the sonar team working out of Grandmother's Bay and contracts them to do the work. They use two pieces of equipment when they search for bodies, a small side scan sonar and a remote-operated vehicle (ROV) with a camera and "claw" that can retrieve specimens. Unfortunately the ROV needs repairs, so we are going to the lake without it. This is not ideal. It means that, even if the sonar picks up an anomaly, we won't get a high-quality photo or sample to confirm what we find. It is, however, the best that we can do.

With a surge of spray, the plane lands heavily, and we step out into another world. Jacques Cousteau chose well, for Beaver Lodge is located on a beautiful sandy beach at the end of an inlet, sheltered from the wind but facing west so that the sun streams in during the long summer evenings. Our host, Randy Olson, is on the dock to meet us. He bought the lodge in 1985 and is a cheerful master-of-all-trades, capable of maintaining a fishing lodge and hosting large groups of tourists. Eric has given him a heads-up about what we're doing, both to explain our lack of fishing interest and because we need the right boat from which to work the sonar.

After putting our gear in the cabin and having breakfast, we waste no more time. The lodge has half a dozen sixteen-footers and one pontoon boat available. Eric, Thompson, and Stanley choose the pontoon. It will comfortably seat all five of us and provides a better working platform for the sonar equipment. As we push off from the dock, Randy calls out, "Good luck. There's a lot of water out there!" "We'll need it," I call back.

We motor down the inlet leading to the main body of the lake, then turn to starboard, to the north. I lean toward Deanna and call over the wind, "We're really doing this!" We smile. I'm pleased to see Mike and Jim from Texas head to the opposite end of the lake, where they won't be able to see where we're working.

Randy was right. There is a *lot* of water out there, and there is no way in the four days we have available that we can scan the entire lake. We have to identify priority search areas. Eric cuts the motor, and we go over our strategy. I've brought the article from *The Northerner* describing the clues that McIvor Eninew found and read the passage out loud to the team: a one-inch-wide mark on a rock and a bundle of moss and reeds where it didn't belong, about 200 feet from a sand beach. We need to find the beach, but Eric's gut instinct is also that anyone who wanted to get rid of dead bodies, knowing that they would float to the surface unless sunk down deep, would choose a trout hole in which to sink them. Now, knowing about the fishing tourist who reportedly snagged a body a few years earlier, we are sure that this "catch" would have occurred in an area where a guide took the fishing tourists: that is, a trout hole. Furthermore, a

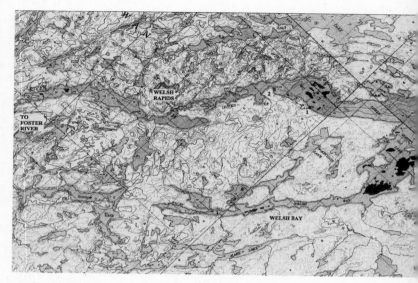

Map of Lower Foster Lake. *Source: Randy Olson, Beaver Lodge Fly-Inn.*

large hook and heavy line would have been necessary to bring a body to the surface, which would be more like lake trout tackle—again suggesting that we should target trout holes. (In contrast, if the guide and tourists were fishing for northern pike instead of trout, they would have been in the shallows close to shore because that is where pike are. But if Jim and Abbie had been dumped in the shallows, their bodies would have floated, and they would have been found long ago. Therefore, the body must have been snagged in or near a trout hole.) This is when Natalie Thompson's bathymetric chart of Lower Foster Lake becomes important: we spread it out looking for the deepest parts of the lake toward the end where Jim and Abbie camped, and it shows two trout holes in the northern third of the lake.

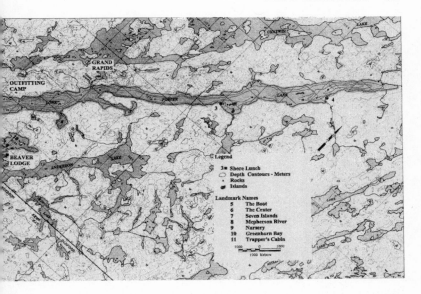

It takes an hour to get to the first location. The search strategy is straightforward in theory. We will tow the sonar from the front of the boat, where there is no engine to interfere with the cable, which means that Eric has to drive the boat backward, because the sonar has to trail behind the direction that the boat is travelling. The sonar has to remain a fairly constant distance from the lakebed to capture a clear image, so the computer operator constantly has to call "down" or "up" to have the cable towing the sonar let farther out or pulled in to maintain this distance.

The sonar that we use is simple in concept and appearance. The object lowered into the water is called a "starfish." It is about a foot long, coated in a bright orange rubber material, has three fins along its entire length, and is connected to a computer via

The sonar expedition, Lower Foster Lake. L to R: Eric Bell, Stanley Roberts, Thompson McKenzie, and Deanna Reder. *Photo credit: Michael Nest.*

a long electrical cable. The starfish sends out soundwaves that bounce off objects, and the bounced-back sounds create images on a computer screen.

Thompson and Stanley prepare the equipment for launching the starfish. The chief problem is reflection from the sky and water on the computer screen that prevents Stanley from seeing it clearly. Deanna ends up draping her jacket over both Stanley's head and the computer to block the light. The computer and sonar are run by a separate portable generator, and with this noise and the boat motor it sounds like a real workstation. The computer records each scan of the lakebed so that there is always an opportunity to review the images at night, but the operator needs to maintain a sharp lookout for anything unusual. Should there be a distraction at the wrong time, a detail might be captured but go unnoticed if it is thought that there is nothing worth reviewing.

Around noon we finally get down to work. Eric marks the four points of a grid over the trout hole, I write down the GPS coordinates, and then he slowly drives the boat back and forth in parallel lines. The team members settle into a rhythm. While Stanley scrutinizes the images in real time, Thompson relays the cable out or in to maintain a steady distance between the starfish and the lakebed. Thompson also advises on interpreting the images.

Being outdoors and seeing the expertise of Eric, Thompson, and Stanley have lifted my mood, and I allow myself some hope. As if reading my mind, Thompson says, "It feels good to be here!" He later tells me that as soon as he heard about this job he wanted to come. He knew about Jim and Abbie and thought it a great injustice that they had never been recovered.

With no specific roles, Deanna and I take turns sitting under the jacket with Stanley. We haven't done this before and think that everything we see on the screen might be a body. "No, that's a rock," says Stanley. "A fish," he says thirty seconds later when I point to something else. "Log," a minute later, before I have time to ask the question.

There are three worlds out there on the lake. The claustrophobic space under the jacket where Stanley scrutinizes images sent up from the lakebed. I still don't know how he maintains such concentration hunched over the computer screen for hours on end. Then, coming out from under the jacket—or up for air, for that is what it feels like—there is the pontoon with its engine noises and work activity; Thompson lowering or raising the sonar and getting in a joke and a smoke in between; waves slapping against the hull; and Eric swivelling around in his chair, reading the wind, and gauging the engine speed to keep the boat in a straight line on its grid. Finally, when I focus away from the boat, there is the long lake surrounded by wilderness. On this day, its grey waters are impassive and the shoreline motionless. Huge fires swept through the area in 2015, so instead of the usual mix of black spruce and jackpine the shore is almost stripped bare of tall trees. Stones and boulders and burned trunks are all that is left.

On day one, we scan the entirety of the first trout hole along nine different lines. Finding nothing, we are satisfied that we can move on to the next one, but we also get a sense of how big a task we have set for ourselves. We have discovered that the lake floor is not filled with debris but is relatively empty. We are looking for something that stands out, but so far there has been nothing. On our way back to the lodge, we speculate on what actually happened in 1967. Thompson wonders if Jim and Abbie stepped willingly into Mason's boat—this had never occurred to me—thus the lack of signs of a struggle on the shore. It makes sense because Jim and Mason knew each other (it is not clear if Abbie also knew Mason, but he probably did given the small size of the community). Or, if Uncle Frank's suspicion about hitmen has any merit, and given the poor weather back in early June 1967, could the killers have approached Jim and Abbie as friendly fishermen and offered to take them to the warmth of the outfitter's lodge, luring them away? This scenario would see the killers sitting aft in their boat, and Jim and Abbie sitting in front of them, probably facing away and hence vulnerable to a blow from behind.

It is almost 6 p.m. when we arrive back at the lodge to fresh coffee and questions from staff and the Texans. Clearly the cat is out of the bag. We remain circumspect about the locations that we are searching and the information that has led us to them, but it feels good to tell them about Jim and Abbie, about who they were and what they had accomplished in life.

Day two brings a change in the weather. It is windy, cool, and cloudy. We decide to go first to the top of the lake to see whether we can spot where Jim and Abbie camped, and we set out at 8 a.m. aware that it will take an hour and a half to get there. The mouth of the creek where their canoe was found is clearly visible, but after the fires the vegetation has completely changed from 1967. There is no tall forest, but a lot of thick brush has grown up. Eric spots a flat area back from the shore, probably where they erected their tent shack.

We then head back down the lake to our second location. We are buoyed by information that we got the night before from Randy. With Eninew's clue in mind, Eric asked Randy if he knew of any small sand beaches. Randy indicated one on the eastern shore near the top end of the lake, just before a granite ridge closed in on the water. We knew that Eninew had walked along the eastern shore, so the spot where he'd found the mark and moss and reeds might well be on this rocky ridge and north of this beach. It is also the location of the second, northernmost, trout hole.

Eric steers the boat along the shoreline as we head up the lake until Stanley spots the small sand beach—Eninew's reference point and now ours. We slow right down and chug slowly north, the motor making a low gurgling sound under the water. Eric knows that any guide working the lake would use landmarks to remember the locations of trout holes, and in this case variations in the steep ridge that looms ahead along the east shore are obvious markers. He and Thompson scrutinize the land and the rock face coming down into the water, and look at the depth chart, before they are satisfied that we are in the right place and make the spot our primary search quadrant.

Because of the wind direction, we have to traverse the lake across its breadth rather than its length, so shorter grid lines but more of them. We improvise to protect the computer against rain and reflection, putting up the boat's canopy to reduce the light and to give us some shelter. Stanley then sticks the computer deep into a cardboard box to further shield the screen. We put a jacket over the box, with the whole contraption sitting on top of a big wooden crate. It's a jumble, but it works. Eric reads the wind to keep the pontoon in a straight line, and we mark the corners of our grid before doing our transects.

The day before the lake felt open. This location is completely different. It *feels* strange: cold black water underneath and the ridge descending precipitously into the lake, creating the sense of working against a wall. Elsewhere we heard loons and saw gulls and an eagle. Here there is nothing. We are talking quietly, bundled up against the chill, when Stanley sits up sharply and says, "Mark the spot!"

31
ANOMALY

Stanley knows straightaway that it is something different.

Thompson says, "That's a body."

Eric says, "It looks like they're lying on their side."

Deanna says, "Give me a cigarette!"

It is the first anomaly that we find, something totally different from the logs, rocks, and fish that have shown up on the screen, a mere fifty metres from the shore. After marking the spot on his GPS—at thirty-four metres deep—Eric completes the rest of the transect and then cuts the motor. We all look at the image.

"It wasn't a coincidence we were in that spot," says Thompson. "The wind blew us right over it." It is just over a kilometre from where Jim and Abbie camped on the other side of the lake.

The sonar images that we obtain are sandy coloured and grainy, which give them their otherworldly look. In this case, the image appears to show six objects in a row, the middle four possibly connected and the top and bottom objects separated from the rest by about a metre. One object is boomerang shaped, and the middle four have an odd geometry of straight lines and round shapes.

For the rest of the afternoon, we scan the hole—an area roughly 200 × 700 metres—along lines perpendicular to the length of the lake. Nowhere else has there been anything strange. It is just that one spot. On the way back to the lodge, we speculate about what else it might be, really just to rule out alternative explanations. A dogsled that sank through the ice? A sunken boat? Old equipment dumped by a trapper?

We agree to say nothing back at the lodge. When we pull up at the dock, we wave hello, quietly unload our gear, and retire to our cabin. Randy, Mike, and Jim surely notice that we all vanish for the hour before supper but don't ask any questions.

In fact, we are unnerved by what we've found and need to reassure each other about the next step. We are worried about word getting out—to family, the community, or the media—before we have a chance to verify the anomaly. Thompson explains that once back home he will send our scans to a consultant in Saskatoon who could give him expert advice in confidence. We also have to do something that I've been putting off for eighteen months: face the reality of what we are likely to find.

Before I left Montreal for Lower Foster Lake, I got advice from Vienna Lam, a forensic anthropologist completing her master's degree at Simon Fraser University. Her thesis was on the decomposition of skeletons in freshwater lakes. How apt. Vienna had doubts that we would find anything other than bones but agreed that such deep, dark, cold water might have minimal bacteria, allowing for the possibility of finding flesh. She counselled me about the need to collect a DNA sample if possible. I also sought advice from Dr. Varsha Pilbrow, a biological anthropologist at the University of Melbourne, about which bones I should be looking for. Varsha advised me that, though the skull, pelvis, and femur are most diagnostic in that they immediately indicate a human, if I could take a photo of something that we found next to a tape measure (for scale) and send it to her, she could likely tell if it came from a human. I wasn't afraid of dead bodies or skeletons, but I wanted whatever we discovered to be peaceful for Jim's and Abbie's families. I finally had to admit that this was unlikely.

Sitting around in the cabin, we realize that there is worse to deal with. The anomaly seems to be composed of separate objects, which bring us directly to stories about what Mason did to Jim and Abbie after he killed them, if that is what happened. There was Knox's theory that the only way to get rid of a body in northern Saskatchewan was to cut it open, fill it with rocks, tie it back up, and sink it. Gene Ralston from Idaho—who performs the charity service of searching for drowned people—had mentioned the possibility of bodies being put into barrels, which would be intact and captured by sonar after fifty years (Gene had been doubtful that sonar would pick up a body after this length of time). My grandfather was a butcher and spent his days sizing up carcasses to work out how to make them more manageable. This is all that I can bring myself to say about the disturbing but frank conversation we have in the cabin that evening.

It takes me hours to fall asleep. I lie curled on my side, tracing in my mind the shapes of those objects. I am one of the most secular people to ever walk the Earth, but that night while the wind sighs in the trees outside I feel that I communed with Jim and Abbie lying at the bottom of the lake. I hope this means that they are no longer alone, no longer lost or missing.

Day three brings a hint of fall. It is cold, there is rain on the horizon, and the forecast is for thunder showers. Unlike the black water of the previous day, however, the lake is alive and reflects a pearl light. Deanna stays back at the lodge to work, and I borrow all-weather gear from Randy.

Our aim is to do a full criss-cross scan of the trout hole. We make the same long trek up the lake, Eric pointing out a solitary birch—green the previous day, it has turned gold, contrasting with the grey rock that frames it. Way up in the sky, a V formation of honking geese fly over us. We manoeuvre into position and get the pontoon's canopy up just as the showers hit.

There is the familiar flurry of activity as we prepare to start the transect: turning on the generator, preparing the computer and cables, protecting them from the rain in the box and under the jacket, putting the starfish overboard, then relaying out the cord. Looking like ocean fishermen in our gear, we settle into the work and brace against the rain. There has been a change in the wind direction, and Eric uses it to help our transects of the area that we scanned the day before. Occasionally I relieve Thompson from relaying the starfish up and down and join Stanley burrowed under the jacket in between stints.

That day we get three more images of the anomaly from a different angle. One of these images is even more curious than that from day two. It has sharp points sticking up and another object off to the side. Whatever the anomaly is, it does not belong there.

Day four sees all five of us back out on the pontoon boat in milder weather. We are pretty sure that we have found Jim or Abbie, but there is another location that we want to scan to satisfy ourselves what a natural lake bottom should look like. It is almost bereft of objects, with a smooth layer of silt covering everything but the occasional rock or log and schools of monster trout.

Randy has arranged a fish-fry lunch on a small hill overlooking the lake, and we sit there in the sun eating beets, potato salad, and fried trout. Being onshore is a welcome change and a chance to focus on the land. It is lush, with the thickest and spongiest moss that I've ever seen, colourful lichen on the rocks, and cranberries and blueberries everywhere. I've never seen wild blueberries before, and I gorge on them like a bear, so preoccupied I wander farther and farther away from our picnic area. I learn that the way to pick blueberries is not to pluck them one by one. Rather, the entire bunch needs to be gently fondled, and the whole lot just falls off into your hand. A high-pitched sound distracts me, and I am puzzled where it is coming from until I realize that a swelling cloud of bugs is coming to gorge on *me*, and I flee back to the lunch area.

Our final stop before heading back to Beaver Lodge is on the opposite shore, near the old outfitter's lodge that sits empty and derelict but was a tourist destination at the time of Jim and Abbie's disappearance. The day before we stopped there briefly to try to identify where Mason and his family might have camped (guides typically camp away from the lodge where they work) and stumbled across a large area covered in stones tightly arranged in concentric circles or spirals. Thompson suspected that it was an old medicine wheel, and we wanted to show Deanna. Blueberries thickly carpet the whole area, cranberries scattered in between, and I even find raspberries and three saskatoon bushes right next to where we've tied up the boat.

The authors and sonar team at Beaver Lodge Fly-Inn. *Photo credit: Lenore Jessop, Beaver Lodge Fly-Inn.*

After four days of concentration and tension, we are simultaneously tired, elated, relieved, and pensive. A chill wind is blowing, and fall is around the corner. It feels good to get on the plane the next morning and fly south to La Ronge.

32
ROAD TO
SASKATOON

Deanna and I planned to have at least a day in La Ronge after the lake trip before heading back to Saskatoon, knowing that we had people to visit and tasks to complete.

We wanted to find out more about Abbie, in particular, and went to the Lac La Ronge Indian Band Council, where he had been a councillor, to ask if they had archives that might hold documents that he wrote or any photos. We had a long conversation with two women in the office and discovered that they have their fingers on the pulse of La Ronge's beating heart. We learned that Annie, the partner of Abbie when he disappeared, was still alive but mentally frail; she still spoke only Cree. They thought that the widow of the owner of Pre-Cam was also still alive and told us where she lived (we dropped in, but she was out of town). One of them, herself an avid researcher, told us that she had also looked into the disappearance of Jim and Abbie at one stage, and we discussed the different murder theories. The women also gave us copies of information that the council had printed about traditional Cree life that included a photo of Abbie.

Throughout the day, Deanna and I discussed how we could fund the necessary next step: returning to Lower Foster Lake with an ROV to take close-up photographs of what we found and to collect a bone specimen for DNA analysis. We knew that Grandmother's Bay Reserve had the experts and the equipment, due back from repairs any day. The problem was paying for it. Eric thought that First Nations or Métis organizations might be willing to contribute funds, but he needed to have formal meetings with them to discuss this. It was neither Deanna's nor my place to make the request, nor was our visit the time to tell them what we had found.

Thompson also heard back from the sonar expert in Saskatoon. Her preliminary opinion was that the anomaly was a human-made object and not natural to that environment. This was encouraging.

The next morning after a visit with Eric and Wanda, we hit the road to Saskatoon. About an hour into our trip, Deanna's phone rang. It was Eric, who had been on the phone to Thompson. The Saskatoon expert had re-examined the images sent to her, and Thompson had forwarded the scans to another expert in Washington, DC. Through the crackling phone, we heard Eric say, "Both experts independently say that a few metres from the main anomaly they could identify a skull and torso. I have to tell the police." The coverage was poor, and we got cut off. What a mix of elation and relief! We still had four hours to drive but didn't want to bother Eric with more questions about what seemed to be evolving news.

Forty minutes out of Saskatoon, Eric called again. "On the basis of what I showed the La Ronge police," he said, "they've referred it to the RCMP's Major Crimes Division. Michael, they've also requested your research notes. Could you send them through?"

We had done it! We had found Jim and Abbie, and the RCMP were now on the case and ready to investigate. They would go in and retrieve the bodies.

The most touching moment of this entire project happened when we visited Uncle Frank immediately upon arriving in Saskatoon. Deanna called his daughter Connie to check if we could drop in and asked for her or Pat to be there when we visited. Because of his age, we thought that we needed to speak to him sooner rather than later, but we were worried about the shock that our news might cause. Uncle Frank looked even more frail than he had the previous week. He said hello in an offhand way and didn't ask us what we'd found. I suspect that he didn't want to be disappointed.

Gently Deanna said, "Uncle Frank, we went to the lake, and we found their bodies. We found Jim and Abbie." We were all stunned when we heard those words said so simply out loud. Deanna wanted to leave out the ambiguity of our need for a follow-up visit and confirmation of their identities, so she cut right to the point.

Uncle Frank bowed his head, then looked up, eyes glistening. "I can rest in peace now."[1]

Our final stop before heading to the airport was to meet Abbie's daughter, Rema Halkett, with whom we had been trying to get in touch for months. She had moved a couple of times, thus the difficulty in tracking her down. Rema was tired, having got up at 4 a.m. to catch the bus to an appointment and then catching more buses to get to work. We met in a hotel after her shift and talked quietly over drinks. Rema never knew her dad. She was initially raised by her grandparents before being separated from the family. A few years earlier she had met her uncle, Abbie's brother, Thompson Halkett, and had a joyous two weeks getting to know him and the family and hearing stories about her father. Rema has had a tough life, moving around Saskatchewan, raising her kids, and still working hard at sixty-one, and she has always wondered about her dad.

We felt awkward meeting Rema. We didn't know her, but we were pretty sure that we had found her dad or Jim. However, without confirmation of what we had found, it would have been wrong to mention our discovery, so we didn't. We said that we'd been to the lake to see where Abbie and Jim had last camped, which was true, and that we would let Rema know when we could confirm anything (which we did[2]).

As we were talking, Tracy Chapman's hit song "Fast Car" started playing in the background. It's about a woman who strives to cope with what fate has dealt her but hangs on to her dreams for living. Prompted by the song's lyrics, I asked Rema if she was happy that we were searching for her dad. "Yes," she replied. "I'm stuck in this place and cannot move on."[3]

Around 6 p.m., Deanna and I crawled into the Courtyard Hotel near Saskatoon's airport for dinner, exhausted by the events of the week. Since arriving in the city, we had been too busy to look at the sonar images to determine whether we could see what the sonar experts saw, but now I could finally turn on the computer.

I found the image, enlarged it, stared at it for a few seconds, then let out an "Oh!" so loud that the people at the bar could hear. There it was: a grainy image of what the experts told us was a body. It looked a bit like a Halloween ghost with a sheet draped over it, revealing an outline but with specific bones obscured—presumably this was the effect of silt on the lakebed. The person was lying on his back, right arm extended over his head. It seemed to be unmistakably human.

33
RECKONING

I t took eighteen months of work from when I first became involved in the search for James Brady and Absolom Halkett, in February 2017, to get to the location on Lower Foster Lake in August 2018 where they had gone missing over fifty years earlier. Deanna had the vision and the contacts, and she organized the funding. I had the skills to research and recognize evidence of what might have happened. (Deanna has these skills too but simply lacked the time to work on the project full time.) Eric has more talents than I have fingers and toes and undertook the logistics necessary for the lake search and was fully involved in it. When finally at the lake, we also had two community members, Thompson and Stanley, who could operate the sonar equipment.

Our breakthrough was the clue found by McIvor Eninew, and he found it because he had the traditional, tested-by-time, skills and knowledge of a northern Cree man. This tiny but immense clue—literally a one-inch-wide mark on a rock and a bundle of moss and reeds that didn't belong there, spotted perhaps *one month* after Jim and Abbie disappeared—was the trigger for everything else. Lloyd Mattson had the smarts to get Eninew involved in the first place, to record what he had found, and then the perseverance to publish the article in *The Northerner* ten years later.

In contrast, the "clues" found by the RCMP and noted in the coroner's inquest—the canoe, the axe blaze, the match, the campfire, and the raft—were nothing of the sort. We don't know whether Jim and Abbie really beached their canoe on the eastern bank of the creek or whether it was positioned there to make it appear that they had headed east from Lower Foster Lake. However, though the axe blaze and match most likely belonged to the two men, it is unlikely that the raft or campfire did. The reality is that, contrary to what the Mounties wanted the coroner to believe, these were not connected clues that indicated anything about the fate of the men or where they were trying to go. It was a botched investigation.

In terms of my role, none of what I did was complicated. I am a methodical researcher and a careful reader, so I paid attention to the clues and the article, and I had the skills to filter out irrelevant information. The snagged body with its hands tied gave impetus to our efforts, propelling us toward a lake search. Importantly I also believed both Eninew and the story of the snagged body, which convinced me that we needed to search the lake. Once Deanna and I arrived at Lower Foster Lake, the rest was done by experts: Eric and the Grandmother's Bay team, Thompson and Stanley, who read the charts, the land, and the lake; found the trout holes; kept the boat on its grid; operated the sonar and the computer; and did the initial interpretation of the images.

Our sonar images and the sonar experts' advice were forwarded to the police, and then we had to wait. To our disappointment and disbelief, we eventually got word that the RCMP's Historical Case Unit would not send in a dive team to recover whatever was there based solely on our sonar images. The reasoning of the RCMP was that, given the remoteness of the search area and on the basis of the sonar images alone, they preferred that we return with the Grandmother's Bay team—this time with an ROV—to photograph whatever was on the lakebed and collect a specimen. They also thought that there was inadequate proof that a crime had been committed. If the ROV confirmed the presence of human remains, they would be more willing to assist us.

So the RCMP's Historic Case Unit for the North didn't want to investigate a historic case in the North even though we had given it the first fresh lead in half a century. It appears that the RCMP didn't believe us.

To be fair, there are probably bodies in many lakes in northern Canada—it can be a dangerous place, and for generations people have fallen through the ice and otherwise drowned—so the RCMP might have doubted any connection to Jim and Abbie. But it was not a fluke that we found this body. We didn't snag it while out fishing for trout; we weren't looking in the wrong lake, or the wrong part of the lake, only to end up accidentally in the right place on the right lake. We investigated evidence that led to two specific locations—the two trout holes—in the north end of Lower Foster Lake. We then found two anomalies that sonar experts ascertained were not from the natural environment. The first, in fact, was probably just rocks lying in an unusual configuration on the lakebed. It was the second anomaly that the two sonar experts subsequently identified as a skull and upper torso. I had no doubt about what we had found: a body on the lake floor waving *help me!*

Perhaps the problem was money. Sending in a dive team would cost a lot, and I assumed that the RCMP didn't want to spend the money. Some would say that it was because Jim and Abbie were Indigenous or because they were northerners; others would note that it was because the RCMP didn't want its wrongheaded investigation in 1967 to be exposed.

But if *we* could not find the money, would the police just let Jim and Abbie lie there at the bottom of the lake in perpetuity? And, if not from the police, then where did the RCMP think the funding would come from for this next stage (the estimated cost was $30,000)? From the Lac La Ronge Indian Band, in the second poorest region of Canada?[1] From Simon Fraser University, where Deanna works, two provinces away? When we were at the lake, we saw formations of geese heading to the prairies to fatten up in the grain fields before migrating south. *In mid-August!* The freeze-up in the North was not far away, and any delay would close the window of opportunity to retrieve the bodies that year.

Then out of the blue—and ironically given the lack of police interest—Eric got confirmation of the story of the guide and fishing tourist who snagged a body on Lower Foster Lake. Hearing about our search, the guide came forward, saying that it had occurred as we had heard—and the body had its hands tied. I asked Eric *where* the guide said his client had snagged the body, because the location was key to its being one of the bodies found in our sonar image and therefore being Jim or Abbie. "Right against the rock wall where we were," Eric said. The only difference from the story that we had heard was that it had actually happened in the summer of 1968 or 1969—the guide couldn't remember exactly—so at most a couple of years after the disappearance. Much longer ago than we had thought. (Although believing the story, I'd always doubted a later date because I couldn't understand how a body could be so intact after so many years.)

So what about the RCMP claim that there was inadequate proof of a crime? Having received our information, the RCMP probably reviewed their file on Jim and Abbie, saw that they were considered missing persons, and noted that there had been a search in 1967. This became the official story—the story in the police records—because it was "confirmed" through the coroner's inquest. However, evidence that Jim and Abbie were lost and tried to walk to the Churchill River is fiction masquerading as fact. If the story of the snagged body with its hands tied was true, then this was further evidence of a crime.

There were three key elements of our investigative project: to look into the disappearance of Jim and Abbie, to ask why they disappeared, and to assess the response by government authorities.

First and foremost, we wanted to find the bodies of Jim and Abbie—to return them to their families if we could. According to sonar experts in Saskatoon and Washington, DC, the sonar image that we obtained during our first lake trip shows a body lying at the bottom of a trout hole in the north end of Lower Foster Lake. Circumstantial evidence suggests that this is likely to be Jim or Abbie. But, as in many cold case investigations, our research did not solve all of the mysteries of their disappearance.

Who was behind the simultaneous break-ins in which Jim's and Cecilia Dorion's (his partner's) business papers were stolen? What was the name of the company co-owned by the five men, if not Foster Lake Mines, and what mining interests did it have? What was the nature of Jim's big find? Where was it located? In the absence of interviews, we can never be sure what motivated the killer, or killers, if Jim and Abbie were in fact murdered. However, the 1960s were a hostile time for Indigenous activists, especially those with the temerity to suggest radical reform, and it would be naive to think that the likes of Jim and Abbie had no enemies beyond La Ronge.

What we did do is expose the RCMP's failure in 1967 to listen to the community, to treat the missing persons case as a potential crime, to interview everyone who should have been interviewed, and to put a more experienced officer in charge of the case. The coroner's inquest was also flawed. It did not explore why the aviation company never acted on Gerald Mitchinson's report about putting the men down on the wrong lake, nor did it push the RCMP on why the things claimed to be evidence should be viewed as such or plausibly used as the basis for theories about Jim and Abbie's supposed actions.

What about Uncle Frank? Was he right or wrong? Not all of his details were correct, including some important ones. But he was right about what lies at the heart of this story: violence against Indigenous people being ignored and police failing to do something about it. His insistence that Jim and Abbie need justice, and his steely moral resolve, are a lesson for us all.

34
FOCUSING

When I look at those wall maps of Canada, the ones with a table of road distances between major cities and a scale in the corner, my eye isn't drawn to the Rockies, the big blue of Hudson Bay, or the Gulf of St. Lawrence, nor does it float up to the Arctic. It goes to Saskatchewan.

I see the dark forest and deep snow of the North, but like those machines for hyper-sensitive focusing in the sci-fi film *Bladerunner* my mind whirrs and clicks, and La Ronge comes into view. A few more clicks of the lens and I see a cabin nestled in the trees. Yet more clicks and there is a warm hearth, laughter, and book-lined shelves. A little more focus and there on a table sits a Bible and *The Communist Manifesto*. I hear the repartee between Jim and Abbie, spending the night together before leaving on a prospecting trip early the next morning. They argue about politics and the best way to emancipate Indigenous people. Abbie talks about spiritualism; Jim tries to persuade him that there is a future in revolution. Both reach for their books to find a reference.

Momentarily the whole scene jars. I'm still a newcomer, but I already know that camaraderie and philosophizing by educated, hard-working, Indigenous men in a book-filled cabin in the North is at odds with the image that Canada portrays to the world. Not a hockey stick, sunburnt homesteading family, handsome Mountie, or chic Montréalaise in sight, let alone a moose or "noble savage" uncontacted by "civilization."

I try to refocus, but Jim and Abbie are gone, released into the ether. Spirits in the clear night air, so cold that when you breathe in it hurts.

PART 4
STEADY GREEN

Steady green: the light signal authorizing a pilot to land if satisfied that no risk of collision exists.

35
PÂSTÂHOWIN:
AS FAR AS YOU CAN GO

Long ago I promised Uncle Frank that I would try to find out what happened to Jim Brady and Abbie Halkett, and I did my best, as his niece, to do right by him and those missing men.

In August 2018, I spent a lot of time sitting at the back of the boat on Lower Foster Lake watching and listening. On day one, I watched as Thompson McKenzie and Stanley Roberts demonstrated to us how to use the sonar and how to set up a grid for a search. I saw my cousin Eric Bell use land markers to steady the boat as he drove backward, doing what he could to limit the effects of the waves and wind that wanted to push us off course. I sat by Stanley and watched the images of the smooth lake bottom that scrolled by on his laptop. I witnessed Michael take photos and collect information from every conversation, consulting the map of the lake and grafting the stories onto locations.

On day two, we sought and located the sandy beach that McIvor Eninew had referenced as well as the cliffs where he had found the scuff mark that he thought was from the prow of a boat. We drove to the end of the lake where Jim and Abbie had been dropped off and where they had set up camp. At that point, Eric cut the engine and pulled out a smoke, giving us some time to go through the various scenarios.

Already some details were clear. There was no way that anyone who saw this thick bush would try to walk out of it. This meant that the bodies of Jim and Abbie must still be there. If they had both perished in an accident, then their remains or at least their gear would have been found during the extensive community search; if they had drowned by falling overboard, then their bodies would have floated to the surface eventually and been recovered. The only other possibility that explained why they had disappeared was that they had been murdered and weighted down, hidden deep in the lake.

I still remember Thompson and Eric talking, imagining Jim and Abbie lured into, or maybe hauled into, a boat that was not theirs on a snowy June day. If the murderer (or murderers) eventually ended up at the cliffs at the northern end of the lake, stopping to clean away any evidence before fleeing even farther away from the murder scene, then the bodies would have been dumped along the way. I remember Thompson and Eric looking at the lake and discussing its deepest parts, scanning in their minds from our position, where we were sitting in the boat, all the way up to the sandy beach; they remarked that en route there was a deep trout hole marked by prominent overhanging bluffs. It was Eric who mentioned that someone fifty years earlier wouldn't have needed a map to find the trout hole, because the bluffs marked that spot. This was after only a day of working together, and already Eric had demonstrated a clear understanding of the impacts over time of the weather, of forest fires, of the seasons. At some point, Thompson said, with a great deal of respect in his voice, "you really know how to read the land."

We headed directly for the trout hole marked by the bluffs, put down the sonar, and within an hour or two found the anomalies that experts later told us were human remains. It wasn't luck. It began with a belief that Jim and Abbie had to be somewhere in the lake. And it was the expertise of Thompson and Eric that determined the most likely place to start.

After getting back to La Ronge, Michael and I left to return to our families, certain that the police would take over; Eric, however, had to contend daily with stirred-up attention in the community and the sense that the police wouldn't help.

A month later he, Thompson, Stanley, and others as part of the Grandmother's Bay team returned to Lower Foster Lake to take underwater video, with the cost of the sonar covered by the Lac La Ronge Indian Band. It was miserable the entire time, windy and rainy, below freezing every morning. The ROV, a remotely operated vehicle, was sent down into the trout hole and found and videoed bones—possibly ribs—though without testing them we couldn't be sure that they were human. The site was more extensive than expected, with additional remains found twenty metres from our original anomaly. Collecting a specimen, however, proved to be impossible. Everything was covered with four to five inches of silt, and when the ROV's claw took hold of something the object fell apart. Given the fragility of the remains, the scattered site, and the challenges caused by silt and weather, the team returned home.

Eric met with the police and showed them the video that the ROV took, but they continued to refuse to retrieve the remains based on what we had found. At this point, winter was setting in, and any further search would need enough funding to involve divers. I didn't tell Uncle Frank all of these details, not wanting to upset him, but he was aware that there was no national announcement of the discovery. Just before he passed away in April 2019 at the age of ninety-two, he asked my cousin Connie to call me with instructions that we not give up.

The evidence that we had collected from the sonar expedition and then the second trip with the ROV was proving to be enigmatic. As a *whole*, it gave us confidence that we had found Jim and Abbie's final resting place, not least because the cluster of unusual objects in this remote location—precisely where we were looking for something—was in such contrast to the surrounding featureless lakebed. The fishing guide whose client had snagged the body also said that it had occurred right where we detected these objects. However, individual experts expressed a range of opinions about what we had found: some thought that the sonar scans were promising but had little interest in the ROV video footage; others were not convinced by the sonar scans but found the video footage compelling in terms of the possibility that it showed human remains.

Throughout this time, I was thinking about how to move forward in a good way, and I remembered Kohkum. Even with her expertise, her knowledge of medicines, she still asked Abbie Halkett to go away when he approached her for a cure for his blindness so that she could dream and find the answer for him. I peered into my own dreams but saw nothing definitive.

I kept finding other indications that we were on the right path. I looked back to a book published in 1988 in which Cree intellectual Stan Cuthand refers to Kohkum by her married name. In this essay, Cuthand shares his memories as a young man in La Ronge about the 1940s: "There were medicine people in La Ronge who were well known for their ability to heal the sick. Mrs. David Patterson and Mr. Jerrimiah McKenzie both have a wide reputation for their healing powers."[1] Could it be, I wondered, that relatives of both of these healers' families—the Pattersons and the McKenzies—were part of the search?

Another good sign appeared unexpectedly when I asked a senior colleague if he knew of any marine archaeologists to whom I could talk. He pointed out that across the hall from my office was Rob Rondeau, who had a long career as a professional diver and was completing his PhD in the Department of Archaeology. Rob had spent years locating the underwater wreckage of ships and planes and other archaeological sites. He was named a Fellow of the Royal Canadian Geographical Society for his contributions to the search for the HMS *Erebus* and HMS *Terror*.

Rob and I met to discuss this project, and I discovered that he had grown up in Saskatchewan and put himself through his first degree teaching scuba diving, which meant that he had trained a lot of diving masters. Although he was reluctant to comment on the evidence that we had gathered, he was sufficiently convinced that he agreed to put us in contact with divers and to accompany us to Lower Foster Lake with an underwater ROV with a high-resolution camera that he was testing for a company based in California.

Things started to fall into place. Earl Cook from the Métis Association of Saskatchewan stepped forward out of respect for Jim Brady and his work for Métis people in the province. He contributed enough to pay for the services of a professional diving team and the twenty-two tanks of oxygen-enriched air, dry suits, flippers, masks, underwater metal detector, and special baskets and bags for retrieving remains that they would need. My university allowed me to access funds to pay for the additional plane required for the extra gear, along with the cost of accommodations at the lodge. Eric, Michael, and I went over the protocols that we needed to follow when uncovering human remains, and Eric had the phone numbers of the appropriate contacts at hand.

There was one detail that did not fall into place, the fact that Michael would not be able to join us. The only week in the summer of 2019 that the lodge had available, which coincided with the time that the divers could go, was the same week that Michael had a family wedding in Montreal that he had to attend. He assured us that he didn't need to be at Lower Foster Lake, that we would keep in touch via email, and that there wasn't much else we could do.

Then, in early August 2019, about a week before the final trip to Lower Foster Lake, I got a call from Thompson. He'd had a dream warning him to stop the search, and after conversations with an Elder he'd decided that he and Stanley couldn't join us. I remember being confused about what to do next. I shared with him Uncle Frank's last wishes and the wishes of the families who wanted to retrieve the remains of Jim and Abbie and bury them closer to home. But I was also sensitive to the fact that Thompson is an Elder himself, and I couldn't ask him to dismiss his dream. So certain about the directions given to me to proceed, I asked him to pray about it some more, in case there was some way that he was mistaken. He shared with me a word that was on his mind—*pâstâhowin*—a Cree word that warns against passing a forbidden point. Implied are the bad effects on the person who goes against the rules in place. Later I read a quotation from Cree language teacher Reuben Quinn, who says that pâstâhowin means to "shatter the future."[2]

Although troubled by Thompson's decision, I still felt the call to proceed, to honour Uncle Frank's last wish, especially since the divers were booked and everything was ready to go. I reminded myself to respect the decision of the Grandmother's Bay team even if we continued the search. I consoled myself that we had Rob's ROV as a backup and that maybe Thompson's dream was a directive for Thompson and Stanley only. On my last day on campus in Burnaby before heading off to Saskatchewan, I discussed the details of the trip with two of my research assistants, Kimberley John and Treena Chambers. I appreciated being able to talk to them about the details of this mystery in conversations that had spanned the summers that they had worked with me, especially since they were sensitive to the significance of this trip. Even though their fields are radically different from mine—Kim in health science, Treena in public policy—we spent a lot of time talking about Indigenous research ethics to make sure that the work we did wasn't driven by our egos or the desire for personal gain. It was reassuring to talk with colleagues who have knowledge of the consequences of not following correct protocol.

I was the last person to leave the office that day, and on my way to the parking lot I was listing everything that I was taking with me on the trip, trying not to forget anything that I might need. As I approached my car, I saw something on my windshield. As I got closer, I saw a pouch of tobacco that Kim had left for me, a reminder to use it as part of the search, to offer tobacco to the spirits of Jim and Abbie, to let them know that we wanted to conduct this work in a good way. I was cheered by this gift and began to think that everything was falling into place.

On August 11, 2019, Eric, two medics who work for him, Rob and his ROV, and I arrived at Lower Foster Lake, almost exactly one year after our first search. For the next few days, the weather was so calm and sunny that the edges of the land were reflected in the water, as though there were mirrors held up to them. It was so perfect that Randy, the lodge owner, told us that, in his thirty years there, he had seldom seen this effect. At some point, Eric remembered a pilot who had flown to lakes all around the North and left plaques on the sides of cliffs, dedicating each lake to a different fallen soldier in the Second World War. He suggested that we return with a plaque dedicated to Jim and Abbie as a way to remember them. And every time we went out onto the water I laid down tobacco and said a prayer.

It was in this place of respect and confident watchfulness that we reminded ourselves of the landmarks on which we had relied the year before while Eric found the GPS coordinates of the anomalies that we had identified. We did not expect anything to go wrong. Then Rob took the brand new ROV out of its case and lowered it from the pontoon boat into the water. It was the ROV's camera that would provide us with an "eye" on the bottom of the lake and help us to relocate the body that we had found a year earlier. The ROV, or underwater drone, went down eighty feet (about twenty-four metres) and then unexpectedly flooded and short-circuited. Within less than a minute, it was clear that it had shorted out and would remain inoperable throughout the rest of the trip.

We were taken aback, mystified, and it took us a while to realize that our only backup now to whatever the divers saw was Eric's Helix depth sounder that had side scanning abilities. Once we recovered from the shock, we began to calculate what to do. We knew the approximate area of the first image that we had obtained and had a GPS coordinate, but the coordinate was for our boat on the surface, not for the object on the lakebed. Because of the length of the tether for our original tow-fish sonar, the difference between the two could be ten to twenty metres, and this complicated things. We used the fishing camera and adjusted as best we could, dropping a descent line into the trout hole with an anchor at one end and a buoy at the other to mark where it was on the surface.

The next day, August 12, Eric shared with me that he had dreamt that Jim and Abbie were welcoming us. I nodded, confident that we were approaching this recovery operation with respect, attentive to the protocols that we knew we had to follow, and careful to keep paying attention. When the divers, George Mueller and Trent Dybvig, arrived, we shared with them the information that we had. As they prepared for the dive, they followed strict protocols of their own, designed by divers to ensure that every procedure is followed to minimize risk. Their first descent was quick, perhaps two minutes to get down to thirty-four metres; the temperature was seven degrees Celsius. Constrained by time, murky vision, and sediment, the divers remained only twelve minutes on the bottom searching an area about nine square metres.

They found nothing.

Again we were mystified. How was it that all this effort, all this expertise provided by consummate professionals, all the careful planning and good luck could come to nothing? Eric and I remained optimistic, certain that we were following the right procedures, with good motivations, that the search was being conducted with respect as we prepared for the next dive.

Again we would locate the spots closest to the GPS coordinates of the anomalies, using Eric's camera to locate the exact spot as best we could, and George and Trevor would go through their practised routines in preparing to continue the search. After three more dives, the total time spent on the lakebed over two days was twenty-seven minutes, and the total area searched was about ten by twelve metres—the size of an ordinary suburban house.[3]

By the time of the fourth dive, Rob started talking about a potential future search, with a battalion of ROVs and additional high-tech, remote-sensing technologies as part of a separate research plan. I knew that it would be possible, that this was a compelling enough story that another search would merit funding. But I couldn't imagine the future because I was feeling a sense of shock, a disbelief that this was all we would find this time around. It was dawning on us that our efforts might have reached their limits. Eric commented that perhaps we had to accept that "the land has reclaimed them."

I recalled all of the good signs that we had, from the continued support of the families and communities, to how we all worked together so well, to the way in which each of us was dedicated to the search but not trying to control everything. We knew that Jim and Abbie were missing from the lives that they ought to have completed, missed by loved ones and by descendants who would have liked to have met them.

I remembered that, as I was leaving home in Vancouver to join this last leg of the search, I had wanted to bring a gift for my cousin Eric. I couldn't think of a single thing I could buy that would communicate the level of respect and gratitude that I had for his amazing efforts. Then I thought of a gift given to me from my friend Alannah Young. Alannah and I had studied together as graduate students, and I had learned that, though she was from Peguis First Nation and Opaskwayask Cree Nation in Manitoba, her beloved stepfather, Wally McKenzie, was originally from La Ronge. It was about that time that I found the passage by Cuthand that talked about two La Ronge healers, one a Patterson—my grandmother—and the other a McKenzie, likely related to Wally. Although I met Alannah's mother, Doris, over the years, on her annual visit to see her granddaughter, Melody, I never got the chance to meet Wally and ask about this possible connection. When Melody turned thirteen, Alannah organized a puberty ceremony, and Doris came to help. I remember the sad moment when Doris got the news that Wally, who had decided to take this time to go to La Ronge to attend a ceremonial fasting camp, had unexpectedly passed on. When I completed my PhD, Alannah gave me a small eagle feather about six inches (or fifteen centimetres) long, beaded at the stem. It was a precious gift from a dear friend who had been a mentor to me. Thinking about how much I had learned from Alannah and the fact that her relative, Wally, had been a member of the same band as Eric, I decided that this feather was the best token of my appreciation that I could give.

On the third day of the search in 2019, needing a chance to stretch our legs, I asked Eric if we could return to the shore where we had found a medicine wheel the year before. Thompson had found the scattered stones, now overgrown with wild blueberries, and I wondered whether we could learn more about them. As we walked at one end, Rob noticed that the stones had likely been subject to a forest fire, confirming that the formation was at least five years old, and we talked about the ways that we could determine how much older it might be.

I recognized the pattern to be not so much a circle as a spiral, built on a clearing with a gradual upward slope away from the lake. I traced the outer loop with my eye as I walked carefully, trying to see past the foliage to trace the path that would lead to the centre. As I began to see the whole outline, I couldn't believe my eyes. Sitting at the centre point, where the terrain was a mound almost like an altar, sat an eagle feather, nineteen inches (or forty-eight centimetres) long. I picked it up, unbelieving, and showed it to Eric. What else could it mean but encouragement? He nodded, and we were reassured.

We returned to our final day of the search; I continued to drop tobacco into the water and pray for guidance. We checked and rechecked the markers so that they were as close to the landmarks we remembered and the coordinates we had recorded as possible, giving the divers the best possible chance to find what the sonar and the ROV had recorded the year before. And before we knew it the dives were completed with nothing found. Eric and I left Lower Foster Lake both certain that we had done all we could but also unsure how this could be the conclusion of the search for Jim and Abbie.

Once we returned from Lower Foster Lake to La Ronge, I sought out my cousin Lillian, a life-long activist and leader, whose work has always been an inspiration to me. She wasn't that difficult to find because she had organized a three-day fair to celebrate Cree healing traditions, right in the middle of town, and I arrived on the last afternoon before it wrapped up. I only needed to go past the group of Elders and the main stage, past the medicines at one station or the beading or birchbark biting at another, from one tipi to the next, in order to find her. I was a bit shell-shocked and fell upon her, wanting to share how confused I still was about the results. She immediately asked me if we had offered tobacco to Jim and Abbie during the search. I was glad to be able to assure her and myself that we had.

In 2005 I had the great honour to hear Cree intellectual Harold Cardinal give one of his last public speeches at the University of British Columbia before his passing. He told us that Cree people, known as *nêhiyaw*, are searchers for knowledge in the four worlds, that no one person can know everything, and that nêhiyaw thus have to rely on ancestors and descendants to work together. Cardinal stated that the Cree "saw the pursuit of knowledge as an unending, continuous, intergenerational exercise."[4]

I began to think of the pursuit of knowledge about Jim and Abbie as an example of Cardinal's point. We were not the first to begin this search, and our efforts relied on the work that others had begun. Perhaps someone in the future might rely on what we have found. In the weeks following our last trip, Eric, Michael, and I talked about the search with our families, trying to make sense of what had happened. One day Eric called me to say that he had spoken to an Elder and wanted to share his words. Eric had asked him about the word *pâstâhowin*, and the Elder had said, "Sometimes you'll get signs that tell you that this is as far as you can go."

Deanna Reder
Vancouver, 2020

ACKNOWLEDGEMENTS

From Michael: From the bottom of my heart, thank you, Deanna, for inviting me to participate in this project. It saved my sanity during that first long year in Montreal when I was wondering what to do with myself, and it opened a door to Canada. Eric, together with Deanna, your collegiality, generosity, patience, and expertise were a humbling—and always fun—experience. *Thank you*. Wanda, you made me feel so welcome in La Ronge and were such a constructive critic of our ideas and theories.

I had the privilege of speaking with family members of Jim and Abbie. Thank you to Anne Dorion, Isabelle Impey, Leah Dorion, Rema Halkett, and Amanda Halkett for being so generous with your time, for sharing memories (some of them painful), and for giving us permission to repeat your stories in this book. Your fathers and grandfathers were remarkable men, and I hope we have done them justice.

This story never would have been brought to the page without Uncle Frank Tomkins. I'm so grateful that I got to meet, and learn, from him. May you rest in peace. Connie and Pat, thank you for your kindness in Saskatoon.

Thompson McKenzie and Stanley Roberts worked with us on our first and second expeditions to Lower Foster Lake. Truly we could not have done it without you! It was such a pleasure to share your company and to learn from you during our time together.

Many people provided expert technical advice on issues on which I needed help, and the manuscript is so much stronger for their input: Sergeant Geoff Bennett of the RCMP, Regina, for advice on missing persons cases; Tony Jones for advice on policing and investigations; Don Belovich for legal advice on points of mining and mining law; Natalie Thompson for advice on prospecting and mining in northern Saskatchewan; Don Bubar for advice on the Canadian mining industry; Carol Bubar for advice on boreal forest tree species; George Xuereb for advice on the Canadian Criminal Code; Richard Nest for advice on aviation and search and rescue techniques; Des Webster for advice on flying light aircraft; Vienna Lam for advice on the decomposition of bodies in freshwater lakes; Varsha Pilbrow for advice on the identification of skeletal remains; Gene Ralston for advice on side scan sonar and recovering bodies; and Heather Marvell for advice on wills and testaments. Without the series of interviews conducted by Murray Dobbin in the 1970s, our book would have been far more difficult to research and perhaps even impossible to produce. He deserves a huge thanks for his work on Jim Brady and Malcolm Norris, for his interviews captured invaluable aspects of their lives and Indigenous history. If there are any errors in the book, however, then they are mine alone.

I received a warm welcome from people in La Ronge and elsewhere who shared background information that helped me to understand the context in which Jim and Abbie lived, who put me straight on some fundamental aspects of the mystery, who were involved in the search in 1967, or who knew Jim and Abbie or were family members of those who did. Thank you to Deborah Charles of Missinipi Broadcasting Corporation, Tom "Tracker" Charles, Graeme Guest, Harold Johnson, Lloyd Mattson, Gerry Mitchinson, Brent Ostwald, Darren Préfontaine, Cathy Quandt, Sid Robinson, Karon Shmon, and Vern Studer. Randy Olsen, along with Lenore and Wayne Jessop and their nephew Ethan, took great care of us at Beaver Lodge Fly-Inn. Arya Boustani and Liza Lorenzetti were wonderful hosts during my research at the Glenbow Museum and Archives in Calgary. We met with several other people who knew details of Jim's and Abbie's lives but wish to remain anonymous—thank you for sharing your stories. Other names have been changed to protect identities.

Lynn Atkinson, Debbie Bell, Syvi Boon, Karen Gillespie, Evalynn Mazurski, Odile Ruijs, and Sara Teachout gave me feedback on the manuscript or helped with specific sections. Thank you so much for your thoughtful comments and advice. The book is clearer, tighter, and better structured because of your input and encouragement. Mahtab Khoshgoo tutored me in explaining in French the themes of the book.

The following institutions generously facilitated my research, tracked down documents, answered questions, gave access to materials, or gave permission to reproduce photographs or other documents in the book: Bibliothèque et archives nationales du Québec, Frances Morrison Central Library in Saskatoon, Gabriel Dumont Institute of Native Studies and Applied Research in Saskatoon, Glenbow Museum and Archives in Calgary, John M. Cuelenaere Public Library in Prince Albert, Judicial Centre of Prince Albert, Pahkisimon Nuye?áh Library in

La Ronge, Prince Albert Historical Society, Provincial Archives of Saskatchewan, Saskatchewan Precambrian Geological Laboratory in La Ronge, Saskatchewan Coroner's Service, Saskatchewan Geological Society, Saskatchewan Mining Association, Saskatchewan Association of Chiefs of Police, University of Regina, and University of Calgary. Chief Tammy Cook-Searson and other staff of the Lac La Ronge Indian Band Council clarified facts, answered questions, and gave up their time to talk to us. I'm also grateful to Randy Olsen of Beaver Lodge Fly-Inn for giving me a superb map of Lower Foster Lake and permission to reproduce it in our book; Craig Neely for the photograph of Abbie Halkett from 1966 taken by his father, Don Neely; the Patterson family for their photo of Abbie Halkett from 1955; and Katherena Vermette for permission to reproduce her heartfelt poem "indians" as the book's epigraph.

Special thanks to the team at the University of Regina Press for taking on this project: Director Kristine Luecker; Managing Editor Kelly Laycock; Acquisitions Editor Karen Clark; and Art Director Duncan Campbell, who designed the wonderful cover. Two terrific freelancers also helped immeasurably to improve the text: Dallas Harrison, our copy editor, and Rachel Taylor, our proofreader.

As always, my greatest debt of gratitude is to Ramin for the love, moral support, and patience.

From Eric: I would like to thank Deanna Reder and Michael Nest for inviting me to join them on this great adventure. It was one of the most unique experiences of my life, and I thoroughly enjoyed it. I would also like to thank my wife, Wanda, for her support and encouragement throughout the whole experience.

I acknowledge Chief Tammy Cook-Searson and the Lac La Ronge Indian Band Councillors for their financial contribution and moral support throughout the project. I would also like to thank Earl Cook and the Saskatchewan Métis Nation for their contributions and for making me realize how important this project was. Thanks to Anne Dorion and the Jim Brady family for their continued support and encouragement, which allowed us to do the job that we needed to do. Thanks also to Thompson McKenzie for his friendship and moral guidance on our expeditions and for ensuring that we respected all cultures and people that we worked with. We appreciated his contributions on search techniques. I also thank the community members of La Ronge, Air Ronge, and Lac La Ronge First Nation who provided encouragement and support on a regular basis and asked numerous questions about the project.

From Deanna: I want to add my thanks to the people and organizations that Michael and Eric list above and to add to this list several others. Thanks especially to Michael Nest, a formidable researcher and generous research partner. We would not have this book in our hands without his efforts. Likewise, I cannot thank Eric Bell enough for sharing his amazing talents that made all of this research possible. Thanks also to Wanda Bell for her generosity, intelligence, and kindness. Thanks to Simon Fraser University President Joy Johnson, who while Vice-President Research offered her personal support; thanks also to Simon Fraser University Dean of the Faculty of Arts and Social Sciences Jane Pulkingham for her support. Thanks to colleague and Squamish archaeologist Rudy Reimer, along with archaeology graduate students Robert Rondeau and Vienna Lam and divers George Mueller and Trevor Dybvig. *Tenikhe* to Thompson McKenzie and to Stanley Roberts. Thanks to the original search team, especially Lloyd Mattson and McIvor Eninew. Thanks to Frank Tomkins for insisting that we find and follow the clues, and to Connie Thompson and Pat Brenyo, who encouraged us despite the disruptions that our search caused as they cared for their dad. Thanks to the various members of the Brady, Halkett, and Patterson families for their support. Special thanks to Brenden Carlson and his father for permission to publish the photo with their grandmother and mother. Also thank you to Susan Farago and Tom Carlson for their help. Thanks to those whom I talked with and consulted about this case over the years, including Alannah Young, Lillian Sanderson, Treena Chambers, Kimberley John, Maddie Reddon, Margery Fee, Suzanne Mathieson Bates, and Rebecca Anderson. And to Eric Davis for conversations, proofreading, and endless support.

NOTES

EPIGRAPH

1   Katherena Vermette, "indians," in *North End Love Songs* (Winnipeg: Muses Company, 2012), 90. Reprinted with permission from Katherena Vermette.

CHAPTER 2: CIRCLING

1   *Affidavit of Beresford Robert Richards in the Matter of the Estate of James Patrick Brady, Late of the District of La Ronge, in the Province of Saskatchewan, Prospector, Deceased*, April 12, 1978, para. 17. The document was obtained with Jim Brady's will from the Judicial Centre of Prince Albert. A copy is held by Michael Nest.

2   "Died This Day," *Globe and Mail*, June 10, 2003, R5.

3   "Photo Gallery: Saskatchewan's Missing People (1969 and Earlier)," *Leader-Post* [Regina], April 23, 2009, http://www.leaderpost.com/Photo+gallery+Saskatchewan+missing+people+1969+earlier/1526336/story.html.

CHAPTER 3: RECOVERY

1   Murray Dobbin, *The One-and-a-Half Men: The Story of Jim Brady and Malcolm Norris, Metis Patriots of the Twentieth Century* (Vancouver: New Star Books, 1981), 9.

2   Clyde Conrad, interview with Murray Dobbin for the oral history project *Biographies of Two Metis Society Founders, Norris and Brady*, August 20, 1976, Provincial Archives of Saskatchewan [PAS], tape IH-361, 19, http://hdl.handle.net/10294/1025.

3   William (Bill) Knox, interview with Murray Dobbin for the oral history project *Biographies of Two Metis Society Founders, Norris*

and Brady, June 21, 1976, PAS, tape IH-383, 6, http://hdl.handle. net/10294/1329.

4   Dan Whitcomb, "Body of Missing Lake Tahoe Diver Found 17 Years Later," August 9, 2011, https://www.reuters.com/article/us-diver-body/body-of-missing-lake-tahoe-diver-found-17-years-later-idUS-TRE7785Wl20110809.

5   "Sherlock of Saskatchewan," *The Globe and Mail*, March 25, 2017, A9.

6   Sergeant Geoff Bennett, RCMP, Regina, email to Michael Nest, March 14, 2017.

CHAPTER 4: NOT JUST ANOTHER INDIAN

1   Jim Brady, interview with Art Davis, 1960, PAS, tape IH-425B, transcript disc 132, 12, http://hdl.handle.net/10294/652. Note that Metis has been spelled without an accent to be consistent with the original historical documents.

2   "Died This Day," *The Globe and Mail*, June 10, 2003, R5.

3   Tony Wood, interview with Murray Dobbin for the oral history project *Biographies of Two Metis Society Founders, Norris and Brady*, July 28, 1984, PAS, tape IH-417A, 2, http://hdl.handle.net/10294/1425.

4   Anne Carrière-Acco, interview with Darren Préfontaine, August 27, 2010, Gabriel Dumont Institute, text document, 4, http://www.metismuseum.ca/resource.php/12915.

5   Ibid.

6   Murray Dobbin, The One-and-a-Half Men: The Story of Jim Brady and Malcolm Norris, Metis Patriots of the Twentieth Century (Vancouver: New Star Books, 1981), 115–16.

7   Wood, interview with Dobbin, 2.

8   James E. Carriere, interview with Murray Dobbin for the oral history project *Biographies of Two Metis Society Founders, Norris and Brady*, August 18, 1976, PAS, tape IH-354, 8, http://hdl.handle.net/10294/1028.

9   Ibid., 5.

10 *Jim Brady: In the Footsteps of the Métis Leader* (TV documentary), Missinipi Broadcasting Corporation, La Ronge, SK, 2011.

11 The CCF ruled Saskatchewan from 1944 to 1961. It rebranded itself as the New Democratic Party and governed for another term from 1961 to 1964.

12   See Reg Whitaker, Gregory S. Kealey, and Andrew Parnaby, *Secret Service: Political Policing in Canada from the Fenians to Fortress America* (Toronto: University of Toronto Press, 2012).

13   James Brady and Malcolm Norris, Various Correspondence 1954–1967, letter of January 20, 1967, Virtual Museum of Métis History and Culture, Gabriel Dumont Institute of Native Studies and Applied Research, http://www.metismuseum.ca/resource.php/12688.

14   Carriere, interview with Dobbin, 8.

15   Helga Reydon, quoted in W.O. Kupsch and S.D. Hanson, eds., *Gold and Other Stories as Told to Berry Richards: Prospecting and Mining in Northern Saskatchewan* (Regina: Saskatchewan Mining Association, 1986), 53.

16   Brady and Norris, Various Correspondence 1954–1967. Metis has been spelled without an accent to be consistent with the original historical documents.

17   Jim Brady, interview with Art Davis, 1960, PAS, tape IH-425, transcript disc 131, 11, https://ourspace.uregina.ca/handle/10294/536.

18   Brady, interview with Davis, 16.

19   William (Bill) Knox, interview with Murray Dobbin for the oral history project *Biographies of Two Metis Society Founders, Norris and Brady*, June 21, 1976, PAS, tape IH-383, 8, http://hdl.handle.net/10294/1329.

20   Ibid.

21   Roberta Quandt, interview with Murray Dobbin for the oral history project *Biographies of Two Metis Society Founders, Norris and Brady*, July 26, 1976, PAS, tape IH-405, 2, http://hdl.handle.net/10294/1400.

22   Ibid.

23   Ibid., 3.

24   Anne Dorion, phone call to Michael Nest, October 10, 2018.

25   Roger Phillips and Alan Hill, "A Picture Story of the La Ronge Claim Staking Rush," *Saskatchewan Mining News* 4, no. 7 (1957): 5–6.

CHAPTER 5: THE ENIGMA OF ABBIE HALKETT

1   "Died This Day," *The Globe and Mail*, June 10, 2003, R5.

2   Amanda Halkett, Facebook post, April 1, 2013.

3   Liora Salter, interview with Murray Dobbin for the oral history project *Biographies of Two Metis Society Founders, Norris and Brady*, February 1978, PAS, tape IH-411, 4, http://hdl.handle.net/10294/1413.

4   Ibid.

5   For more about this story, see Deanna Reder, "Writing Autobiographically: A Neglected Indigenous Intellectual Tradition," in *Across Cultures/Across Borders: Canadian Aboriginal and Native American Literature*, ed. Paul Depasquale, Renate Eigenbrod, and Emma LaRocque (Peterborough, ON: Broadview Press), 153–69.

6   Lloyd Mattson, "Disappearance in 1967 Still Causing Controversy," *The Northerner* [La Ronge, SK], August 4, 1977.

7   Gwendoline Beck, interview with Murray Dobbin for the oral history project *Biographies of Two Metis Society Founders, Norris and Brady*, July 20, 1976, PAS, tape IH-421, 8, http://hdl.handle.net/10294/1429.

8   W.O. Kupsch and S.D. Hanson, eds., *Gold and Other Stories as Told to Berry Richards: Prospecting and Mining in Northern Saskatchewan* (Regina: Saskatchewan Mining Association, 1986), 52.

CHAPTER 6: PRECAMBRIA

1   Andrew M. Miller and Evelyn Siegfried, "Traditional Knowledge of Minerals in Canada," *The Canadian Journal of Native Studies* 32, no. 2 (2017): 35–60.

2   See Arn Keeling and John Sandlos, eds., *Mining and Communities in Northern Canada: History, Politics and Memory* (Calgary: University of Calgary Press, 2015).

3   Mike Denner, *Prospectors' Schools* (Regina: Saskatchewan Geological Survey, 1976), 146, http://publications.gov.sk.ca/documents/310/85070-Denner_1976.pdf.

CHAPTER 7: THE DROP-OFF

1   Gerald Mitchinson gave Michael Nest copies of relevant pages of his logbook.

2   As reported by Murray Dobbin, *The One-and-a-Half Men: The Story of Jim Brady and Malcolm Norris, Metis Patriots of the Twentieth Century* (Vancouver: New Star Books, 1981), 244.

CHAPTER 8: THE SEARCH

1   Frank Tomkins, in conversation with Michael Nest, March 26, 2017.

2   "Assist Search Parties," *Prince Albert Daily Herald*, June 30, 1967, 3, PAS, call. no. micro A-1.575.

3   Saskatchewan Coroner's Service (Office of the Chief Coroner), *Inquiry: Re: James Brady and Absolom Halkett* (La Ronge, SK, March 27, 1969), PAS, accession no. R78-132, call no. R-E177, 6.

4   William (Bill) Knox, interview with Murray Dobbin for the oral history project *Biographies of Two Metis Society Founders, Norris and Brady*, June 21, 1976, PAS, tape IH-383, 8, http://hdl.handle.net/10294/1329.

5   The following chronology is based on Berry Richards, interview with Murray Dobbin for the oral history project *Biographies of Two Metis Society Founders, Norris and Brady*, June 14, 1976, PAS, tapes IH-408, http://hdl.handle.net/10294/1406; Art Sjolander, interview with Murray Dobbin for the oral history project *Biographies of Two Metis Society Founders, Norris and Brady*, March 9, 1976, PAS, tape IH-415, http://hdl.handle.net/10294/1422; and Saskatchewan Coroner's Service, *Inquiry*.

6   Saskatchewan Coroner's Service, *Inquiry,* 17.

7   Ibid.

8   Harold Johnson, in conversation with Deanna Reder and Michael Nest, August 16, 2018.

9   Ibid.

10 Lloyd Mattson, in conversation with Michael Nest, March 27, 2017.

11 Eric Bell, in conversation with Michael Nest, June 11, 2020.

12 Saskatchewan Coroner's Service, *Inquiry*, 44.

CHAPTER 9: MISGIVINGS

1   Philip Carriere, interview by Murray Dobbin for the oral history project *Biographies of Two Metis Society Founders, Norris and Brady*, August 2, 1976, PAS, tape IH-355, 10, http://hdl.handle.net/10294/1017.

2   Art Sjolander, interview with Murray Dobbin for the oral history project *Biographies of Two Metis Society Founders, Norris and Brady*, March 9, 1976, PAS, tape IH-415, 7, http://hdl.handle.net/10294/1422.

3   Clyde Conrad, interview with Murray Dobbin for the oral history project *Biographies of Two Metis Society Founders, Norris and*

Brady, August 20, 1976, PAS, tape IH-361, 13, http://hdl.handle.net/10294/1025.

4   Ibid.

5   Murray Dobbin, *The One-and-a-Half Men: The Story of Jim Brady and Malcolm Norris, Metis Patriots of the Twentieth Century* (Vancouver: New Star Books, 1981), 89.

6   Conrad, interview with Dobbin, 19.

7   Saskatchewan Coroner's Service (Office of the Chief Coroner), *Inquiry: Re: James Brady and Absolom Halkett* (La Ronge, SK, March 27, 1969), PAS, accession no. R78-132, call no. R-E177, 41.

8   Conrad, interview with Dobbin, 19.

9   Sjolander, interview with Dobbin, 7.

10   Saskatchewan Coroner's Service, *Inquiry*, 10.

11   Anonymous, in conversation with Michael Nest, August 8, 2017.

12   Anonymous, in conversation with Michael Nest, March 17, 2018.

13   Jacob McKenzie, interview with Murray Dobbin for the oral history project *Biographies of Two Metis Society Founders, Norris and Brady*, 1976, PAS, tape IH-391, 2, http://hdl.handle.net/10294/1422.

14   Conrad had been promoted to the rank of sergeant by the time of Dobbin's interviews in the mid-1970s.

15   Carriere, interview by Dobbin, 3.

16   Sjolander, interview with Dobbin, 4.

CHAPTER 10: FINDING THE TRUTH IN STORIES

1   Paul Watson, "Ship Found in Arctic 168 Years after Doomed Northwest Passage Attempt," *The Guardian*, September 12, 2016, https://www.theguardian.com/world/2016/sep/12/hms-terror-wreck-found-arctic-nearly-170-years-northwest-passage-attempt.

2   Ibid.

3   Garrett Hinchey, "Sir John Franklin's Long-Lost HMS *Terror* Believed Found," September 12, 2016, http://www.cbc.ca/news/canada/north/hms-terror-found-1.3758400.

4   Frank Tomkins, interview with Deanna Reder and Michael Nest, March 25, 2017.

5   Liora Salter, interview with Murray Dobbin for the oral history project *Biographies of Two Metis Society Founders, Norris and Brady*, February 1978, PAS, tape IH-411, 4, http://hdl.handle.net/10294/1413.

6   Tomkins, interview with Reder and Nest, March 25, 2017.

7   Fatal wolf attacks on humans are exceedingly rare in North America. Prior to 1967, when Jim and Abbie disappeared, the previous *confirmed* fatal attack was in 1893 in Michigan (there were three *unconfirmed* fatal attacks, all in Canada, two in 1922 and one in 1923). It was only in 2005, thirty-eight years after Jim and Abbie's disappearance, that another fatal wolf attack on a human was documented, in Points North Landing, Saskatchewan. For the story of this attack and subsequent inquest, see Harold R. Johnson, *Cry Wolf: Inquest into the True Nature of a Predator* (Regina: University of Regina Press, 2020). In all of these cases, human remains were found, suggesting that, if Jim and Abbie had been killed by wolves close to their campsite or where they were working, their remains would likely have been found by search parties.

8   Lloyd Mattson, "Disappearance in 1967 Still Causing Controversy," *The Northerner* [La Ronge, SK], August 4, 1977.

CHAPTER 11: UNCLE FRANK'S THEORY

1   *Statement of Frank Tomkins of Yellow Creek, Sask., Concerning His Witnessing of the Will of James P. Brady of La Ronge, Sask.*, October 10, 1974, 1, posted on Facebook's Jim Brady–Abbie Halkett Disappearance Public Group, July 14, 2010.

2   Frank Tomkins, in conversation with Deanna Reder and Michael Nest, March 25, 2017.

3   Ibid. This is a summary of the conversation.

4   Ibid.

5   *Statement of Frank Tomkins, 2.*

6   W.O. Kupsch and S.D. Hanson, eds., *Gold and Other Stories as Told to Berry Richards: Prospecting and Mining in Northern Saskatchewan* (Regina: Saskatchewan Mining Association, 1986), 43–44.

7   Tomkins, in conversation with Reder and Nest, March 25, 2017.

8   Frank Tomkins, in conversation with Michael Nest, March 27, 2017.

9   Jim Brady–Abbie Halkett Disappearance Public Group, Facebook.

10   Ibid.

CHAPTER 12: PERSONS OF INTEREST

1 Sergeant Geoff Bennett, RCMP, Regina, email correspondence with Michael Nest, November 22, 2017.

2 Frank Tomkins, in conversation with Deanna Reder and Michael Nest, March 25, 2017.

3 *Jim Brady: In the Footsteps of the Métis Leader* (TV documentary), Missinipi Broadcasting Corporation, La Ronge, SK, 2011.

4 For a discussion of the RCMP's surveillance of citizens, see the eight volumes of *R.C.M.P. Security Bulletins*, ed. Gregory S. Kealey and Reg Whitaker (St. John's: Canadian Committee on Labour History, 1993–97).

5 See Reg Whitaker, Gregory S. Kealey, and Andrew Parnaby, *Secret Service: Political Policing in Canada from the Fenians to Fortress America* (Toronto: University of Toronto Press, 2012), 107.

6 Lloyd Mattson and Eugénie Thomas, *Cuba Libre* (Regina: Clarion Publications, 1962), 141.

7 Whitaker, Kealey, and Parnaby, *Secret Service*, 248–49.

8 "Local RCMP Seek Direction," *Prince Albert Daily Herald*, July 5, 1967, 3.

CHAPTER 13: THE FLYING PREACHER

1 "Flying Preacher Means Vital Contact with Outside World to Northern Parish," *The Ottawa Citizen*, August 20, 1983, 42.

2 Gerald Mitchinson, email to Michael Nest, March 30, 2017.

3 W.O. Kupsch and S.D. Hanson, eds., *Gold and Other Stories as Told to Berry Richards: Prospecting and Mining in Northern Saskatchewan* (Regina: Saskatchewan Mining Association, 1986), 124.

4 Gerald Mitchinson, letter to Michael Nest, May 20, 2017.

5 Mitchinson, email to Nest, March 30, 2017.

6 Gerald Mitchinson, letter to Michael Nest, May 20, 2017.

7 Jim Parres, "Lost . . . Never Found," *Cottage North* 9, no. 2 (2011): 20–22.

8 Gerald Mitchinson, letter to Michael Nest, May 20, 2017.

9 Michael Nest uses the Swiss cheese model as part of corruption risk management training.

10 Kupsch and Hanson, *Gold and Other Stories*, 144.

11 Murray Dobbin, *The One-and-a-Half Men: The Story of Jim Brady and Malcolm Norris, Metis Patriots of the Twentieth Century* (Vancouver: New Star Books, 1981), 245.

CHAPTER 14: AMERICANS

1   Frank Tomkins, in conversation with Michael Nest, March 27, 2017.

CHAPTER 15: ZOMBIES IN TORONTO

1   Manitou Lake Gold Mines, *Prospectus*, March 26, 1979, 12–13.
2   William (Bill) Knox, interview with Murray Dobbin for the oral history project *Biographies of Two Metis Society Founders, Norris and Brady*, June 21, 1976, PAS, tape IH-383, 2–3, http://hdl.handle.net/10294/1329.
3   Adam Ross, *No Reason to Hide: Unmasking the Anonymous Owners of Canadian Companies and Trusts* (Toronto: Transparency International Canada, 2016), 6.
4   Bob Holt, "Good Day Garry" [email], *The Explorationist*, February 2004, 4, http://ontarioprospectors.com/publications/0402-Explorationist.pdf.

CHAPTER 16: THE CAPITALIST

1   Frank Tomkins, in conversation with Deanna Reder and Michael Nest, March 25, 2017.
2   W.O. Kupsch and S.D. Hanson, eds., *Gold and Other Stories as Told to Berry Richards: Prospecting and Mining in Northern Saskatchewan* (Regina: Saskatchewan Mining Association, 1986), 57–58.
3   William (Bill) Knox, interview with Murray Dobbin for the oral history project Biographies of Two Metis Society Founders, Norris and Brady, June 21, 1976, PAS, tape IH-383, 2, http://hdl.handle.net/10294/1329.
4   Lloyd Mattson, letter to Berry Richards, October 19, 1974, 2, posted on Facebook's Jim Brady–Abbie Halkett Disappearance Public Group, August 17, 2010.
5   James Brady and Malcolm Norris, "James Brady and Malcolm Norris, Various Correspondence, 1954–1967," letter of February 12, 1967, Virtual Museum of Métis History and Culture, Gabriel Dumont Institute of Native Studies and Applied Research, http://www.metismuseum.ca/resource.php/12688.
6   Ibid.
7   Knox, interview with Murray Dobbin, 2.

8   Lloyd Mattson, note of phone call to Don Hooton, Selco Mining Corporation, October 24, 1974, posted on Facebook's Jim Brady–Abbie Halkett Disappearance Public Group, July 16, 2010.

9   Knox, interview with Dobbin, 2–3

CHAPTER 17: THE BOSS

1   Lloyd Stinson, *Political Warriors* (Winnipeg: Queenston House, 1975), 105–06.

2   W.O. Kupsch and S.D. Hanson, eds., *Gold and Other Stories as Told to Berry Richards: Prospecting and Mining in Northern Saskatchewan* (Regina: Saskatchewan Mining Association, 1986).

3   Berry Richards, interview with Murray Dobbin for the oral history project *Biographies of Two Metis Society Founders, Norris and Brady*, June 14, 1976, PAS, tape no. IH-408, transcript disc 100, 14,http://hdl.handle.net/10294/1406.

CHAPTER 18: TOUGH OLD NORTHERNERS

1   Joanna Jolly and Georgia Catt, "My Partner Vanished without Warning. I Had to Find Him," August 26, 2017, https://www.bbc.com/news/magazine-40966867.

2   Lloyd Mattson, "Disappearance in 1967 Still Causing Controversy," *The Northerner* [La Ronge, SK], August 4, 1977.

3   Anonymous, in conversation with Eric Bell and Michael Nest, March 17, 2018.

4   Amanda Halkett, email to Michael Nest, February 20, 2018.

5   Royal Canadian Mounted Police, *Missing and Murdered Aboriginal Women: A National Operational Overview* (Ottawa: RCMP, 2014).

6   Darren Préfontaine, in conversation with Michael Nest, March 17, 2017.

7   Vern Studer, in conversation with Deanna Reder and Michael Nest, August 27, 2017. Further quotations from Studer are from this conversation unless otherwise noted.

8   This is a summary of the conversation.

9   James Brady and Malcolm Norris, "James Brady and Malcolm Norris, Various Correspondence, 1954–1967," letter of February 12, 1967, Virtual Museum of Métis History and Culture, Gabriel Dumont Institute of Native Studies and Applied Research, http://www.metismuseum.ca/resource.php/12688.

CHAPTER 19: LA RONGE, LATE SUMMER

1   Liora Salter, interview with Murray Dobbin for the oral history project *Biographies of Two Metis Society Founders, Norris and Brady*, February 1978, PAS, tape IH-411, 7, http://hdl.handle.net/10294/1413.

2   Jim Brady, interview with Art Davis, 1960, PAS, tape IH-425D, transcript disc 132, 5, https://ourspace.uregina.ca/handle/10294/556.

3   Salter, interview with Dobbin, 7–8.

4   Brady, interview with Davis, 5.

5   Anne Dorion, in conversation with Deanna Reder and Michael Nest, August 27, 2017.

CHAPTER 20: THE GUIDE

1   Anonymous, in conversation with Deanna Reder, Eric Bell, and Michael Nest, August 28, 2017.

2   Maya Angelou, *All God's Children Need Travelling Shoes* (New York: Random House, 1991), 155.

3   William (Bill) Knox, interview with Murray Dobbin for the oral history project *Biographies of Two Metis Society Founders, Norris and Brady*, June 21, 1976, PAS, tape IH-383, 4, http://hdl.handle.net/10294/1329.

4   Ibid., 7.

5   Saskatchewan Coroner's Service (Office of the Chief Coroner), *Inquiry: Re: James Brady and Absolom Halkett* (La Ronge, SK, March 27, 1969), PAS, accession no. R78-132, call no. R-E177, 41.

6   This lodge eventually ceased operations, but a new commercial fishing lodge—the Beaver Lodge Fly-Inn—was established on the opposite shore in the mid-1970s.

7   Frank Tomkins gave Michael Nest a copy of the document.

8   Eric Bell, in conversation with Michael Nest, March 17, 2018.

CHAPTER 21: RIVER ICE

1   William (Bill) Knox, interview with Murray Dobbin for the oral history project *Biographies of Two Metis Society Founders, Norris and Brady*, June 21, 1976, PAS, tape IH-383, 4, http://hdl.handle.net/10294/1329.

2   Deborah Charles, phone conversation with Michael Nest, January 18, 2018.

3   Eric Bell, phone conversation with Michael Nest, February 14, 2018.

4   Louise Penny, *Glass Houses: A Novel* (New York: Minotaur Books, 2017), 6.

CHAPTER 22: IN PLAIN SIGHT

1   Lloyd Mattson, "Disappearance in 1967 Still Causing Controversy," *The Northerner* [La Ronge, SK], August 4, 1977.

2   Michael Nest is indebted to Tom Charles of the Lac La Ronge Indian Band for these insights. Tom Charles, phone call to Michael Nest, April 17, 2017.

3   Mattson, "Disappearance."

4   Doug Horner, "Bring Up the Bodies: The Retired Couple Who Find Drowning Victims," *The Guardian*, January 16, 2020, https://www.theguardian.com/science/2020/jan/16/bring-up-the-bodies-gene-sandy-ralston-drowning-victims-sonar.

5   Gene Ralston, email correspondence with Michael Nest, February 23, 2018.

CHAPTER 23: JIGGING FOR TROUT

1   Natalie Thompson, in conversation with Michael Nest, March 15, 2018. Further quotations from Thompson are from this conversation unless otherwise noted.

2   Testimony by Corporal Clyde Conrad, Saskatchewan Coroner's Service (Office of the Chief Coroner), *Inquiry: Re: James Brady and Absolom Halkett* (La Ronge, SK, March 27, 1969), PAS, accession no. R78-132, call no. R-E177, 19.

3   Ibid.

4   Eric Bell, in conversation with Michael Nest, March 16, 2018.

5   Reply by "Mr. Taylor" to Brent Ostwald's financial advice request in 2007, URL now defunct; and Brent Ostwald, email to Michael Nest, May 20, 2020.

CHAPTER 24: DREAMS

1   Frank Tomkins, in conversation with Deanna Reder and Michael Nest, August 16, 2018. Further quotations from Tomkins in this chapter are from this conversation.

2   Clyde Conrad, interview with Murray Dobbin for the oral history project *Biographies of Two Metis Society Founders, Norris and Brady*, August 20, 1976, PAS, tape 1H-361, 7–8, http://hdl.handle.net/10294/1025.

3   Deborah Charles, in conversation with Michael Nest, March 18, 2018.

CHAPTER 25: THE FRIEND

1   Jim Brady, interview with Art Davis, 1960, PAS, tape 1H-425A, transcript disc 131, 10, https://ourspace.uregina.ca/handle/10294/555.

2   Testimony by Allan Quandt, Saskatchewan Coroner's Service (Office of the Chief Coroner), *Inquiry: Re: James Brady and Absolom Halkett* (La Ronge, SK, March 27, 1969), PAS, accession no. R78-132, call no. R-E177, 38.

3   Allan Quandt, interview with Murray Dobbin for the oral history project *Biographies of Two Metis Society Founders, Norris and Brady*, August 21, 1976, PAS, 1H-404B, transcript disc 99, 1, http://hdl.handle.net/10294/1399.

4   Allan Quandt, in conversation with Harold Johnson, recorded in his notebook, January 16, 2004.

5   Ibid. On several occasions the authors heard speculation that Corporal Conrad, the officer in charge of the search, was inexperienced. In June 1967, Conrad was about thirty-one years old and had been a police officer for around nine years, including at least four years—possibly more—in northern Saskatchewan. Nevertheless, to older locals who had lived much of their lives in the area, spending four years in the North by the time one was thirty-one might hardly amount to "experience" and probably still qualified one as "young.".

6   Cathy Quandt, in conversation with Michael Nest, March 16, 2018. Subsequent quotations are from this conversation unless otherwise noted.

7   Roberta Quandt, in conversation with Harold Johnson, recorded in his notebook, January 16, 2004.

8   Allan Quandt, in conversation with Harold Johnson, recorded in his notebook, January 16, 2004.

9   Sid Robinson, email to Michael Nest, August 28, 2019. Quandt had relayed this episode to Robinson, a long-time friend.

10   Roberta Quandt, in conversation with Harold Johnson, recorded in his notebook, January 16, 2004.

11   See *Renunciation by Beneficiary in the Matter of the Estate of James Patrick Brady*, April 26, 1978. The document was obtained with Jim Brady's will from the Judicial Centre of Prince Albert. A copy is held by Michael Nest.

12   See *Affidavit of Execution of Will by Subscribing Witness in the Matter of the Estate of James Patrick Brady*, April 26, 1978. The document was obtained with Jim Brady's will from the Judicial Centre of Prince Albert. A copy is held by Michael Nest.

13   Jim Brady, interview with Art Davis, 1960, PAS, tape IH-425D, transcript disc 132, 4, http://hdl.handle.net/10294/556.

CHAPTER 26: THE BIG FIND

1   William (Bill) Knox, interview with Murray Dobbin for the oral history project *Biographies of Two Metis Society Founders, Norris and Brady*, June 21, 1976, PAS, tape IH-383, 2, http://hdl.handle.net/10294/1329.

2   Frank Tomkins, correspondence with Donald E. Worme, QC, October 23, 2013. This document is held by Michael Nest.

3   J. Robinson, Saskatchewan Department of Mineral Resources, to Lloyd Mattson, October 9, 1974, 1–2. Document posted on Facebook's Jim Brady–Abbie Halkett Disappearance Public Group, July 14, 2010.

4   J.A. Gribben, Selco Mining Corporation, to Lloyd Mattson, October 17, 1974. Document posted on Facebook's Jim Brady–Abbie Halkett Disappearance Public Group, July 16, 2010.

5   Frank Tomkins, in conversation with Deanna Reder and Michael Nest, March 25, 2017.

6   Anonymous, in conversation with Michael Nest, March 16, 2018.

CHAPTER 27: A TIP-OFF

1   Amanda Halkett, email to Michael Nest, April 17, 2018.

CHAPTER 28: "MY ANSWER IS NO"

1 Anne Dorion, in conversation with Michael Nest, October 10, 2018.

CHAPTER 29: OMENS

1 "Beavers of the North Country," episode 31 of *The Undersea World of Jacques Cousteau* (TV documentary), Metromedia Productions, January 6, 1975.

2 Harold Johnson, in conversation with Deanna Reder and Michael Nest, August 16, 2018.

3 We donated the portfolio to the Gabriel Dumont Institute of Native Studies and Applied Research in Saskatoon.

CHAPTER 32: ROAD TO SASKATOON

1 Frank Tomkins, in conversation with Deanna Reder and Michael Nest, August 22, 2018.

2 Once we had confirmation of the sonar experts' opinion that our scan showed a body, Deanna contacted Rema and let her know.

3 Rema Halkett, in conversation with Deanna Reder and Michael Nest, August 22, 2018.

CHAPTER 33: RECKONING

1 Cassandra Kyle, "Study Names Northern Saskatchewan Canada's Second-Poorest Region," *Leader-Post* [Regina], July 31, 2010, A6.

CHAPTER 35: PÂSTÂHOWIN: AS FAR AS YOU CAN GO

1 Stan Cuthand, "On Nelson's Text," in *"The Orders of the Dreamed": George Nelson on Cree and Northern Ojibwa Religion and Myth, 1823*, by George Nelson, vol. 3, ed. Jennifer S.H. Brown and Robert Alain Brightman (St. Paul: Minnesota Historical Society Press, 1988), 194–95.

2 Quoted in Angela Van Essen, "*Pêyâhtik* (Giving Something Great Thought; to Walk Softly): Reading Bilingual *Nêhiyaw*-English Poetry" (PhD diss., University of Alberta, 2019), 55.

3 Information about the dive is from Rob Rondeau, "Survey Report: Lower Foster Lake Project, August 11–15, 2019," Simon Fraser University, Department of Archaeology, August 14, 2019.

4   This lecture has been archived at the University of British Co-
     lumbia's Xwi7xwa library as an article titled "Indigenous People's
     Knowledge = Einew kiss-kee-tum-awin."

REFERENCES

Angelou, Maya. *All God's Children Need Travelling Shoes*. New York: Random House, 1991.

"Assist Search Parties." *Prince Albert Daily Herald*, June 30, 1967, 3 PAS, call. no. micro A-1.575..

"Beavers of the North Country" [television documentary]. Episode 31 of *The Undersea World of Jacques Cousteau*. Metromedia Productions, 1975.

Beck, Gwendoline B. Interview with Murray Dobbin for the oral history project *Biographies of Two Metis Society Founders, Norris and Brady*. July 20, 1976. PAS, tape IH-421. http://hdl.handle.net/10294/1429.

Brady, James (Jim). Interview with Arthur Davis. 1960. PAS, tape IH-425, transcript disc 131. https://ourspace.uregina.ca/handle/10294/536; https://ourspace.uregina.ca/handle/10294/555; https://ourspace.uregina.ca/handle/10294/556; https://ourspace.uregina.ca/handle/10294/652; https://ourspace.uregina.ca/handle/10294/655.

Brady, James, and Malcolm Norris. "James Brady and Malcolm Norris, Various Correspondence, 1954–1967." Virtual Museum of Métis History and Culture, Gabriel Dumont Institute of Native Studies and Applied Research. http://www.metismuseum.ca/resource.php/12688.

Carriere, James E. Interview with Murray Dobbin for the oral history project *Biographies of Two Metis Society Founders, Norris and Brady*. August 18, 1976. PAS, tape IH-354. http://hdl.handle.net/10294/1028.

Carriere, Philip. Interview with Murray Dobbin for the oral history project *Biographies of Two Metis Society Founders, Norris and Brady*. August 2, 1976. PAS, tape IH-355. http://hdl.handle.net/10294/1017.

Carrière-Acco, Anne. "Carrière-Acco, Anne Interview." With Darren Préfontaine. August 27, 2010. Virtual Museum of Métis History and Culture, Gabriel Dumont Institute of Native Studies and Applied Research. http://www.metismuseum.ca/resource.php/12915.

Conrad, Clyde. Interview with Murray Dobbin for the oral history project *Biographies of Two Metis Society Founders, Norris and Brady*. August 20, 1976. PAS, tape IH-361. http://hdl.handle.net/10294/1025.

Cuthand, Stan. "On Nelson's Text." In *"The Orders of the Dreamed": George Nelson on Cree and Northern Ojibwa Religion and Myth, 1823*, vol. 3, edited by Jennifer S.H. Brown and Robert Alain Brightman, 189–198.. St. Paul: Minnesota Historical Society Press, 1988.

Denner, Mike. *Prospectors' Schools*. Regina: Saskatchewan Geological Survey, 1976. http://publications.gov.sk.ca/documents/310/85070-Denner_1976.pdf.

"Died This Day." *The Globe and Mail*, June 10, 2003, R5.

Dobbin, Murray. *The One-and-a-Half Men: The Story of Jim Brady and Malcolm Norris, Metis Patriots of the Twentieth Century*. Vancouver: New Star Books, 1981.

"Flying Preacher Means Vital Contact with Outside World to Northern Parish." *The Ottawa Citizen*, August 20, 1983, 42.

Gribben, J.A., and Lloyd Mattson. "Letter, October 17, 1974." Jim Brady–Abbie Halkett Disappearance Public Group, Facebook. Posted July 16, 2010.

Hinchey, Garrett. "Sir John Franklin's Long-Lost HMS *Terror* Believed Found." CBC News, September 12, 2016. http://www.cbc.ca/news/canada/north/hms-terror-found-1.3758400.

Holt, Bob. "Good Day Garry" [email]. *The Explorationist*, February 2004, 4. http://ontarioprospectors.com/publications/0402-Explorationist.pdf.

Horner, Doug. "Bring Up the Bodies: The Retired Couple Who Find Drowning Victims." *The Guardian*, January 16, 2020. https://www.theguardian.com/science/2020/jan/16/bring-up-the-bodies-gene-sandy-ralston-drowning-victims-sonar.

Jim Brady: In the Footsteps of the Métis Leader [television documentary]. Missinipi Broadcasting Corporation [La Ronge, SK], 2011.

Johnson, Harold. Interview notebooks. January 16, 2004. Held by Michael Nest.

Jolly, Joanna, and Georgia Catt. "My Partner Vanished without Warning. I Had to Find Him." BBC News, August 26, 2017. https://www.bbc.com/news/magazine-40966867.

Johnson, Harold R. *Cry Wolf: Inquest into the True Nature of a Predator*. Regina: University of Regina Press, 2020.

Kealey, Gregory S., and Reg Whitaker, eds. *R.C.M.P. Security Bulletins*. St. John's: Canadian Committee on Labour History, 1993–97.

Keeling, Arn, and John Sandlos, eds. *Mining and Communities in Northern Canada: History, Politics and Memory*. Calgary: University of Calgary Press, 2015.

Knox, William (Bill). Interview with Murray Dobbin for the oral history project *Biographies of Two Metis Society Founders, Norris and Brady*. June 21, 1976. PAS, tape IH-383. http://hdl.handle.net/10294/1329.

Kupsch, W.O., and S.D. Hanson, eds. *Gold and Other Stories as Told to Berry Richards*. Regina: Saskatchewan Mining Association, 1986.

Kyle, Cassandra. "Study Names Northern Saskatchewan Canada's Second-Poorest Region." *Leader-Post* [Regina], July 31, 2010, A6.

"Local RCMP Seek Direction." *Prince Albert Daily Herald*, July 5, 1967, 3.

Mahood, Robert. Interview with Murray Dobbin for the oral history project *Biographies of Two Metis Society Founders, Norris and Brady*. September 10, 1976. PAS, tape IH-394. http://hdl.handle.net/10294/1408.

Manitou Lake Gold Mines. *Prospectus*. March 26, 1979.

Mattson, Lloyd. "Disappearance in 1967 Still Causing Controversy." *The Northerner* [La Ronge, SK], August 4, 1977.

———. "Note of Phone Call with Don Hooton, Selco Mining Corporation, October 24, 1974." Jim Brady–Abbie Halkett Disappearance Public Group, Facebook. Posted July 16, 2010.

Mattson, Lloyd, and Berry Richards. "Letter, October 19, 1974." Jim Brady–Abbie Halkett Disappearance Public Group, Facebook. Posted August 17, 2010.

Mattson, Lloyd, and Eugénie Thomas. *Cuba Libre*. Regina: Clarion Publications, 1962.

McKenzie, Jacob. Interview with Murray Dobbin for the oral history project *Biographies of Two Metis Society Founders, Norris and Brady*. 1976. PAS, tape IH-391. http://hdl.handle.net/10294/1422.

Miller, Andrew M., and Evelyn Siegfried. "Traditional Knowledge of Minerals in Canada." *The Canadian Journal of Native Studies* 32, no. 2 (2017): 35–60.

Mitchell, Ken. "The Trouble with Helping the Metis." *Maclean's*, June 18, 1966, 1–2.

Parres, Jim. "Lost . . . Never Found." *Cottage North* 9, no. 2 (2011): 20–22.

Penny, Louise. *Glass Houses: A Novel.* New York: Minotaur Books, 2017.

Phillips, Roger, and Alan Hill. "A Picture Story of the La Ronge Claim Staking Rush." *The Saskatchewan Mining News,* July 1957, 5–6.

"Photo Gallery: Saskatchewan's Missing People (1969 and Earlier)." *Leader-Post* [Regina], April 23, 2009. http://www.leaderpost.com/Photo+gallery+Saskatchewan+missing+people+1969+earlier/1526336/story.html.

Quandt, Allan. *Affidavit of Execution of Will by Subscribing Witness in the Matter of the Estate of James Patrick Brady.* April 26, 1978. Document is available from the Judicial Centre of Prince Albert. A copy is held by Michael Nest.

———. Interview with Murray Dobbin for the oral history project *Biographies of Two Metis Society Founders, Norris and Brady.* August 21, 1976. PAS, IH-404B, transcript disc 99. http://hdl.handle.net/10294/1399.

———. *Renunciation by Beneficiary in the Matter of the Estate of James Patrick Brady.* April 26, 1978. Document is available from the Judicial Centre of Prince Albert. A copy is held by Michael Nest.

Quandt, Roberta. Interview with Murray Dobbin for the oral history project *Biographies of Two Metis Society Founders, Norris and Brady.* July 26, 1976. PAS, tape R-A1118. https://ourspace.uregina.ca/handle/10294/1400.

Reder, Deanna. "Writing Autobiographically: A Neglected Indigenous Intellectual Tradition." In *Across Cultures/Across Borders: Canadian Aboriginal and Native American Literature,* edited by Paul Depasquale, Renate Eigenbrod, and Emma LaRocque, 153–69. Peterborough, ON: Broadview Press, 2009.

Richards, Berry. *Affidavit of Beresford Robert Richards in the Matter of the Estate of James Patrick Brady, Late of the District of La Ronge, in the Province of Saskatchewan, Prospector, Deceased.* April 12, 1978. Document is available from the Judicial Centre of Prince Albert. A copy is held by Michael Nest.

———. Interview with Murray Dobbin for the oral history project *Biographies of Two Metis Society Founders, Norris and Brady.* June 14, 1976. PAS, tapes IH-408. http://hdl.handle.net/10294/1406.

Robinson, J., and Lloyd Mattson. "Letter, October 9, 1974." Jim Brady–Abbie Halkett Disappearance Public Group, Facebook. Posted July 14, 2010.

Rondeau, Rob. "Survey Report: Lower Foster Lake Project, August 11–15, 2019." Department of Archaeology, Simon Fraser University, Burnaby, BC, August 14, 2019.

Ross, Adam. *No Reason to Hide: Unmasking the Anonymous Owners of Canadian Companies and Trusts*. Toronto: Transparency International Canada, 2016.

Royal Canadian Mounted Police. *Missing and Murdered Aboriginal Women: A National Operational Overview*. Ottawa: RCMP, 2014.

Salter, Liora. Interview with Murray Dobbin for the oral history project *Biographies of Two Metis Society Founders, Norris and Brady*. February 1978. PAS, tape IH-411. http://hdl.handle.net/10294/1413.

Saskatchewan Coroner's Service (Office of the Chief Coroner). *Inquiry: Re: James Brady and Absolom Halkett*. La Ronge, SK, March 27, 1969. PAS, accession no. R78-132, call no. R-E177.

"Sherlock of Saskatchewan." *The Globe and Mail*, March 25, 2017, A9.

Sjolander, Art. Interview with Murray Dobbin for the oral history project *Biographies of Two Metis Society Founders, Norris and Brady*. March 9, 1976. PAS, tape IH-415. http://hdl.handle.net/10294/1422.

Stinson, Lloyd. *Political Warriors*. Winnipeg: Queenston House, 1975.

Van Essen, Angela. "*Pêyâhtik* (Giving Something Great Thought; to Walk Softly): Reading Bilingual *Nêhiyaw*-English Poetry." PhD diss., University of Alberta, 2019.

Watson, Paul. "Ship Found in Arctic 168 Years after Doomed Northwest Passage Attempt." *The Guardian*, September 12, 2016. https://www.theguardian.com/world/2016/sep/12/hms-terror-wreck-found-arctic-nearly-170-years-northwest-passage-attempt.

Whitaker, Reg, Gregory S. Kealey, and Andrew Parnaby. *Secret Service: Political Policing in Canada from the Fenians to Fortress America*. Toronto: University of Toronto Press, 2012.

Whitcomb, Dan. "Body of Missing Lake Tahoe Diver Found 17 Years Later." Reuters, August 9, 2011. https://www.reuters.com/article/us-diver-body/body-of-missing-lake-tahoe-diver-found-17-years-later-idUSTRE7785Wl20110809.

Wood, Tony. Interview with Murray Dobbin for the oral history project *Biographies of Two Metis Society Founders, Norris and Brady*. July 28, 1984. PAS, tape IH-417A. http://hdl.handle.net/10294/1425.

INDEX

Page numbers in italics represent maps/photos.

ABOUT THE AUTHORS

MICHAEL NEST is a freelance researcher and award-winning author whose work focuses on mining and corruption. Michael lives in Montreal.

DEANNA REDER is a Cree-Métis literary critic and an associate professor in English and Indigenous Studies at Simon Fraser University. Deanna lives in Vancouver.

ERIC BELL is a member of the Lac La Ronge Indian Band and the owner of La Ronge Emergency Medical Services. He served for twenty-two years as a park warden. Eric lives in La Ronge, Saskatchewan.

Printed by Imprimerie Gauvin
Gatineau, Québec